AMERICAN CRISIS DIPLOMACY

AMERICAN CRISIS DIPLOMACY

The Quest for Collective Security
1918-1952

RICHARD W. VAN ALSTYNE

Foreword by
GRAHAM H. STUART

STANFORD UNIVERSITY PRESS
STANFORD, CALIFORNIA

STANFORD UNIVERSITY PRESS
STANFORD, CALIFORNIA

LONDON : GEOFFREY CUMBERLEGE
OXFORD UNIVERSITY PRESS

———

THE BAKER AND TAYLOR COMPANY
HILLSIDE, NEW JERSEY

HENRY M. SNYDER & COMPANY
440 FOURTH AVENUE, NEW YORK 16

W. S. HALL & COMPANY
457 MADISON AVENUE, NEW YORK 22

———

COPYRIGHT 1952 BY THE BOARD OF TRUSTEES
OF THE LELAND STANFORD JUNIOR UNIVERSITY

PRINTED IN THE UNITED STATES OF AMERICA
BY STANFORD UNIVERSITY PRESS

Library of Congress Catalog Card Number: 52-6349

American Foreign Policy in the Making

It is paradoxical but true that the phenomenal progress of science threatens mankind with a return to the Dark Ages. The new agencies of destruction are so deadly that the human race can now destroy itself. Science has unleashed the secrets of the radar-controlled rocket, the atomic bomb, and bacteriological warfare. Can man control these evil genii of destruction?

Only two avenues of escape lie open: either to eliminate the disputes which cause war or to settle these disputes by peaceful means. This is particularly vital to democracies because they are badly handicapped in a modern war. Their governments are not geared to take immediate and drastic action. The autocracy acts while the democracy debates. The aggressor has all the advantage of the offensive. Therefore peace is vital to democratic security.

The primary causes of war are conflicts in foreign policy. Our first line of defense, therefore, is the machinery for the conduct of foreign relations. We still need the best army, navy, and air force to support our foreign policy, but this policy must merit defense. It must be a policy so wisely formulated that its execution will appeal to the citizen as both reasonable and necessary.

Since the President is wholly responsible for the conduct of American foreign policy he must choose able advisers to help him formulate such policies and able agents to execute them.

Even with the soundest advice the dangers are great. Isolationists still fear commitments abroad. Politicians seek selfish partisan advantage in disregard of national interest. Minorities raise their claque, giving a fictitious value to their importance. In spite of these handicaps the United States has had to rebuild Europe, protect the Near East, try to keep China from disintegration, and save democracy from communism. Never has the United States more needed able makers of foreign policy.

There is also need of an informed and intelligent public opinion to support a wisely formulated foreign policy. But to devise a wise foreign policy is not a simple problem, nor is it easy for the public to be intelligently informed. The maze of complex factors which control the making of foreign policy can puzzle even the expert. But underlying principles are easily understood and their maintenance is fundamental. Faith in ideals must go hand in hand with so-called practical politics.

The politically biased attacks upon the Department of State for its alleged failure to formulate a successful foreign policy in the Far East because of Communist infiltration is a question of facts. But facts can be concealed or distorted. The hit-and-run tactics of Senator McCarthy are discreditable but effective. The defense never catches up with the accusation. Problems of policy vital to the safety of the state become subjects for partisan dispute and personal attack.

Since public opinion plays such an important role in a democracy, the only satisfactory solution is to make the facts easily available. Problems such as the recognition of Communist China, the future status of Formosa and Korea, the rearming of Germany, regional security arrangements, such as NATO, are still to be discussed and solutions found. But the facts regarding such issues can easily be distorted for partisan advantage. Political campaigns can be won or lost by the way these facts are presented to the public. The nation's safety may depend upon the informed and objective attitude of its body politic. A clear presentation of the facts by a trained historian is an excellent stimulant to clear thinking on the subject.

Mr. Van Alstyne's brilliantly written volume is an effort to untangle the skeins of American foreign policy in Europe and the Far East in this period of crisis diplomacy. The facts are logically and accurately presented so that the reader can form his opinion intelligently and honestly. The author has explored all the documents which have now become available and studied the first-hand reports of the men who played the principal roles in the drama.

The United States has had one goal to achieve—security of the Western Hemisphere. No longer is isolation a solution. The role of the United States has been to throw its strength on the scales in defense of democracy at the time when it would count most. National sovereignty is expendable provided its sacrifice can achieve an effective organization of peaceful and law-abiding states. The United Nations as conceived by its makers could have achieved a better world based upon the principles of fair dealing and justice. But the shadow of Soviet power brought it into temporary eclipse. We have won the

war but have yet to win the peace, and no solution is evident on the
horizon.

But before any solution is possible the facts must be known, their
implications considered, and judgment be based upon them. This
volume attempts to present the facts in their logical sequence and
such conclusions as are drawn are based upon these facts. The reader
may at times object to the author's conclusions but he cannot criticize
the remarkable presentation of all relevant material upon which they
were based. The reader will unquestionably be compelled to agree
that the United States has at least had a definite goal in the conduct of
its foreign policy—a world where the nations and their governments
are merely instrumentalities for the protection and the advancement of
the individual. He will also be convinced that such an ideal can only
be achieved by the co-operation of states working toward its realiza-
tion. Whether this interpretation is true or false it is vital for the
citizen to be informed of the issues in order to decide intelligently.

GRAHAM H. STUART

STANFORD, CALIFORNIA
January 1952

Preface

A FRENCH SCHOLAR, in an essay published in Paris in 1949, gives voice to this troubled thought: The United States is now the directing power (*la puissance directrice*). But a very great difficulty arises. "It so happens that for the first time in many years in diplomatic history the international behavior of the directing power is an unknown quantity." So long as we are content with mere generalities and expressions of visionary objectives, we confess our inability to rise to this criticism. It is no answer to say that American foreign policy adheres to the Truman Doctrine, supports the United Nations, and seeks to "contain" the Soviet Union. We shall have to be more explicit.

This book is a history. That is to say, it treats the issues in American foreign policy from the standpoint of experience not of theory. Or, to make the point in slightly different language, it summons experience, notably the experience of the last thirty years, to testify in regard to the international behavior of the United States. The doubt that this French critic has raised is the same as that so commonly heard in this country: does the United States have a foreign policy? The response is in the affirmative, but it cannot be given in simple declarative sentences. We shall have to scrutinize the record. In fact we shall have to do more. We must achieve that which the great historian Edward Gibbon credited to the Roman historian Tacitus: the capacity for applying the science of philosophy to the study of facts.

We are now at about mid-passage through the aftermath of World War II. But crisis diplomacy, the theme of this short volume, is a concept applicable, I believe, to the international issues affecting Europe and the Far East since 1918. Wars, even small ones, are social upheavals sure to have long-range effects. World wars, conducted on the scale of the last two, injure society organically and lead to long periods of readjustment which inevitably spell new frictions. One of the long-range effects of World War I was to place Japan and the United States in a position of rivalry involving China and the Pacific, a situation which the British naval writer, Hector C. Bywater, grasped with crystal clearness at least by 1920 and perhaps before. The signals for the great war in the Pacific were set in 1918, not in 1931 as too many hasty writers would have us believe. In Western Europe and the Atlantic the change in the balance of power was equally profound, although more hidden from view because Germany was temporarily down and out. The lesson of World War I was that Britain and France could not keep the peace of Europe without aid from the United States. In 1918 the United States *redressed the balance of power* in their favor, and with that accomplished, the coalition fell apart. The point here is that the significant alteration in the international equation, putting the United States in the position of keeper of the peace of Europe, took place in 1918, not in 1940. This being the case, we shall in this book make a survey of the aftermath of World War I and bring it into context with the aftermath in which we are now laboring.

In writing this volume, I have taken the pains to draw definite conclusions, as Mr. Stuart has pointed out in the Foreword. During the aftermath that followed the First World War a very large number of historians, publicists, and journalists, who styled themselves "revisionists," gave way to their disappointments and frustrations and indulged in a widespread witch-hunt for nations, groups, and individuals whom they could charge with the crime of causing the war or, if Americans, of dragging the United States in. This resulted in badly warped history which unfortunately received wide acceptance. It introduced a number of red herrings, and unquestionably it was an important influence confirming the pathological isolationism that palsied American foreign policy during the 1930's. A few historians and publicists, writing in the present aftermath, have surrendered themselves to the same psychology of bitterness and frustration. With them President Roosevelt is the favorite villain. But there are many others who can do naught but vent their rage upon Russia, Communism, and Stalin. They too are taking a warped view, one indeed so extreme that it too is pathological. Relief from difficult situations, whether domestic or international, cannot be gained through misguided leadership of this kind. The historian can do very little to mitigate tension, but at least he can be careful about his facts and composed in his judgments. Otherwise the voice of history, to resort again to the great Edward Gibbon, is "little more than the organ of hatred or flattery."

The present work draws on two chapters of my larger book *American Diplomacy in Action* and another source mentioned below. These have been revised for this book, and Part III, "New Worlds, New Quarrels," is entirely new. I close this Preface with thanks to Professor Graham H. Stuart of Stanford University for his

interest and practical help in the writing of this volume; to Mr. D. G.
Redmond, the editor of *Current History*, for permission to use portions of the several articles which I have contributed in recent years
to his magazine; and to Professors Ross N. Berkes, acting director of
the School of International Relations, University of Southern California, and Richard W. Leopold of the Department of History, North-
western University, for giving me their critical advice respecting
portions of the manuscript.

RICHARD W. VAN ALSTYNE

LOS ANGELES, CALIFORNIA
January 1, 1952

Contents

I

The Pacific Becomes
a Crisis Area, 1918-1941

Security in Eclipse at Pearl Harbor

O N THE MORNING of December 7, 1941, the armed forces of
the Mikado suddenly and without warning swept down from the skies
on the great American naval base at Pearl Harbor, Territory of Hawaii. The fruit of this brilliant though treacherous assault was the
quick achievement of mastery over the entire Western ocean from
Hawaii to the China coast. In rapid succession the following points
fell to the Japanese: (1) the American outpost of Guam, recognized
by naval men since 1898 as the strategic center between Hawaii and
the Philippines; (2) the British island of Hong Kong, the sole remaining obstacle to the control of China's coastal waters since October 1938 when the Japanese had cut in behind and occupied the
city of Canton; (3) the entire Malay Peninsula and the British base
of Singapore, the southwest bastion of the Pacific guarding the en-
trance to the Indian Ocean; (4) the Philippine Islands, including the
fortified harbor of Manila; (5) the whole of the massive East Indian
archipelago, known as Netherlands India; (6) British Burma and its
tributary islands of Nicobar and the Andamans in the Indian Ocean;
and (7) a foothold on Attu and Kiska islands, near the western ex-
tremity of the Aleutians in the far northwest corner of the Pacific.

Superb planning, familiarity with the geography and the character of the defenses of the places at which major thrusts were aimed,
complete audacity and recklessness in attack, and utilization of the
most modern weapons and techniques of warfare thus accomplished
for the Japanese in less than six months the subjugation of an area
so rich and vast that nowhere in the history of warfare could a case
be found to equal it. But this was by no means all. In the three and
a half years prior to the attack on Pearl Harbor the Japanese had
obtained control of the principal rivers, the greater share of the rail-

1

way mileage, and the whole of the coast of China from the borders of French Indo-China in the south to the boundary of Russian Siberia in the north; they had taken the Spratly Island and Hainan, the natural shield to French Indo-China from aggression by sea; taking advantage of the extremities of France, at the time under the heel of the German conqueror, they had then absorbed French Indo-China itself; and from threats to the independence of the adjoining state of Thailand they had swiftly passed to action, once the general attack on the American, British, and Dutch empires had commenced.

The zenith of Japanese ambition, openly depicted since 1938 as aimed at establishing a "Co-Prosperity Sphere in Greater East Asia," had thus nearly been reached. On the mainland of Asia the greater part of China proper was directly or indirectly in Japanese hands; only the interior provinces of the central and western sections were left to the Chinese Republic, still intact and resisting desperately from its capital at Chungking. Some succor still reached the Chinese from the West by way of India, but clearly whatever the Chinese accomplished in defeating the invader had to be done on their own resources. The Western Powers, on whose support China had long been accustomed to lean, were effectually excluded; the mass of property rights, personal privileges, and concessions which had long constituted the tangible evidence of their interests in China had vanished; and Japan had attained, at least until the scales could be turned against her, the supremacy of the Far East. She had tipped the balance wholly in her favor; she had triumphed over both the Western Powers and China.

Further Japanese advances were in the summer of 1942 checked as follows: (1) in India and the Indian Ocean by British naval power, based upon the islands of Ceylon and Madagascar, and by the British-commanded Indian army; (2) by combined American and Australian forces which succeeded in keeping the lines of communication open between the United States and the Australian Commonwealth, and which also thwarted Nipponese efforts to capture the necessary island outposts preliminary to an invasion of the subcontinent; (3) by the Chinese army of Chiang Kai-shek, which showed no sign of collapse; (4) by an effective American defense of Midway Island, an exposed outpost of American power eleven hundred miles west of Pearl Harbor; and (5) by the American naval base at Dutch Harbor, Unalaska, some eight hundred miles east of the Japanese-held islands of the Aleutians.

These points, as it were, constituted the last line of defense on the part of the United Nations, the new international alliance of anti-Hitlerian forces; the capture of any single one of them would under-

mine the immediate independence and territorial integrity of them all:
(1) The conquest of India and the Indian Ocean would be preliminary to a successful junction of the German-Japanese partners and
the "mopping-up" by them of the unconquered portions of Europe,
Asia, and Africa. (2) The breaking of the Australian-American line
of defense would mean the advance of the Japanese into Australia
itself, the probable conquest of that dominion and its sister, New Zealand, and the inevitable retirement of the Americans to a weak line
of defense passing from Samoa in the south through the Hawaiian
Islands to Dutch Harbor in the north. Forays by enemy air and sea
forces to the east of this line into the waters and coastal belts of
North and South America would be at the enemy's choice; their
number and extent would probably be conditioned far more by the
strength or weakness of his rear than by American ability to prevent
the line from being pierced.

The Anglo-Japanese Alliance

The disastrous experience of 1942 therefore begs consideration
of the historical question: what was the character of the security
problem in the western Pacific area prior to December 7, 1941? What
was the relative sense of safety felt by the principal powers having
territories or interests in this region, and how were their policies
toward one another formulated with a view to maintaining the general peace? Australia and New Zealand first posed the question in
the last quarter of the nineteenth century; competition among the
French, Germans, and Americans for islands between Samoa on the
east and New Guinea on the west aroused the fears of the older
British colonies, and they clamored for the annexation to the British
Empire of a chain of islands including the southeastern portion of
New Guinea, the Fijis, and western Samoa. Behind this screen the
British colonies, which became self-governing dominions at the turn
of the century, felt reasonably secure. Nevertheless, at the outbreak
of the World War in 1914 they made assurance doubly sure by over-
running all of the island colonies south of the Equator that Germany
had taken up. This projection of the security zone of the two British
dominions was ratified by the Peace Conference of 1919, with the
sole qualification that the colonies so appropriated should be conducted as mandates under the League of Nations.

So far as the United States was concerned, the security of the
region scarcely became a live issue until 1918. The historic interest
of the United States in this section of the ocean involved only the
safety of the China route; to this had been added after 1898 the re-

sponsibility for the defense of the Philippine Islands. The Spanish Empire in the Pacific was at that time partitioned, the Germans balancing the American acquisition of Guam and the Philippines with the purchase of the remaining Spanish islands. These comprised three groups north of the Equator—the Marshalls, the Carolines, and the Marianas. The Americans distrusted German intentions toward the Philippine Islands at the time of their conquest, but despite the fact that the German purchases after the Spanish-American War sat squarely astride the American route the United States interposed no obstacle to their transfer from Spain. Nor does it seem to have feared this strategic disadvantage to its route so long as Germany remained in possession.

Probably the United States appreciated the extreme exposure to which these distant German colonies were subject. They were hostages of the Anglo-Japanese alliance, which after 1902 held the peace of the western Pacific in safe keeping. Germany's inability to retain any of her possessions in the Pacific, once they were challenged by British and Japanese sea power, justified the previous American indifference to their presence. It was beyond Germany's strength to use them for purposes of aggression. The shift in the balance of power which took place in the western Pacific in 1915, however, altered the American outlook. By the withdrawal of the British naval forces, by the dependence of the British Empire upon its ally for convoy duty and patrol service as far west as Suez, and especially by the easy Japanese conquests of the German islands north of the Equator, Japan became the predominant sea power of the Far East. Secret suspicions of Japanese intentions, harbored by the American government as far back as 1905, came to life when Japan slid into the seat of Germany on the flank of the American route to China and the Philippines.

American reactions to the Japanese island acquisitions were slow —much slower than they were to the forward policy pursued by the Japanese in China. The American government protested the Twenty-One Demands in 1915 but ignored the potential freedom which expanded sea power gave to Japan to develop her policies in China. And when Viscount Ishii, the Japanese special ambassador in 1917, reached the United States, he found the Secretary of State solicitous concerning the open door in China but apathetic toward the altered naval situation in the western Pacific. Not even the knowledge, freely given by the Ambassador, that the British had agreed to Japan's keeping the islands disturbed the State Department. Not until the Peace Conference did the American government awaken to the strategic importance of the islands. It then demanded that they, in company with other captured enemy colonies, be converted into mandates, which meant that they would be unfortified and theoretically open to the trade of all nations. It is curious to recall that Woodrow Wilson fought his battle over this issue with the two British dominions, and not with the Japanese. The latter offered no opposition to the plan for mandates, whether as a matter of discretion or one of genuine indifference it is impossible to say. The facts remain that the Japanese mandates formed a great rectangular area in the ocean, twelve hundred miles from north to south and twenty-five hundred miles from east to west; that the security system for the western Pacific which was erected after the war rested on the assumption that all of the mandatory holdings, British and Japanese, would comprise a vast neutral zone; that Japan regularly reported to the League of Nations on the condition of her mandates even after she had withdrawn from the League in 1935; but that in 1942 Japanese sea and air power combined to make an impenetrable barrier of the mandated area.

Geography and the distribution of naval power in 1918 functioned to make Japan the predominant power in the Far East. Practically speaking, the shift had taken place in the years before the war under the guise of the Anglo-Japanese alliance, in which Britain leaned more and more heavily on her partner for protecting her East Asiatic interests. West of Hawaii the American route to the Far East was unguarded; for the first time in its history the United States based a portion of its battle fleet at Pearl Harbor; but, though proposals were made to fortify Guam and the Philippines, neither Congress nor the administration was conciliatory to the idea.

The U.S. Plans a Navy Second to None

Another factor, however, was designed to offset the advantages held in 1918 by Japan. During the war then ending the United States had set out to build the largest navy in the world. The expansion of the American Navy dates from 1916 at a time of intense irritation against Great Britain. Building programs laid before Congress two years later aimed at putting the United States in first place by 1925. The emphasis was on large capital ships displacing 43,000 tons, a battle line that would outdistance and outfight any other fleet in the world. Woodrow Wilson, the president who promoted the principles of collective security and who spoke so eloquently about the need for reducing armaments to "the lowest point consistent with national safety," put himself at the head of the movement to build a navy bigger than the British and establish an American supremacy of the high seas. All the signs point to the conclusion that Wilson was aiming more at the British than he was at the Japanese. A devotee of "freedom of the seas" and the classical rules of American neutral rights, the offenses allegedly committed by the British on the high seas rankled in his memory. There had been bitter moments, particularly in 1916, when it seemed as though the United States would be driven into war with England.

At the end of the war Wilson had another reason for building a navy second to none. He meant to make good on the enforcement provisions of the League Covenant. But what if the aggressor should turn out to be the strongest naval power, Great Britain? The logical answer was supplied by Admiral Benson, Wilson's naval adviser at Paris: "The League of Nations must be strong enough to restrain, if necessary, its strongest member." But "no international navy made up of ships of heterogeneous types, training, language, custom, and command could hope to cope with the British fleet." The argument had force and the conclusion was obvious: the United States must have a fleet at least equal to the British. Being a satiated power, Benson added, the United States could be trusted by the League to carry out the obligations of the Covenant. Reduced to plain English, this meant that the United States would assume for itself the leading role of world judge and world policeman.[1]

Wilson's motivation at Paris appears to have been most complex. He intended to enforce "freedom of the seas" and in this respect had Great Britain chiefly in mind. In the future Britain would have to wage war on the terms and under the conditions prescribed by the United States. In the realistic sense, of course, "freedom of the seas" meant mastery of the seas on the part of the United States. But Wilson intended also to hold Japan in her place, to crowd her out of Shantung particularly, and to force her to obey the principles of Chinese independence and integrity. The mandated area gave Japan regional supremacy for the time being. But Wilson apparently expected to overcome that advantage by a concentration of naval power at Pearl Harbor.

The effect of Wilson's naval policies was to inspire both the British and the Japanese with fear and to stimulate a three-cornered naval race. The Japanese naval budget of 1921 tripled that of 1917, while the British ruefully reflected that they had overcome one rival in the Atlantic only to be faced with a larger and wealthier antagonist, on the other side of the ocean. Neither Wilson nor his successor, Harding, showed an inclination toward any alternate solution. The Executive branch of the government was clearly headed for a struggle for the command of the seas. The race, however, was averted in 1921 through the pressure of organized public opinion; a coalition of various elements among the people and in Congress, which challenged the need for the largest navy, repudiated the ambition to replace Great Britain as mistress of the seas, believed that the proper road to peace lay in the direction of disarmament, and demanded economy and reduction of taxes on the part of the federal government. The isolationist Senator, William E. Borah, sponsored the demand in Congress that an arms conference be held with Great Britain and Japan; powerful support for the cause came from the *New York Times* and from both Generals Bliss and Pershing, strong advocates of the League of Nations but not supporters of the ambition to outbuild the British navy; and the Senate refused to approve the administration's navy bill.

Just how the Harding administration felt about the matter is very obscure. It held out against the popular demand for a conference, but one need not jump to the conclusion that it favored a race with England merely for the satisfaction of winning the race. Wilson in 1918 and popular sentiment later interpreted the movement for a big navy as a gesture directed against the British. Both the British government and the British public thought likewise. Thoroughly alarmed over the situation, the First Lord of the Admiralty managed to convey privately to the American Navy Department the knowledge that Britain would abandon her traditional two-power standard and concede parity with the United States. He furthermore suggested that the two countries share the responsibility for policing the oceans between them, the United States to take the Pacific and Britain the Atlantic. The United States, let us recall, had already transferred the greater share of its fleet to the Pacific, and it is quite possible that this is the kind of a proposal for which the administration was waiting. It had had a sharp brush with the Japanese over the status of the island of Yap, one of the mandated islands which controlled the cable crossings in the Pacific. It also appears to have been eager to succeed in China where Wilson had failed. Senator Lodge, the Republican majority leader, made this clear in arguing for the big-navy bill in 1921; to make good on its China policies the United States must have the necessary capital ships. In other words, so far as the American government was now concerned, the main motive for a big navy was the implementing of its program in the Far East. This again was not primarily a question of security for the insular possessions of the United States, but rather a determination to forbid

Japan from gaining mastery on the mainland of Asia. Furthermore, by 1921 the issue of "freedom of the seas" in the Atlantic was purely an academic matter, and the Republican administration had no intention of playing policeman in Europe. In its view that responsibility should be resumed by Great Britain, while the United States would turn its attention to keeping the balance in the Far East.

There was one other point to be settled. The Anglo-Japanese alliance had been the vehicle on which Japan had ridden to power in eastern Asia. The British had carefully guarded themselves against involvement in a possible war between the United States and the Japanese; nevertheless, the alliance stood in the way of a free and independent China. In American eyes China was the right bulwark against Japan. Throughout the British Empire there was wide difference of opinion over the worth of the alliance; the public, especially in the Dominions, shared the racial dislike of the Japanese; on the other hand, men like Premier Hughes of Australia regarded China as Japan's best safety valve. If she were kept busy in Asia, she would be less likely to cast eyes on the southwest Pacific. This view was common to British statesmen, who, with the exception of Premier Arthur Meighen of Canada, were committed to a renewal of the alliance. In the imperial Conference of 1921 Meighen stood out against it. At the same time in Washington Secretary Hughes was urging the British Ambassador to get a definite decision from his government whether it intended to side with the United States or with Japan. Britain too had always paid lip service to the principle of Chinese integrity. A combination of forces finally brought the desired result, and it was understood that the United States would call a conference which would take in both the arms-limitation question and Far Eastern problems.

1921: Naval Disarmament

With British collaboration thus assured in advance, the American government issued invitations to Japan, France, and Italy as the principal naval powers and also to China. Since the Far East was to be an important subject at the conference, Belgium, who had commercial interests there, complained of the omission of herself from the list. In consequence invitations were extended to three smaller powers, Portugal, the Netherlands, and Belgium. Soviet Russia was brusquely ignored in spite of her protests. Fear of Communism ran high in both Britain and America at the time, and it was one of the favorite pleas of apologists for the Anglo-Japanese alliance that Japan was the best possible buffer to Russia in Asia. As for Japan herself, she was well aware that one purpose of the conference was to isolate her. The Japanese were willing to talk naval limitation, but they realized the implications of the American effort to dissolve their tie with Great Britain. They could hardly afford to absent themselves from the conference, however, and a last-minute effort to get Chinese questions excluded from the agenda was simply overruled.

The Conference of the Nine Powers convened at Washington on November 12, 1921. There had been a general prayer for disarmament, echoed even in Japan, and that was the feature of the Conference that held the public interest. Two years previously the United States had seemed to be rushing into a race with Great Britain, with no issue at stake except to see who could put the biggest fleet on the ocean and run the League of Nations. Prompted by extreme navalists, like Admiral Benson, Woodrow Wilson had allowed his ambitions for world leadership to outrun his discretion. The two countries which had done the most to bring the League into existence in the hope of promoting a better world would now fight it out for the leadership of the pack! That was the logical end of the Wilsonian policies. To be sure, there was actually little danger of putting such logic into practice. The popular drift was all the other way in both countries, in each of which there spread a cry for relief from the burden of armaments and a conviction that a race was the surest road to war. Few Americans, even in the professional services, desired more than parity with England; few Englishmen cared to tease the United States into wanting more.

Secretary Hughes gave the Washington Conference at the very outset a dramatic quality that few such gatherings are privileged to enjoy. Without previous announcement or advance consultation of any sort with any other government, he pledged the United States to a program of scrapping thirty capital ships displacing a total of over eight hundred thousand tons. He then turned to the British delegation and calmly "sank" four of their new capital ships and nineteen older ones—"more than all the admirals of the world had destroyed in a cycle of centuries," as one writer described the scene. As for Japan, she was to scrap seven ships partly built and ten others. The proposal was in perfect keeping with the popular feeling in all three countries, and was received with the utmost acclaim even in Japan. Hughes proposed also a ten-year holiday on capital-ship construction and the establishment of a ratio of naval strength, based on capital-ship tonnage, of five to five for the United States and Great Britain, three for Japan, and one and three-quarters for France and Italy each. In actual capital-ship tonnage this meant 500,000 tons for the United States, 600,000 for Great Britain (the difference being due to the greater age of some British ships), and approximately 300,000 for Japan.

Ultimately Hughes's proposals were accepted in the face of considerable opposition from professional naval and military circles. The Japanese and French especially were affronted by what they regarded as a stamp of inferiority imposed on them by the lesser ratio. The French finally accepted with bad grace, and the Japanese were offered compensation in the form of a second treaty based upon the principal of nonaggression against each other's possessions in the Pacific. The original suggestion came from Baron Kato, the Japanese delegate, in the form of a standstill agreement on island fortifications in the Pacific. Japan had two desires: to be insulated against attack by another fleet, and to hold the naval supremacy in China waters. Both were attainable by means of a limitation on American capital ships and an agreement to leave Guam and the Philippines unfortified. If neither of these places could be used as bases, Japan would be beyond the striking power of her rival. In the United States there was as little enthusiasm to fortify Guam and the Philippines as there was to build new capital ships. Consequently Japan's proposal was well received.

The orginal idea was to have a three-power treaty among Japan, Britain, and the United States and to so word it as to extend the principle of nonaggression to one another's interests on the Asiatic mainland. In Japanese and British eyes this was intended to mean that the United States would not interfere with Japanese interests in China or Manchuria. Mr. Hughes would have nothing to do with this, however, and insisted on two changes. He wanted France a member of the pact, probably for appearances' sake; moreover, her presence would head off any charge that the treaty gave Britain and Japan the opportunity to outvote the United States. But the really important part of the pact had to do with its scope. Mr. Hughes limited it to the *insular possessions* of the four powers in "the region of the Pacific Ocean." The parties agreed not to attack one another's islands. The pact had the merit of giving the United States protection against attack on the Philippines or Guam without the expense of fortifying them. By definition the powers agreed that the term "insular possessions" would apply to the American islands, including the Aleutians; to the Japanese islands of Formosa (Taiwan) and the Loo Choos (now the Ryukyus) ; and to the British island of Hong Kong. Specifically excluded from the neutralized area were Singapore on the southwest, the British Dominions and Crown Colonies south of the Equator, Hawaii and the coasts of Canada and the

United States, and the Japanese "homeland," a term which apparently meant the main islands of Japan. In these areas the powers were free to increase or decrease their fortifications at will.

The Power Balance in the Western Pacific Passes to Japan

In sum, the Four-Power Pact, for such it came to be called, meant the extension of the neutralized zone already established in the mandated area so as to bring in those American possessions from which an offensive campaign could be conducted against Japan. Unless a fleet could be based on Dutch Harbor in the Aleutians, or on Guam and the Philippines, Japan was beyond the reach of the United States. Since majority opinion in this country at the time was strongly opposed to fortifying these places anyway, no sacrifice was apparent. What the United States really did give up was its ability to make good on its policies in China. Only overwhelming sea power could do that. True, Japan became an unwilling subscriber to the formal obligations of the Nine-Power Pact, which restated in forcible language the time-honored principles of the open door and the independence and integrity of China; but, as pointed out in the previous case, the responsibility for seeing that the treaty was enforced devolved upon China alone. In like manner the Philippines were beyond the Japanese reach, so long as Formosa and the Loo Choos were not developed as bases.

Locked together, the three treaties formed a seemingly perfect security system for the Pacific and Eastern Asia. None of the Great Powers could attack the others, provided that each respected the neutralized zone. The weakness of the whole fabric lay in the facts that geography was all in Japan's favor, that China was too frail a rod to support the balance of power alone, and that Japan was an unsatiated power with a "mission" to fulfill in China. The Japanese were left with the natural supremacy of the entire western Pacific; except on paper the Washington treaties did not weaken the preponderance of sea power in that region that they had inherited from the First World War.

In reality the United States was faced with a dilemma from which the Washington treaties offered the only escape. In common with Britain it was in search of a method for averting the threatened naval race. The public in both countries clamored for disarmament. The building of costly installations in Guam and the Philippines was not in accord with the trend of the times. It would have been branded in both Japan and the United States as a direct challenge to the former, and the American people frowned emphatically upon the offer of such a challenge. They wanted to encourage China, but not at the sacrifice and expense of a collision with Japan. There was no imminent threat to the American island possessions, and the disposition to place confidence in Japan's good faith was widespread. Hence the resolution to follow a collective system where the use of force was made all but impossible.

Actually the Four-Power Pact contained the implications of a sort of mild substitute for the Anglo-Japanese alliance. It authorized any one of the parties to summon the others into conference in case an issue arose out of "any Pacific question." This clause was interpreted as laying the ground for a common Anglo-American front on Pacific questions, though the term was not defined and there was no suggestion that it applied to China. On the contrary, the absence of reference to China in this treaty would make it appear that the agreement was intended to apply only to the insular possessions of the respective powers. Nevertheless, the treaty attracted the suspicions of the extreme isolationists in the Senate, the same who had fought the League of Nations to a standstill. At their insistence the Senate added a reservation aimed to destroy whatever value stemmed from the consultative stipulations of the pact. The United States, it declared, "understands that . . . . under the terms of this Treaty there is no commitment to armed force, no alliance, no obligation to join in any defense." If this dictum were followed literally, it would mean that the United States would loftily refuse co-operation with Britain, even though its own possessions in the Pacific were directly threatened. A more gratuitous bid to Japan to regard the western part of the ocean as her own preserve can scarcely be imagined.

The Power Balance in Western Europe Passes to the U.S.

The Washington treaties yielded one considerable compensation: they checked a sinister naval race between the English-speaking countries, though unfortunately they fell short of a permanent solution. Britain acknowledged the principle of parity in capital ships only, and even in that category American naval authorities complained that the treaty restrictions on replacements would keep the United States from achieving actual equality for twenty years. The tendency of the decade was to accentuate the naval rivalry with the British in technical matters and with respect to the different categories of ships, particularly cruisers. A conference held at Geneva in 1927, at which the admirals predominated in contrast to their relegation to the background at Washington, advertised the sharp sense of rivalry between the navies of the two countries. The General Board at Washington had openly set forth its demands for a navy second to none in all types of vessels, and equipped for operations of any kind in either ocean. In general this was a challenge to the British view that the Royal Navy must have superiority in cruisers so as to defend the long lines of empire communications.

The British also remained uncertain of the American attitude in case of another European war; would the United States revert to its classic thesis of the defense of neutral rights, or would it follow the precedents of the First World War in allowing the British Navy untrammeled action against its enemies on the high seas? No one in either country could give the answer, and the question mark in Anglo-American relations weakened the British will to stand back of the collective system on the European continent. There was in fact a fundamental contradiction between the traditional American concept of freedom of the seas, meaning respect for neutral rights, and the principle of collective security being evolved from the Covenant of the League of Nations for the benefit of stabilization on the Continent. The heights of economic and naval power to which the United States had risen were factors recognized by the British as decisive in any future conflict. If the United States, a neutral in a second European war, insisted on its legal rights of trade with Britain's enemies on the Continent, the British questioned their capacity to fight a war in Europe. In 1914–18 Wilson had allowed the British a free hand on the high seas, though he and a section of the American public had complained bitterly of being bereft of their rights; at the end of the war Wilson returned belligerently to the time-honored doctrine of freedom of the seas in the name of the League of Nations. British aggressions against maritime rights, in other words, might be interpreted as a violation of the Covenant and hence might call for retaliation at the hands of the United States. Failure to join the League did not alter the situation, because the United States still paid allegiance to the nineteenth-century rules restricting blockade. Britain risked American displeasure in 1914–17; but if the United States actually achieved parity in naval strength, her position on the Atlantic would be so jeopardized as to render impossible a revival of the practices of 1914–18.

In other words, the United States, despite its alleged isolation, really held the balance of power in western Europe. The First World War had wrought a revolution in the position of this country; it was idle to suppose that the British could defy it, as they did in the Napoleonic wars, or that they would even commit themselves to defend France against German aggression without knowing in advance the attitude of the United States toward warfare on the seas. In spite of the interrelationship of the collective system, each of the major powers persisted in treating its own interests as isolated and exclusive. The United States clung to "neutral rights"; as a makeweight in a European conflict its economic power had been proved beyond a doubt in 1914–18; now it wished to build a navy "second to none." With such a combination of forces it would have little trouble in striking the weapon of sea power from British hands and thereby determining the course of victory in a European conflict.

The public discussions of the 1920's focused upon the possibilities of an Anglo-American war, with "neutral rights" as the issue. During that decade the United States planted an enormous stake in the trade and investment of the European continent. Japan and the Orient were all but forgotten. It was these considerations that underlay the British jealousy of the American Navy, the fear of insecurity even in their own waters. The specter of neutral rights now had real claws and real teeth, and the issue was a vital one. By 1929 Senator Borah so far set aside his isolationism as to state the point: the naval controversy waited upon a comprehensive and definitive agreement respecting neutral rights. Navies were means to an end, not an end in themselves, and if Britain and the United States were to reach an understanding on the size of their respective forces, each had to know where the other stood on matters considered of vital national interest. This attempt to clarify the main issue was a distinct improvement over the contradiction in aims emphasized by Wilson. Freedom of the seas as conceived by him meant a return to the system of armed neutrality practiced by the European neutrals during the American Revolution, with the United States occupying the front seat among the armed neutrals.

When Japan overran Manchuria in 1931 and detached it from China, she upset the equilibrium of the Washington system. Immediate proof of the connection between this aggression and the general problem of the Pacific was lacking, however, though Secretary Stimson pointed out the relationship in an open letter to Senator Borah. The pledge of the United States to leave Guam and the Philippines unfortified was predicated upon the self-denying covenants of the Nine-Power Treaty respecting China. Nevertheless, the Manchurian incident was treated as a moral problem; American diplomacy under Stimson had rejected any other approach, and the several proposals that had been submitted for international action by the League or by the Nine-Power Treaty nations had all come to naught. In May 1934 the Japanese government, through its Ambassador in Washington,

sounded the new Roosevelt administration on the possibility of divid-
ing the Pacific area between them, Japan to have the western Pacific as
her sphere of influence and the United States to confine itself to the
"eastern Pacific regions."[2] President Roosevelt, however, had already
decided to rest on Stimson's nonrecognition doctrine, and the Japanese
were rebuffed.

This attitude of detachment on the part of the United States,
tempered only by moral indignation, toward the tragedy of China
continued to be characteristic of American policy through the decade
of the 1930's. The steady encroachment of Japan in North China,
her increasing pressure on the treaty rights of the Western Powers,
her open repudiation of the Nine-Power Treaty, and even her fero-
cious onslaughts after 1937 against the very heart of China were
met almost with a shrug. The popular inclination seemed to favor
not only leaving China in the lurch and abandoning the treaty rights,
but evacuating the western Pacific and retreating, if necessary, to
Hawaii. The Philippines Independence Act of 1934 was so interpreted. The measure pleased the farming interests in the United
States particularly, because it would rid them of the annoying competition of Philippine products. The Island people were to be piloted
toward complete independence within twelve years, at the end of
which time the United States would cease to be responsible for their
defense. It is true that the President was empowered to promote an
international agreement for the neutralization of the Islands; but
clearly there was no intention of permitting him to negotiate an
armed alliance to defend them. Considering the Japanese activities on
the mainland and the veiled announcements from Tokyo of the right
to rule the Pacific, such pious gestures unsupported by force were futile. Committed apparently to withdrawal, the American government
set itself to the task of training a native draft army capable of
standing off an invasion. This was as far as the public at home,
passionately devoted to isolationism, would allow it to go.

The Pathology of Isolationism

This is not the place to examine the isolationist obsession that
held the American public spellbound during the decade of the 1930's.
Pathological in its devotion to the empty slogan of "Keep out of
war!" the public was fascinated and frightened by the growing spec-
tacle of violence and lawlessness in Europe. Its education in the
strategy of the western Pacific was yet to come. Pearl Harbor proved
to be the best teacher. China's sorrows were treated as moral issues,
painful to most Americans but pointing no object lesson in inter-

national politics. Generally speaking, the treaty rights and investments in China were held in contempt. Their monetary value was known to be scanty and hardly worth defending, but the public refused to accept any other practical reason for going to China's assistance. Furthermore, Japan shared in the sympathy loudly expressed by the pacifists and "intellectuals" for Germany and Italy as "have-not nations." It was the unfailing excuse for the lawlessness of the dictators. There was a faint consciousness of American dependence on the rubber and tin of the East Indies, and some uneasiness over the possibilities of Japan's attacks in their direction. It was usually silenced, however, by the easy confidence in the magic of South American resources and by the assurance that, even if Japan should conquer the Indies, she would have to sell the products anyway. The popular imagination simply rejected pictures of the opportunities for world conquest open to Nippon, once such an aggregation of natural wealth and power as only the East Indies could offer was within her clutches.

Stirrings of Strength in the U.S.

Such in brief was the general popular estimate of the situation—skepticism, faint-heartedness, a deep sense of futility shared even by the most ardent friends of China, a complacent belief that Japan's strength was limited, and a false sense of American national security. There were a few indications that the United States did not plan an abject withdrawal. One was the reiterated firmness with which the American government greeted each new Japanese aggression, its consistent refusal to recognize changes brought about by violence. Such announcements of policy, approved by the American public, infuriated the Japanese without defeating them. A second was the establishment of an air-mail and passenger route to the Orient in 1936 via Midway, Wake, Guam, and the Philippines, leading directly over the unfriendly waters of the Japanese mandates. A third was the ostentatious "colonization" of a group of small islands and atolls in the Phoenix archipelago in the South Pacific in 1937, followed by a window-dressing agreement with Great Britain for joint occupation. The location of these atolls suggested the establishment of an alternate air route to Australia and the East Indies in case the Japanese cut off the direct line.

Naval Rearmament Under Roosevelt

Most important of all, however, was the naval rearmament program inaugurated by the Roosevelt administration in 1933. For the first time since the Washington treaties the duty of building up the Navy to treaty limits was undertaken. The pace was accentuated greatly in 1936. Japan had given formal notice that she intended to repudiate the ratio system. At a third great naval conference held in London early in the year she demanded full parity with Britain and the United States. This was of course refused, and the Japanese delegation walked out of the conference just as they had done three years before from the League of Nations. Britain and the United States then reached a limitation agreement between themselves, confirming the principle of parity in all categories of ships and limiting the battleship to 35,000 tons. Persistent rumors that Japan was secretly building two ships of 45,000 tons brought inquiries but no satisfactory information. Consequently even this limitation had to be abandoned, and the naval appropriation bills enacted successively in 1937, 1938, and 1939 provided sums that satisfied the fondest wishes of the Navy Department. The act of 1939 called for an outlay of $1,300,000,000 on 127 ships within four years. At the end of that period the American Navy was scheduled to possess a global tonnage of 2,154,000.

Conspicuous at the London Conference of 1936 and thereafter was the growing rapprochement between the British and American governments. The bickering of the 1920's had given way to teamwork, as close as the jealous watch of American isolationists would permit. Letters were publicly exchanged at the end of the Conference declaring that the two countries would not engage in competitive building, and each government thereafter regarded additions to the other's fleet as increased security for itself. In so far as domestic politics would allow, the static conceptions of the Washington system were repudiated. In February 1938 three American cruisers put in an appearance at the formal opening of the completed British base at Singapore, a gesture showing that the American government appreciated the common interest in the southwest Pacific. Nothing adequate was accomplished by either power, however, to overcome the advantages long held by Japan. The British were unequal to equipping and maintaining the separate fleet for which the Singapore base was intended; the Americans succeeded in increasing the defenses of the Philippines, but they failed to fortify Guam. A bill to accomplish this purpose was debated in Congress in 1939, after the European war had begun; it was strongly endorsed by the administration and by the Naval Affairs Committees of both houses; but the majority drew back from the obvious challenge intended for Japan, and the measure was beaten. Without a heavily fortified Guam it was out of the question to hold the route to the Philippines. By 1939 it was definitely too late so much as to try.

War in Europe, and Japan Allied with the Axis Powers

Meanwhile the Japanese prepared to take immediate advantage of the outbreak of the war in Europe. They had, it will be remembered, already correlated their program with Hitler's. Hankow and Canton were in their hands in October 1938; then early in 1939 came the occupation of the large island of Hainan, the Paracels, and the Spratly Island group in the China Sea, and the negotiation of a suspicious non-aggression treaty with Thailand that put Japan in a position to move into French Indo-China at her own pleasure. In September, five days after war began in Europe, she gave Britain and France "friendly advice" to get out of China; and the United States received a broad hint to do likewise. In their desperation the British and French were inclined to throw in the towel, but the American government flatly rejected the "advice" and thus encouraged the British and French to keep at least token forces at their stations in China to bear company with the small American garrisons. In the State Department's opinion the potential threat from Russia in the north would hold Japan in check for the time being. In January 1940 the Trade Treaty of 1911 expired, and the Roosevelt administration was now free to use punitive measures on the Japanese. It had previously applied a "moral embargo" on the sale of aircraft to Japan; and as far back as December 1938 it had started bolstering Nationalist China with direct government loans. Further than these steps, however, it was decided for the time being not to go: a policy of forebearance might help save the Japanese government from falling completely under the control of the army extremists.[3] Actually the Japanese advance showed no tendency to slow down: in March the puppet regime in Nanking was formally constituted, and the following month, as if in anticipation of Hitler's ruthless blow at the Netherlands, the Japanese Foreign Office made its first bold cast for the Dutch East Indies. In pursuit of the "Co-Prosperity Sphere of Greater East Asia," which was now official Japanese doctrine, a sounding was taken at Washington on the American attitude if Japan should attempt to bring these valuable islands under her influence.

The fall of France in June brought in its wake a fresh train of events. First, the Japanese demanded of the British that they evacuate Shanghai and close the Hong Kong and Burma doors to intercourse with China. The British Ambassador, Lord Lothian, advised Secretary Hull of these demands and submitted two alternative proposals for concerted action with the United States: (1) a full embargo by both countries on exports to Japan or the sending of American warships to Singapore to stiffen British resistance; (2) a joint approach to Japan to induce her to make peace in China, to pledge her neutrality in the European war, and to promise to respect the possessions of Occidental powers in the Orient. In return Britain and the United States would give the Japanese financial and economic assistance.[4] But the American government was unready at this time for a policy of resistance, such as the first of these proposals required, and Mr. Hull also proved unwilling to take a hand in bringing peace to China. He had already tried, without success, to get the Japanese Foreign Office to commit itself to respect the territories and possessions of the powers "in all parts of the Pacific Ocean." Mr. Arita, the foreign minister, showed plainly he dared not take this step because it would compromise a fundamental national policy. As for China, it was made clear that in Japan's view Chiang Kai-shek would fall as soon as he was deprived of foreign aid.[5] The American government, on its part, had no intention of recognizing any Chinese government other than Chiang's, yet its support of Chiang at that time could hardly be called substantial. From what amounted to a do-nothing policy on the part of the United States, Japan, it would appear, hoped eventually to benefit. She would force the British and French out, doors would thus be closed to Chiang Kai-shek, and he would fall; and the United States would face an accomplished fact.

Japan won a seeming victory over the British: the latter cut off access to China through Burma, but since the rainy season in that country was now on, there was no hope of sending supplies to China anyway. After three months the British felt confident enough to reopen the road. The submission of France was much more ominous. In September the abject regime at Vichy was cornered into admitting Japan into "protective occupation" of the northern part of French Indo-China; and on the twenty-seventh, coincidental with this move Japan announced she had signed an alliance with Germany and Italy. The latter recognized her leadership in the New Order of East Asia in return for her recognition of theirs in Europe. Furthermore, the three Axis powers undertook "to assist one another with all political, economic and military means when one of the contracting powers is *attacked by a power at present not involved in the European war or in the Sino-Japanese conflict.*"[6] This alliance was an attempt to intimidate the United States. It was negotiated in Berlin between Ribbentrop and the Japanese Ambassador, Saburo Kurusu. Back of Kurusu stood Yosuke Matsuoka, the foreign minister in Tokyo, who was convinced that Germany would win the war and that Japan should act accordingly. If she failed to seize this opportunity, she might lose out in the grand division of the spoils.

Neither Ribbentrop nor Matsuoka appear to have expected the Tripartite Pact to be invoked at once. The alliance was Hitler's answer to the recently concluded deal concerning destroyer-island bases whereby the United States had come out openly in support of Britain in the Atlantic; and the mere hope that the threat of war in the Pacific would distract American attention satisfied the Germans for the time being. Ribbentrop wanted to make Russia a member of the alliance, and in November he sent to Moscow a grandiose plan for carving up the British and French empires among the four powers. The United States was to be ignored. Moscow set conditions, however, which the Germans tabled; and Hitler at this very time, December 1940, ordered the German Army to begin secret preparations for Operation Barbarossa, the great invasion which was designed to crush the Soviet Union before the war with Britain had been won.[7] With this change in their plans the Germans began urging the Japanese to attack the British at Singapore. They argued that Japan could well afford to take the risk because the United States would not come to the aid of Britain in Southeast Asia. In March 1941 Matsuoka, using the Trans-Siberian Railway in both directions, journeyed to Berlin to see for himself. Both Ribbentrop and Hitler plied him with arguments, but Matsuoka declined to be definite. He was not so ready as Hitler to believe that Germany had won; neither were Stalin and Molotov, who cautioned him on his return through Moscow and rewarded him with a nonaggression pact. This pact meant that, if Japan were to strike at all, it must be to the south against the British, Dutch, or American possessions; and it protected Japan from a Russian attack from the north. With this new card to play, Matsuoka returned to Tokyo determined to throw all his influence in favor of an attack on Singapore. But Prince Konoye, the premier, had different ideas. Even while Matsuoka was lending an ear first to Hitler, and then to Stalin, Konoye resolved upon an approach to the United States. Reluctant to tie up with Nazi Germany, he refused to implement the Tripartite Pact and his influence carried the day in Tokyo. In July Matsuoka was forced to resign. Meanwhile the Prince hoped to get from the United States a free hand at least in China. Some valuable concession from the United States in favor of the New Order for Greater East Asia was, from the Japanese viewpoint, absolutely indispensable.[8]

The Tripartite alliance never demonstrated its usefulness to any of the Axis powers. Its value depended upon the meaning of the word "attack," and the Japanese reserved for themselves the sole right to make the definition. For the Nazis the alliance never yielded any results. It did not even slow down the American program of assistance to Britain in the Atlantic. When in December 1941 Japan did attack the United States, she did not inform the Nazis in advance and she did not justify herself under the Tripartite Pact; the act was her own choice and had no reference to the alliance. Nevertheless, she put a certain nuisance value on it during the tortuous negotiations that were to ensue in Washington during the first eleven months of 1941. Mr. Hull tried without success to get her to cancel it. While the Emperor and the premier declined to follow Matsuoka into the arms of Hitler, they evidently thought the Pact had some bargaining power in extracting a settlement with the United States. In this they were wrong. The Pact appears to have had no real influence on American policy, and we are entitled to dismiss it as a bluff that failed to work.

Throughout 1941, between February and December, Japan tried various methods of winning America over to her proposed New Order for Greater East Asia. Her new Ambassador, Admiral Nomura, was a congenial and honest envoy, and with him Secretary Hull carried on a series of lengthy conversations in the privacy of Hull's apartment. The obstacles to an agreement, however, were fundamental: Nomura admitted that whatever he did would probably be vetoed by the military clique in Tokyo. Japan was ready to make peace in China, but only if Chiang Kai-shek agreed to "merge" with the puppet regime in Nanking and to recognize the regime in Manchukuo. To bring this about, pressure on the Nationalist leader by the United States would be necessary, but this the Roosevelt administration was utterly unwilling to do. On the contrary, as early as January it initiated a series of conferences with the British on naval co-operation in the Pacific in the event of war, and in May it put China on the eligible list of Lend-Lease.[9] Then suddenly on July 12 Japan served an ultimatum on the Vichy government to hand over eight air fields and two naval bases in southern Indo-China. Washington had foreknowledge of this move as early as July 2, and the details were in its hands by the fifteenth.[10] In the meantime the United States had occupied Iceland, a move which created a considerable stir in Japan. It justified her, so she held, in her proposed seizure of Indo-China. To the State Department Nomura raised the encirclement issue and listed the reasons for Japanese fears of the United States: the aid being given Chiang Kai-shek, the despatch of supplies to Malaya and Netherlands India, the visits of American squadrons to Australia, and the rumors of American eagerness to acquire air bases in Siberia.[11] But to Matsuoka the Ambassador revealed his own feeling that if southern Indo-China were invaded a settlement with the United States would become impossible. For his part, Matsuoka wanted to follow Germany into the war against Russia, but General Tojo and the Army chiefs decided in favor of Indo-China first. They would at the same time strengthen the Kwantung Army in Manchuria; and when Russia and the British Empire both collapsed, an event which they counted on happening not later than the coming winter, Japan could scoop up both Russia's eastern provinces in the north and Malaya and the Dutch East Indies in the south.

Crisis, and the Resolution at Pearl Harbor

Relations between Japan and the United States now entered the crisis stage. On July 21 Washington was apprised of Vichy's surrender to the Japanese ultimatum. Three days later came the report that Japanese warships were about to enter Camranh Bay, where the French maintained their principal naval base in Indo-China. To Ambassador Nomura, President Roosevelt offered to get a solemn declaration from Britain, China, and the Netherlands neutralizing Indo-China provided that Japan would give up her adventure in that country.[12] On the same day, however, the administration reached a decision to freeze all Japanese funds in the United States—a move which Morgenthau of the Treasury had been urging ever since the preceding December.[13] The freezing order was issued on July 26, but what it meant in terms of a stoppage of exports to Japan of oil and gasoline, bauxite, cotton, and other materials no one was able to say. Export licenses in these commodities could still be granted, and funds released. To a committee of three lawyers, representing respectively the State, the Treasury, and the Justice departments, the President gave this power; and the committee by refusing to grant licenses for the export of oil put into effect a complete embargo on this precious commodity. Some licenses for the export of cotton and food products continued to be granted, but it was the oil embargo that aimed a mortal blow at Japan's power. The British and Dutch governments meanwhile, without knowing exactly how far the Americans intended to go, followed suit as best they could.[14]

As a result of its Indo-China policy the Japanese Army General Staff all but captured control of the government in Tokyo. To Roosevelt's neutralization offer it countered with a proposal for a military standstill agreement with the United States, Japan to remain in Indo-China until Chiang Kai-shek had been overthrown and even thereafter to be accorded a special status in Indo-China.[15] The Army was now ready for eventualities with the United States; and the Navy, though still hopeful of peace, agreed that if war were to come, it should not be postponed beyond December. After that the monsoons would make landing operations impossible. With this end in view the Navy began practicing for the raid on Pearl Harbor. Meanwhile the British Prime Minister, Winston Churchill, was convinced that Japan would soon move against Singapore and that, unless the United States gave help at once, the British would be driven from the Pacific and the Indian Ocean and the life line to Australia be cut. At the Atlantic Conference, August 10, 1941, he urged Roosevelt to warn Japan against further encroachment in the southwestern Pacific on pain of war. The President was unwilling to be as direct as this and, moreover, he wanted to lend a hand to Russia. But the statement which he personally made to Ambassador Nomura only seven days later assuredly contained possibilities. Its final paragraph read:

. . . . this Government now finds it necessary to say to the Government of Japan that if the Japanese Government takes any further steps in pursuance of a policy or program of military domination by force or threat of force of neighboring countries, the Government of the United States will be compelled to take immediately any and all steps which it may deem necessary toward safeguarding the legitimate rights and interests of the United States . . . . and toward insuring the safety and security of the United States.[16]

Unlike Churchill, who feared the worst and who wanted the United States to enter the war at once, the President believed the declaration would restrain Japan for at least thirty days, giving the British a breather; and when he returned to Washington, Roosevelt learned from his Secretary of State that there was one more chance for peace. Prince Konoye had asked for a personal conference.

We need not doubt Konoye's sincere desire for peace. But it was a peace to be based on American recognition of Japan's co-prosperity sphere, which the premier fully supported, and not on a Japanese retrenchment and eventual withdrawal from China, on which the American government was prepared to stand firm. The American position required that Japan withdraw at once from French Indo-China; the Japanese position was that peace must first be made in China on the basis of the puppet government in Nanking and the permanent maintenance of a Japanese army in China, and that only after this had been accomplished would Japan retire from Indo-China. Konoye believed there was a chance of winning over Roosevelt personally and that, if he should fail, he would at least have squared himself with the Japanese people. Roosevelt evinced enthusiasm for the meeting and proposed that it take place about October 15 at Juneau, Alaska. Hull, however, persuaded the President against meeting unless an agreement based on the American position was reached in advance. Consequently the proposed conference never took place.[17]

Where Konoye had failed to make a start, the Tojo government, which succeeded him on October 18, determined on trying. Considering General Tojo's previous convictions—his Indo-China policy, his opposition to Konoye's desire to meet Roosevelt, his intransigence respecting the full program of Japan's co-prosperity sphere—it is remarkable that he should now make any attempt at all to keep the peace with the United States. Admiral Nomura, worn out and utterly discouraged by his long, fruitless negotiations in Washington, had asked for help and had suggested the name of Saburo Kurusu, the former Ambassador to Berlin. Tojo refused Nomura permission to resign, but why he sent Kurusu with authority to make the American government an offer that went further than any previous Japanese offer since the occupation of southern Indo-China, we do not know. Kurusu, however, was given the deadline of November 25 to make a settlement with the United States. Later this was extended to the twenty-ninth, but Kurusu was warned that after that date "things are automatically going to happen." Meanwhile the Japanese government continued to strengthen its forces in Indo-China and dispatched a force to Palau in the Caroline Islands, the nearest point of vantage for an attack on the Dutch East Indies. Long before this the American Intelligence Service had broken the secret Japanese code; messages from Tokyo to its embassy in Washington had been regularly intercepted, and whenever Admiral Nomura asked for an interview, the Secretary of State actually knew what he was going to say before he had said it. Information given by the British and Dutch and by the American consular services in southeast Asia, moreover, kept the administration advised of the latest Japanese troop movements in the Far East. On November 17, the day on which the special envoy, Saburo Kurusu, reached Washington, Hull solemnly warned the cabinet to expect a critical attack. The official American attitude henceforth was governed by a conviction that war would soon begin, that the Japanese would fire the first shot, but that, because American military and naval preparations were not ready for the emergency, the longer it could be held off the better. The negotiations that ensued between November 17 and December, 7, 1941, were from the American standpoint at least, only a play for time.

Kurusu on November 20 offered to withdraw from the southern part of French Indo-China at once and from the remainder ultimately, *provided* the United States (a) would lift the embargo, furnish Japan

with a required quantity of oil, and restore normal trade relations, and
(b) would adopt a hands-off policy toward China. Furthermore, the
Japanese envoy left with Hull a letter which virtually repudiated the
Tripartite alliance. Japan, he declared, was in a position to interpret
her obligation under this pact as she chose. She was not obligated to
become "a collaborator or co-operator in any aggression whatever by
any third Power."[18]

The first official American reaction to these proposals was to offer
Japan a *modus vivendi* calculated to stave off hostilities for three
months (Roosevelt at first advocated six months). During this period
(1) the United States would resume limited trade relations with
Japan, including some shipments of oil; (2) Japan would evacuate
southern Indo-China and limit her forces in northern Indo-China to
twenty-five thousand men; and (3) she would open peace negotiations
with Chiang Kai-shek, the United States to bring the two parties together but to take no part in their conversations. At the same time a
ten-point peace program was prepared which, according to Hull, was
intended to *accompany* the *modus vivendi*. But its terms did not agree
with those of the *modus vivendi*. It demanded that Japan withdraw
all military, naval, air, and police forces *from China* as well as from
Indo-China. And it required Japan to pledge herself not to support
"—militarily, politically, economically—any government or regime in
China other than the National Government of the Republic of China
with capital temporarily at Chungking." On its part the United States
would remove the embargo and negotiate a new trade agreement.[19]

At this point the conduct of Cordell Hull becomes very curious. In
his *Memoirs* he describes Kurusu's proposal as an ultimatum (although it comes reasonably close to the *modus vivendi* the American
government had in mind); and he dismisses Kurusu's implied repudiation of the Tripartite alliance as valueless, an opinion which is hard
to reconcile with the Secretary's previous efforts to induce Japan to
void the alliance. Certainly he could not expect Japan to repudiate the
Pact openly. Stranger still is the fact that he submitted the Japanese
proposals of November 20 and the American *modus vivendi* to the
British, Australian, Dutch, and Chinese envoys, but he did not inform
them of the ten-point note. It will be remembered that Churchill at
the Atlantic Conference had tried to persuade Roosevelt to send Japan
a virtual ultimatum. Being shown only the *modus vivendi*, he frankly
records in his book that he thought it "inadequate," but fearing now
that he would be accused of pushing the United States into war, he
sent the President a guarded reply. Chiang Kai-shek showed no such
restraint. He protested vehemently to Churchill and brought all the

pressure he could muster against the American government's relaxing the embargo on Japan. Owen Lattimore, then Chiang's political adviser, and T. V. Soong, the Generalissimo's brother-in-law who was in Washington, were foremost in this move. As Chiang read the *modus vivendi*, he seems to have feared the United States was getting ready to abandon him.

Only a corner of the veil that hangs over this episode can yet be lifted. Cordell Hull's account of the *modus vivendi* and its fate is singularly unsatisfactory. He makes no attempt to explain his original intention to submit simultaneously to the Japanese two documents that contradicted each other. It is not clear that the President understood this intention, and apparently General Marshall, like Churchill, did not even know of the existence of the ten-point note. Churchill, Roosevelt, Marshall, and Admiral Stark wanted hostilities postponed, and they were all agreed that the embargo was driving Japan into war. Marshall had set the figure of twenty-five thousand men which the Japanese were to be allowed in northern Indo-China so as to enable Japan to accept the *modus vivendi*. Probably for the opposite reason the Chinese insisted that the number be reduced to five thousand, and they passionately opposed granting any economic relief whatsoever to Japan. Lattimore from Chungking tried to reach the President direct through his secretary, Lauchlin Currie; Dr. Hu Shih, the Chinese Ambassador, interviewed Hull; while T. V. Soong denounced the *modus vivendi* to Stimson, the Secretary of War, who was an all-out embargo advocate. Soong also worked on other pro-Chinese groups in and out of the government in Washington.

Apparently it was Chinese pressure that defeated the *modus vivendi*, though the British too showed themselves opposed to it. Secretary Hull frankly admitted the weight of Chinese and British opposition and the dangers of unfavorable publicity in the United States against the *modus vivendi*, and the President agreed with him. Accordingly the *modus vivendi* was pigeonholed, and the Japanese envoys on November 26 received only the ten-point program. Kurusu was surprised and depressed. He had expected to conclude a *modus vivendi*, and after receiving the ten-point note he again asked Hull whether the American government was not interested in a *modus vivendi*. An abrupt negative was the response.

Thus all doors to compromise were closed. The ten-point note, as Kurusu declared to Hull, "meant the end." Whether the Japanese government would have agreed to receive it along with the *modus vivendi* may be doubted, but it was not given the chance. The stumbling block was China. Kurusu had come not merely to get a truce, but also to persuade the United States to change its attitude toward that country. In this respect he was up against odds that he did not grasp. If the United States would retreat from its traditional support of Nationalist China and give Japan a free hand in that country, Japan would, so far as words were concerned, give up her ambitions for the mastery of Greater East Asia. But we must remember how far Nippon, having gone since 1931 from success to success, had identified her national fortunes with the Co-Prosperity Sphere of Greater East Asia. Kurusu's mission was a peace mission, but at most Japan expected to gain from it a breathing spell. She had to have relief from the embargo; the alternative was war. Both sides were playing for time. Marshall and Stark for the United States were conscious of weakness and prophetic of military disasters if war came quickly. Since Japan could get no relief short of a surrender of her fundamental position, she chose war. Her government was neither able nor willing to compromise itself and yield the leadership in the Far East again to the United States and China as it had in 1922.[20]

All sides—Japanese, American, British, Australian, Chinese— now expected war. The Tojo government, we recall, had given Kurusu until the twenty-ninth to come to an agreement. But pursuant to its determination to make war otherwise, it secretly dispatched on the twenty-fifth the naval force and carrier fleet on the mission against Pearl Harbor. The expedition, of course, was subject to recall should a settlement arrive from Washington. The American ten-point note was not regarded as a settlement either in Tokyo or in Washington. On November 29 Secretary Hull informed Lord Halifax that "the diplomatic part in our relations with Japan is now virtually over"; and on the same day he warned the President to expect an imminent attack. On December 1 an Imperial conference in Tokyo made the final decision. But Japan kept her military secrets well. The British and Americans continued to believe that the first blow would fall on British or Dutch possessions. And until the actual blow at Pearl Harbor, no one in authority was able to say what the United States would do. At the Atlantic Conference in the preceding August, Roosevelt had said to Churchill: "I may never declare war; I may make war. If I were to ask Congress to declare war they might argue about it for three months." But on November 30, when Lord Halifax asked what action the United States would take if the Japanese invaded the Kra Isthmus, which was part of the territory of Thai, the Secretary of State could give no reply.[21] The administration knew the meaning of such a move, but the only decision the President had reached down to this point was the tentative one to send a special message to Congress asking authority to use force against Japan. The administration had exhausted its constitutional prerogatives. The Japanese strategic choice of striking first at American territory, rather than British or Dutch, saved it from what it had come to regard as its awful dilemma.

The Pearl Harbor attack took the American government completely by surprise. But decoding delays in the Japanese embassy kept the two envoys from delivering the final note from Tokyo in advance of the report of the attack as planned. Hull had the news from the President himself at 2:05 P.M.; Kurusu and Nomura entered his chamber at 2:20 P.M. In the excitement of the moment it was forgotten that Roosevelt himself had dispatched a message the night before addressed to the Emperor personally. The President's message reverted to the *modus vivendi* which Hull and others had smothered. It said not a word about China. It only asked that Japan withdraw her forces from Indo-China and agree to neutralize that country. Such an undertaking, read the message, "would result in the assurance of peace throughout the whole of the South Pacific area."[22] We do not know what prompted this last-minute intervention of the President. It was, of course, too late.

The final note from Tokyo which Nomura and Kurusu handed to Secretary Hull on the afternoon of December 7, the contents of which the Secretary already knew, was an angry retort to the American ten-point note of November 26. It was a bitter accusation leveled at the United States for conspiring with Great Britain and other powers to defeat Japan's efforts "toward the establishment of peace through the creation of a new order in East Asia . . . ." Japan insisted that she was the proper stabilizing power in the Far East. By conspiring with the Chiang Kai-shek regime the American government was indicted for trying to keep up the war in China and strengthen its own dominant position in the Far East. The repressed bitterness and feeling of being thwarted harbored for years in the Japanese breast broke forth in this torrent of official wrath. Aroused by the extraordinary news that he had just received and clinging to the formulas which he had forever been preaching, Hull burst forth in unrestrained indignation. But a dispassionate view of the origins of the war with Japan, of even the immediate origins, will accept neither Hull's outburst nor Roosevelt's subsequent charge of treachery and deception. It will take into consideration the multiple factors that had been accumulating since 1906, when American diplomacy had begun to play Japan off against Russia, and especially since 1922, when Japan unwillingly agreed to the paper peace system of the Washington treaties. These factors, coupled with the unfortunate immigration exclusion policy of the United States, bred in the Japanese mind a psychology of frustration.[23]

II

The Holocaust
of 1939-1945

Finance in the Aftermath of World War I

AMERICAN statesmanship emerged from the First World War with a relish for world leadership and with an instrument for getting it—the League of Nations. But the ambition died quickly. Neither did the war teach any lessons. In Europe Britain and France again had the balance of power firmly in their grip, and American eyes could feel easy when wearing the glasses of prewar days. Only in the Pacific had the power relationship definitely shifted—Japan had put the United States on its guard. In 1921 the American government responded aggressively by organizing a collective system for that region and edging its rival there into membership in it.

The American position in relation to Europe was not the duplication of 1914 that it superficially appeared to be, however. Financially it was the reverse; the United States was now a gigantic creditor, in contrast to its earlier and historic status of debtor to Europe. The Allied Powers had a problem in redeeming the seven billion dollars in bonds they had given in payment for American supplies during the war. In addition Europe needed capital for reconstruction; several major governments on the Continent were willing to offer 7 per cent or more. Their bank accounts swollen by an unexcelled wave of prosperity during the 1920's, American investors continued to meet this demand; additional billions in private capital were poured into Europe, and into Latin America, Australia, and Asia as well. The decade witnessed one of the greatest speculations in foreign and domestic securities that the world had ever seen.

Realistically the financial relations of debtor and creditor were the same, regardless whether the loan came from the private investor or from the United States government. The latter had furnished the capital to its European allies during the eighteen months in which it was at war; in addition it supplied three billions after the war, which were spent for reconstruction. The combined sums, amounting to about ten billion gold dollars, constituted the so-called "war debts," the greatest share of which had gone for munitions and supplies purchased in America. Over the whole lending period from 1915 to 1929 the American private investor more than matched the capital loaned by his government. A portion of this was reflected in exports from the United States, all of it loaned while the Allies were at war, and the remainder was spent on the rebuilding of industry in Europe itself. The problem that baffled every European country was how to find the dollars necessary to meet the mounting interest and amortization payments on its American debts. The "war debts" became a political issue; the private debts did not. The former fanned popular hatred on both sides of the ocean; like Calvin Coolidge, the average American saw only the dollar sign and shrugged his shoulders over the difficult problem of international payments; the average European, burdened with taxes and an inflated currency, grumbled bitterly about "Uncle Shylock."

Great Britain, followed by the Continental debtors, made regular payments in gold under a series of funding agreements negotiated early in the 1920's. Far from working a cure, however, this form of payment only aggravated the problem; it stimulated the fever in this country for speculation in foreign bonds. Blindly the United States refused to follow the rules prescribed for a good creditor; thrice during the 1920's it built its tariff walls higher, thus hampering and eventually destroying the only sound means of international payment in the form of goods and services. By 1929, the financial relationship had become so unbalanced as to make disaster a certainty; more than twenty-one billion dollars were owing. The colossal Smoot-Hawley tariff was the last straw; it brought retaliation in Europe, the speculative bubble burst in October, and debt payments from abroad, on both the private obligations and the "war debts," tapered off to almost nothing. Only the sour looks and the impulse to call names were left. In 1934 a measure useful only as an exhibition of the spleen of its authors issued from Congress—the Johnson Act, which prohibited private citizens from lending money to governments which had defaulted on their "war debts." Except as an expression of spite against the former allies of the United States, the act was innocent of meaning. It took no account of the widespread default of other nations, in South America for example, and of course it had no cure for the serious economic disease which had infected the entire world.

Fundamentally the altered financial position of the United States at the close of the war was symptomatic of the immense power that the country was capable of wielding. But unfortunately the attitude on the war debts was characteristic of the general failure of the American public to appraise the responsibilities the United States would ultimately be obliged to assume toward pressing problems of peace and order in the world. In 1918 the United States had successfully redressed the balance of power against German threats of world domination; that had been its immediate war aim, but its larger purpose had been to introduce a new order in the world based on a collective interest in keeping the peace, by force if necessary. It was elementary with the men of 1918 that success in this effort rested on the continued solidarity of the three powers that had won the war, Britain, France, and the United States. The makers of the League Covenant were conscious of acting in the interests of American security. That was the lesson which their successors so hastily repudiated. Appearances after 1918 were deceiving; the victory was so crushing that the German menace seemed to have been dispelled for good. Republican leaders of the 1920's felt entirely safe in retreating into the country's traditional isolation, having no doubt of the British and French ability to control the Continent. Toward Soviet Russia they indulged in an attitude of studied hostility. So long as Germany remained weak and Central Europe disintegrated, they had little incentive for behaving otherwise.

It is not to be assumed, however, that the United States was satisfied with the manner in which Britain and France managed the League and dominated the Continent. Gratuitous advice flowed continuously from an American public much more sensitive to European conditions than in 1914. In general the criticism focused on the British and, especially, the French disposition to maintain the status quo at the expense of the ideals to which the Allies had pledged themselves during the war. Having shaken off the responsibility for assisting in world reform, American opinion felt free to pass lofty moral judgments on the selfishness of its former associates. The issue which attracted particular comment was disarmament. Disarmament was accepted almost universally in the United States as the true panacea against war. Herbert Hoover, a president especially zealous in behalf of this cause, openly complained of the seeming hypocrisy of nations that spent large sums on armaments and yet shrank from meeting their debts. But Hoover had not the slightest interest in checking the wave of speculation in foreign securities that crested during his administration. Far from shedding light on the realities of international problems, Hoover only contributed to the popular bewilderment and ill-will. He put no check on the widespread promotion of the sale of dubious foreign securities; on the contrary, he did all he could to push the export of American goods, payment for which was tendered from the proceeds of the bond sales in America.

Nor was there the simple connection between the French outlay on armaments and the capacity to pay war debts that Hoover encouraged his countrymen to believe. Armaments represented an investment in terms of francs on goods and labor produced and consumed in France; they created no problem in foreign exchange. Americans could not expect the French to be impressed with the argument against armaments as a cause of war. Universal service and a standing army were the traditional instruments of security for a country facing more populous rivals across artificial frontiers. If the French were at fault, the Americans were equally so. Isolation, based on geography and the existing balance of power, was the traditional American method. Plainly each nation forsook the proposed new order in favor of tested tradition, and the United States was the first one to do so.

Outlawing War: The Kellogg Pact

Recrimination over war debts and disarmament, mutual chiefly between France and the United States, was a token of the forces which kept the world disunited. Sharp trade rivalry and ill feeling over the size of their respective navies kept the British and Americans apart in much the same manner. Britain and France, of course, kept the League going, although their domination of it was greatly to the American distaste; they even secured the temporary reconciliation of Germany, and for a few brief years the League functioned as a true collective system. During this period even the United States showed considerable enthusiasm for it through the support it gave to the several nonpolitical activities conducted by the Geneva organization. A small but influential minority continued to hold up the League before the American people; and from an attitude in 1922 so timid that it would not even acknowledge formal communications from the Secretariat, the Department of State by 1930 acquired enough confidence to station official "observers" in Geneva. But efforts to explore possible roads back to the program of 1918 had to be pursued most cautiously. The philosophy of isolationism held the people spellbound. Even such modest attempts at international cooperation as a movement to join the World Court met with defeat.

The closest the United States came to the collective system was in

1928, when it seized the initiative in negotiating at Paris an "anti-war pact," which most of the other nations of the world agreed to. This was the famed Kellogg Pact, which really originated with Professor James T. Shotwell of Columbia University. The central meaning of the pact was the pledge to "renounce war as an instrument of national policy" and to settle disputes only by pacific means. Professor Shotwell had in mind the setting up of a minimum international obligation to which all nations, members of the League or not, could subscribe. With this as a point of departure, he felt, the United States could officially declare itself toward a nation that violated its pledge.

The Kellogg Pact caught the imagination of the American public and even divided the isolationists concerning its merits. William E. Borah displayed the greatest enthusiasm for the treaty and piloted it through the Senate without a single reservation. He felt certain the moral obligation was enough: no government, having given its plighted word to settle the dispute by pacific means, would dare now to resort to force. It would not dare defy the organized moral sentiment of mankind. This opinion appears to have reflected the general popular view which wheeled the treaty through the Senate with almost a unanimous vote. It crystallized the conception of an "aggressor nation" as one which refused to come into conference or otherwise settle its quarrel peacefully. "Here is a method," said Borah, " . . . . by which to test any government which might be acting not in good faith under the treaty, and to place it in a position before the world where it would be practically impossible to defend its course or conduct."[1] The distinction in fact was one inherent in the League method; the Kellogg Pact simply underscored it.

By indirection the Kellogg Pact dealt a heavy blow at American isolationism. It accustomed the public to thinking in terms of the difference between the aggressor and his victim and to expecting the government to do likewise. Like Woodrow Wilson, Borah really believed that the appeal to "a decent respect to the opinions of mankind" would be enough to stay any aggressor. He lived to learn otherwise, but not to alter his view against implementing the pact. Shrewder men than he saw that if the pact were to mean anything, it had to be accompanied at least by consultation among the powers in case any state repudiated it. Practical politics kept from the text of the treaty any hint that it created an obligation to consult; the United States was free to act or not to act under it, just as it had been before. Agitation during the ensuing four years in favor of a formal consultative pact to supplement the Kellogg treaty reached such proportions that it got the endorsement of both political parties in the presidential campaign of 1932. Once in office, however, the Roosevelt administration thought it "good politics" to bury the proposal.

The moral sanction was put into practice through the doctrine of nonrecognition which the United States had formerly utilized against undesirable governments in Latin America. The Japanese puppet state of Manchukuo, formally constituted in 1932, was the leading object of this sanction. The precedent was important in defining an attitude which the American government reaffirmed consistently in subsequent years. Italy and Germany were in their turn marked with the same brand of aggression as Japan; and however loath they were to try more forceful measures, the American people readily endorsed their government's refusal to recognize the repeated acts of lawlessness for which the names of Hitler and Mussolini soon were to become bywords.

Hitler's Successes

There were three great areas of conflict during the 1930's, each with a background in the previous World War. The one centering in eastern Asia has already been discussed in connection with its relationship to American security. The other two were in the Mediterranean and in Central Europe, respectively. Under Mussolini Italy revived her hope of aggrandizement in the Mediterranean, which had been dashed in 1918. The Italian dictator made no secret of his ambition to convert the Middle Sea into an Italian lake: he not only proclaimed it openly, but he took the steps necessary to bring it about. In 1935 he invaded and subjugated Ethiopia, thus creating an Italian colony able to threaten Egypt from the rear and to challenge the British control of the route through the Red Sea. His next move was to intervene in Spain in 1936; civil strife in that country gave the opportunity to help one party, the Fascists, on such a scale that Spain would become a virtual puppet of Italy. Mussolini in fact all but took over the war in Spain, with some help from Germany; but though his aid probably was decisive he nevertheless failed to become the master of Spain. He did not even compel General Franco, the man who had profited from his assistance, to enter a treaty of alliance. The outcome of this adventure established one point: alone and dissociated from other scenes of conflict, Italy was incapable of wresting the Mediterranean from the British and French, who had shared its control for the period of a century.

The third and by far the most ominous threat of all came from

Germany. Under Hitler the Nazis perfected the blueprints for world domination drawn by the Pan-Germans of the previous generation: the preparation of the entire German population for war; the creation of a Great Germany in the heart of Europe, armed with the manpower, the material resources, and the strategic positions which would give it command of the Continent and the use of air power as a means of nullifying the natural advantages possessed by British sea power. Once he achieved supremacy in the air, Hitler could undermine Britain's independence, perhaps even conquer her, and reduce her to the position of a German province in fact if not in name. That would give him the master key to world power that he so avidly desired.

Hitler's tactics show that he expected to succeed by intimidation, by exploiting the disunity among the former Allies, by playing on their fears of war, and by making specious appeals to their consciences concerning the mistakes of the Versailles Treaty. The complete regimentation of Germany for war on a scale unapproached in any other country was to bring victory without actually striking a blow. Germany's enemies would be so confused, divided, and helpless that they would not dare call a halt. The regime was completely unaffected by considerations of morality or good faith. If a pledge not to attack or a proffer of an alliance could be used to deceive or distract another country even temporarily, it was freely given only to be broken on the instant that it ceased to serve the interests of the German Reich. No power was more prolific in the making (and breaking) of nonaggression pacts with its neighbors than was Germany.

The complete lack of solidarity among Great Britain, France, and the United States and the isolation of Soviet Russia were the fundamental factors in Hitler's successes. Of the three Western countries the French alone identified the security of Germany's neighbors to the east with their own; they had binding alliances with Czechoslovakia, Poland, and Rumania. Nevertheless, the French were torn among themselves and pitifully anxious for peace. They realized too well that without at least British support, they could not grapple successfully with Nazi Germany. By building the Maginot Line of fortifications along their northern frontier they showed they had no intention of pursuing an aggressive policy toward Germany.

Munich, and the American Re-entry into European Affairs

In England the situation was even more doubtful. Hitler was disliked there unanimously, but the Treaty of Versailles was unpopular too. To make excuses for the Nazis was for a while almost an act of conscience. Furthermore, there was an important section of British opinion that openly preached appeasement. The dominant wing of the Conservative Party feared the spread of Russian Communism, and it tended to echo the Nazis' loud denunciations of the Soviet Union. Germany was regarded as a bulwark against Communist pressure from the east. Under Neville Chamberlain the British government followed this line of policy to the very brink of disaster. It had never been willing to join the French in guaranteeing the integrity of Germany's eastern neighbors, in this respect being scarcely less isolationist than the United States. Many British and some Americans openly expressed the opinion that Germany ought to become the master of the European Continent, that National Socialism was the only bulwark against Communism, and that Germany alone had the capacity to maintain the peace. The Nazi conception of world empire, frankly discussed in Hitler's *Mein Kampf* and popularized on countless maps circulated throughout Germany, was almost everywhere taken with a grain of salt. If the Germans were granted a free hand in eastern Europe, so it was assumed, they would leave the rest of the world alone. These beliefs the Chamberlain government acted upon through the great crisis at Munich in September 1938. Hitler was given an advance signal that he might annex Austria, which he did in March, following this with the annexation of the Sudetenland of Czechoslovakia. Both of these steps were taken on the plea of the common German nationality of the people of these regions. What was overlooked was the fact that Austria and the Sudetenland were strategically the heartland of Europe; once they were under his thumb, Hitler could make short shrift of Poland and the countries of the Danube.

It was too late at Munich to retrieve the ground lost during the previous years. Czechoslovakia had been weakened beyond repair and the most strategic and industrially valuable territory in Europe delivered into German hands. With it went the balance of power and the traditional leadership which Britain had exercised over European affairs. There was a definite war crisis; encouraged by past successes and the wide margin of his military superiority, Hitler pushed his demands beyond the limit of the original bargain. In pursuing the dangerous policy of appeasement the British had failed to attend to their own rearmament. German air power, the new and terrifying factor in military affairs, had more than a fifty per cent advantage over the Royal Air Force. This factor, plus the shudder at the prospect of another terrible war that ran through two nations that had not forgotten their sacrifices in the last, decided the issue. Hitler now had the lead; an empty promise to commit no more aggressions was all that he gave in exchange.

The Munich surrender was determined by the attitude of Great Britain. France was a follower, pathetically relieved that British diplomacy had saved her the embarrassments of her treaty obligations to Czechoslovakia. The crisis marked the re-entry of the United States into European affairs. The gravity of that crisis was universally recognized, and it drove every other thought from the American mind. President Roosevelt sent two messages in quick succession to Hitler, and he lined up Mussolini on the side of compromise. The issue was really not one of making a stand against the German; the Czechs alone showed confidence in their defenses, and all they needed was solid support from the Western Powers. But the British government had already warned them not to expect its help, and American diplomacy took the same line. Hitler was told he would get what he wanted if only he would be patient. But he did not have long to wait: his timetable called for Czech evacuation of the Sudetenland by October; two days previously the Allies formally signified their accord, and the Czechs were granted a delay of ten days in which to complete their withdrawal. It was an ominous exhibition of the weakness of the Western Powers, a final proof of Britain's inability to hold the balance, and a tempting invitation to Hitler and his Axis partners to still greater boldness in the future.

Aims of the Axis

Germany and Japan had had an understanding since November 1936, in which Italy joined one year later. They declared they were making common cause against Communism, and thus gave the elements of appeasement in the Western democracies a ready-made reason for justifying themselves. Russia was virtually an exile from European diplomacy during these years, in sharp contrast to her traditional role of leader of the Slavic peoples. She was ignored at Munich, and she kept a close silence. The full price of this folly had yet to be revealed; desperate last-minute efforts in the summer of 1939 to persuade her to enter a "Stop Hitler" partnership led by Britain resulted in failure.[2]

The Rome-Berlin-Tokyo Axis, as the three Fascist powers were now coming to be called, at first advertised itself as Anti-Communist. Actually it was a loose combination of powers which had a common interest in conquest. Japan hoped to make herself the mistress of Greater East Asia, an ambition which she lost no time in proclaiming once the Western Powers had made their fatal surrender at Munich.[3] Italy dreamed of a new Roman Empire in the Mediterranean, and she too became bolder after Munich. Germany expected to be lord of them all at the end, but found it very convenient to utilize the services of her fellow thieves until she had completed the downfall of Britain and France in the West. The collective aim of the Axis was to bring about a complete revolution in world power, to terrorize or to force the British and the French to give up the control of the vital trade routes on the high seas, and ultimately to isolate the United States and force it back to the limits of its own continental domain. To advance this ambition, the Axis, and especially the Germans, displayed an astounding ingenuity in exploiting feelings of jealousy and distrust among the peoples of the Western Powers toward one another; in capitalizing the discontent to be found in every Western country during the years of a harrowing economic depression; in playing upon the pathetic longing for peace and the spirit of disillusionment that proved the masters of popular feeling in Britain, France, and the United States; and in losing no opportunity to impress the world with German unity and military might.

A catalogue of Nazi activities to this end would exceed the scope of this volume. We have mentioned the Western fear of Communism; we might also expand upon the latent mistrust of the British Empire prevalent among certain elements in the United States, especially in the Middle West, and the easy disposition to accept the Fascist argument that the "have-not nations" ought to have a new deal. Where this argument struck home in the United States it invariably implied sacrifices by Britain and France, the cession of colonies for example. Rarely if ever did it take into consideration the possible weakening of the American position in the Western Hemisphere. Only belatedly did the American public awaken to the fact that the Axis was intriguing for advantage in South America.

Munich flashed a definite warning. It was that Great Britain had lost control, that the peace of Europe henceforth lay in Hitler's hands. Having realized their mistake, the British set doggedly to work to repair the disaster. They waited till Hitler closed in on the remainder of Czechoslovakia, a feat easily accomplished in March 1939. With the Czechs in his pocket, the German dictator at once turned his fury on the Poles. This time the British countered by handing Poland a blank check: she could resist the Germans on any point she chose and get British support.

The crucial question, however, was the attitude of Russia. The British sent an eleventh-hour delegation to conciliate the Soviet dictator. It was too late. For reasons of his own Stalin threw in his lot with the Nazis. On August 23, 1939, the Nazi Foreign Minister, von Ribbentrop, performed the crowning act of German diplomacy; he signed a virtual partnership with Soviet Russia, which led to the partition of Poland. Hitler had succeeded in repeating the achievement of Napoleon in 1807; a Russo-German pact meant that Europe was at the mercy of these two powers and Hitler was free to ignore the British and French in the West. Britain and France were left with the weak Polish alliance as their very dubious asset. So overpowering were the odds against them that Hitler appears to have taken another Munich surrender as a foregone conclusion. Instead the Allies stood by their agreement: the Germans attacked Poland on the first of September, and after a vain gesture at persuading them to withdraw their troops the British and the French launched into war.[4]

In the Grip of Isolationism

Through this period of increasing danger the American government had remained no passive spectator. From the reports of its agents in Europe it pieced together an accurate blueprint of Axis plans, and it did its best to shape American policy to thwart them. One of the first reports came from George S. Messersmith, the consul-general in Berlin, in June 1933. The United States, he wrote,

must be exceedingly careful in its dealings with Germany as long as the existing [Nazi] government was in power, as that Government had no spokesman who could readily be depended upon and those who held the highest positions were "capable of actions which really outlaw them from ordinary intercourse." He reported that some of the men who were running the German Government were "psychopathic cases"; that others were in a state of exaltation and in a frame of mind that knew no reason . . . . that the leaders of Germany had no desire for peace unless it was a peace in complete compliance with German ambitions; that Hitler and his assocates really wanted peace for the moment, but only to have a chance to prepare for the use of force if it were found essential.[5]

Mr. Messersmith's opinion was fully shared by other American observers in Germany. Douglas Miller, the commercial attaché, declared:

The real emotional drive behind the Nazi program was not so much love of their own country as dislike of other countries. The Nazis would never be content in merely promoting the welfare of the German people; they desired to be feared and envied by foreigners and "to wipe out the memory of 1918 by inflicting humiliations in particular upon the French, the Poles, the Czechs and anybody else they can get their hands on."

From the military attaché in Berlin in May 1934 came a report that foreshadowed the German-Japanese alliance:

Evidence was accumulating which tended "to show the existence of unusually close and friendly relations between Germany and Japan even to the extent of a possible secret alliance." This report stated further that these friendly relations between the two countries were dependent entirely upon self-interest; that the Germans usually expressed themselves to the effect that "we are encouraging . . . . relations with Japan because it is to our advantage to do so but we must never forget that we are white people and they are not."

A few months later a dispatch arrived from Ambassador Grew in Tokyo discussing similar symptoms among the Japanese. He said:

The aim of certain elements in the Army and Navy, the patriotic societies, and the intense nationalists throughout the country was "to obtain trade control and eventually predominant political influence in China, the Philippines, the Straits Settlements, Siam and the Dutch East Indies, the Maritime Provinces and Vladivostok, one step at a time, as in Korea and Manchuria, pausing intermittently to consolidate and then continuing as soon as the intervening obstacles can be overcome by diplomacy or force."

And, commencing in September 1934, reports flowed in from Ambassador Long in Rome outlining the shape of things to come according to the Italians:

The entire population, both military and civilian, was in complete accord with Mussolini's policies; that the press in every issue gave expression of the national determination to proceed to war and not to tolerate interference from any source. There was every indication of a carefully prepared, well-calculated, "hard, cold and cruel" prosecution of pre-conceived plans by the use of an army and navy which were almost fanatic in their idolatry of and devotion to one man and which were worked up to an editorial pitch unique in modern times. Italy must either be defeated "now" and prevented from realizing its ambitions in East Africa, "or trouble will continue on through for a generation as an additional irritation to European politics and an additional menace to world peace."

Faced with these ominous reports, the administration in Washington was long convinced that the United States should throw its weight into the scale against the aggressors. It especially wanted legislation from Congress that would enable the President to co-operate with other nations in a general arms embargo. Such a measure would help restore the United States to the position of leadership desired in 1919, 1928, and 1931. Secretary Hull promised the Senate Foreign Relations Committee that the power contemplated in a bill before them would be used with the utmost caution and that effective guaranties of co-operation would be required from other governments so as to avoid leaving the United States in an exposed position. The Committee, however, stultified the whole measure by introducing an amendment requiring that any embargo be applied to all belligerents alike. The amendment was exactly contrary to the most rudimentary principles of collective security, and the administration had no choice but to drop its attempt.

The dominant sentiment in the United States was a militant type of isolationism which crystallized about the time that Hitler invaded the Rhineland. Its battle cry was the slogan "Keep out of war!" and Congress, not the President, was entrusted with the task. A group of younger Senators, mostly representing the Middle West, seized the initiative; led by Gerald P. Nye of North Dakota, they got the Senate to appoint a Munitions Investigating Committee in 1934. The move was immensely popular; it was thoroughly in line with the existing bitterness toward bankers and industrialists, who were considered responsible for the depression. The Munitions Committee acted in accordance with certain preconceptions, and it accumulated a mass of circumstantial evidence to prove that bankers and munitions makers had driven the United States into war in 1917. It passed lightly over the basic factors of American participation, and pictured the people as victims of British propaganda and profit-seeking financiers and industrialists. Its report was a perfect reflection of the cynicism and unbelief characteristic of the depression years, and it blamed everybody but the Germans for the war. Even the German submarine campaign came in for a word of approval.[6]

The Munitions Committee overdid itself and aroused considerable criticism. Nevertheless, the pattern of 1917 became a fixture in the American mind. There was an all but unanimous belief in the "war-mongering" influence of private business. The real purpose of the war in 1917 was forgotten—the need for breaking Germany's chances of victory—and the disappointments and futility of that struggle alone were remembered. The feeling was especially intense in the Middle West, one of the sections of the country most hard-hit during the depression; furthermore, this section, it will be recalled, had never accepted wholeheartedly the fear of German domination that ruled the East. The traditions of the Middle West were isolationist and anti-British; in so far as the large German communities were concerned, they were also pro-German. But the Middle West also harbored a hatred of Eastern financiers and industrialists, whom it accused of having dragged the country into war in 1917. If these men could be kept by law from repeating in the next war what they had done in the last, the country would be saved from involvement.

The Neutrality Act of 1935 was the fruit of this mood. Fresh aggressions by the dictators in 1936 and 1937 brought new legislation; but the original determination to control American business remained unchanged. The principal features of these acts were as follows: (1) an automatic embargo on the export of arms and munitions to nations at war; (2) a like embargo on the extension of private loans to belligerents; (3) a prohibition against American ships entering the ports of belligerents or even navigating sections of the high seas which the President should define as war zones; (4) a prohibition against American citizens taking passage on ships of belligerents. Even the Nye committee quailed at the prospect of prohibiting *all* trade with belligerents, for food and raw materials were too important in the American economy to suffer a sudden embargo. Nevertheless, through a "cash and carry" plan, it was thought that the United States would escape the consequences of continuing the general trade. If the belligerents bought the goods before leaving American shores, and carried them across the Atlantic at their own risk, there would be neither financial loss to the United States nor food for controversy with a belligerent. The theory of the law was that involvement in European wars had arisen in the past from violations of American neutral rights and that the same pattern would reappear in the next war. Therefore the isolationists who followed Nye would give up neutral rights. This was too much for the old-fashioned isolationists, like Hiram Johnson, and at their instance a provision was inserted to the effect that the United States gave up none of its rights on the high seas. It was a case of having one's cake and eating it too.

The weakness of this legislation lay in the fact that it was based on a fallacy. The arms trade was not the cause of the German submarine campaign in the First World War, and the Germans did not wait until the arms embargo was repealed in 1939 before commencing submarine operations in the next; neither were the private loans to the Allies in 1914–16 a cause of American entry in 1917. Even the theory that neutral rights were the root cause, either then or in 1812, was open to serious doubt. But the crowning fallacy of the neutrality laws lay in the supposition that there was no connection between the security of the United States and the balance of power in Europe. It took the catastrophe in France in 1940 to stultify this theory.

The isolationists labored under the illusion that they could use the law-making power to project a policy that would fit a certain imaginary pattern of the future. What they succeeded in doing was to add to the general uncertainty and bewilderment and to sap the influence of the United States abroad. The arms-embargo section of the Neutrality Law was particularly vicious, a fact which became evident after Munich. Germany then was not only far ahead in the armaments race; she had potential supremacy in the air, and she held the Continent's richest industrial storehouse in her grasp. Britain and France were at a hopeless disadvantage. Germany's reputation for sudden, treacherous attack was firmly established, and Hitler's ambitions were excited by his great triumph of September. The statutory provision for an arms embargo by the United States was a standing invitation to him to commit further outrages. It was neutrality in reverse inasmuch as it practically insured in advance a British and French defeat.

Roosevelt and a Forward Foreign Policy

President Roosevelt correctly gauged the danger after Munich. It was then that he successfully instituted a forward foreign policy. In April 1939, when Hitler had given further proof of his depravity by liquidating the Czech Republic, the President formally proposed the repeal of the arms embargo. Party politics, pacifism, isolationist stupidity, and the covert desire of several of the leading isolationists to see Germany become the master of Europe stood in his way, however.[7] The Republicans as a body refused to be budged. Senator Borah, with magnificent self-assurance, declared in July that his own private information was better than the State Department's and that there would be no war in 1939. Knowing the real situation, the President used his best efforts to persuade Congress to prolong its session into the summer for the express purpose of repealing the arms embargo. It was understood that a majority of the Republicans would vote for repeal, but only if a war actually broke out. Mr. Roosevelt stated to them his conviction that further delay on the part of Congress would hasten Hitler's decision to attack.

Meanwhile there were several weak spots in the isolationist fort which the administration had succeeded in breaching. Few of the isolationists cared to cross swords on the question of recognizing the

German, Italian, and Japanese despoilment of other countries. Mussolini and the Mikado continued to be given the cold shoulder so far as their foreign conquests were concerned. When Hitler marched into Austria, ostensibly with Austrian consent, the American government could do naught but close its Vienna legation. But when the Nazis violated the body of Czechoslovakia, the case was different. The Czech minister in Washington defied the German order to turn over his legation, and he was given protection and continued recognition as the representative of an independent state. The Nazis got the same kind of reception over their persecution of the Jews. One of the worst horrors in the history of the regime occurred in November 1938, about six weeks after Munich; it was a pogrom of unexampled severity, and it brought expressions of indignation and loathing from all over the United States. The President himself declared he "could scarcely believe that such things could occur in a twentieth century civilization." The criticism struck home: the German chargé in Washington demanded an apology for the language used by the fiery Secretary of the Interior, Harold Ickes; but the State Department not only refused to receive the protest but made counter-complaints against the violent anti-American language of Nazi officials. The American Ambassador was called home to report, and from that time forward the relations of the United States and Germany continued in a state of suspended hostility. The moral sanction anticipated by the Kellogg Pact, was fully at work; and so completely did the acts of the administration in this respect square with the opinions of the American public that it took a bold person to utter a criticism of the government's policy.

Completely at variance with the policy laid down by the Neutrality Acts was the program of naval expansion, which the termination of the naval treaties in 1936 had greatly accelerated. Obviously the United States was building chiefly against Japan. Obviously, too, American naval strategy required action parallel with the British. This became marked in the western Pacific by 1938, after the Japanese attack on China. Munich made the administration fearful for British security in the Atlantic; consequently in December it announced its determination to re-establish a permanent Atlantic squadron, and early in 1939 the entire Pacific fleet was temporarily transferred to the Atlantic for maneuvers. In spite of isolationist efforts to bait the administration with charges of a British alliance, Congress fully supported the program. Indeed a declaration of basic naval principles drawn up by Chairman Vinson of the House Naval Affairs Committee to accompany the Naval Bill of March 1938 gave

THE HOLOCAUST OF 1939-1945

the direct lie to the theory of inaction. The Navy, declared the bill, should be of sufficient strength to guarantee the national security not for aggression but to afford protection to the coast line "in both oceans at one and the same time"; to protect outlying possessions and "our commerce and citizens abroad"; to insure "our national integrity"; and to support "our national policies."

2. An adequate naval defense requires not only the protection of outlying territories, "but also a defense that will keep any potential enemy many hundreds of miles away from our continental limits."[8]

Moreover, there were four other ways in which the United States served notice that it did not intend to be outdistanced by the dictators. (1) In August 1938 Mr. Roosevelt publicly associated his country with the defense of Canada. Less than two years later this declaration developed into a definite alliance. (2) In November 1938 reciprocal trade treaties were signed with Great Britain and Canada. A similar treaty had already been completed with Czechoslovakia. When coupled with the score of less important commercial treaties the administration had already negotiated, this treaty system covered the greater portion of the world's trade and confronted the Axis with an imposing economic front. (3) At Lima in December 1938 the American government emerged with a generalized promise of mutual consultation from its Latin-American neighbors. And (4) in April 1939 it put the direct question to Hitler and Mussolini whether they would promise not to attack any of the independent states of Europe and the Near East for a period of ten years. In exchange for such a pledge the United States would sponsor an international conference at which the dictator countries would have a chance to present their grievances and take part in the abatement of the world's ills. The question of course was purely rhetorical; the appetites of these countries were hardly capable of adjustment to the conference method; and Hitler resorted in reply to the cheap trick of publicly quizzing his weak neighbors on whether or not they were afraid of him.

Undoubtedly these gestures on the part of the United States encouraged the British and French to make a stand against Germany. Completely isolated in August 1939, their declaration of war was an act either of supreme folly or of sublime faith, depending on one's point of view. The United States was their only possible source of large-scale support, and the Neutrality Law appeared designed deliberately to prevent such an outcome. Only the mobilized might of American industry was capable of redressing the balance against the tremendous aggregation of military power and economic wealth that Adolf Hitler had at his command. Moreover, not only were Russian resources available to Hitler, but Russia was a back door through which Germany might receive supplies from the United States. Never was a solemn act of Congress more ironical in its operation and more contrary to the nation's historic policies and elementary needs than the Neutrality Act. In fact it provided something not far short of partnership with the dictators.

The movement to repeal the arms-embargo section was renewed immediately after the opening of the European war. Mr. Roosevelt summoned a special session of Congress for the purpose. Fifty per cent of the people, as measured by the Gallup poll, showed they had a healthy appreciation of the importance of the Anglo-French cause. If, they agreed, it appeared that Britain and France would suffer defeat within a few months, then the United States should declare war and send troops. On the other hand, the great majority, ignoring the disadvantages of the Anglo-French positions, were content to believe blindly in an Allied victory. With this sentiment as a background Mr. Roosevelt was able to secure from Congress a repeal of the arms embargo. The majorities in both houses were more than two to one. But the isolationists still possessed enormous braking power. They had two months in which to repeat the stereotyped opinions which they had vented many times before. Moreover the new measure retained the other features of control and provided for the proclamation of combat areas where American ships might not operate. To all appearances it was a new declaration of faith in isolationism.

Nevertheless, the lifting of the arms embargo was some compensation for the time being. The British and French had accumulated several billion dollars in American investments prior to the coming of the war. They now mobilized these resources and under the cash-and-carry provisions of the act purchased what they needed from the American market. They even furnished the capital with which to build and expand the factories of American aircraft companies. For reasons best known to themselves the Germans did not institute an aggressive war in the West during the fall or winter of 1939. Except for some ship sinkings and the presence of massed troops along the French border, the scene in Western Europe was hardly different during the first six months of war from what it had been previously. There was a bloody side-show going on in Finland from January to March 1940, with Russia the aggressor. Praise and sympathy were lavished upon the Finns by the American people, but no move was made to put arms in their hands against the Russians. A material interest in the independence of Finland was lacking. It was otherwise when the integrity of Britain and France was placed in jeopardy.

Holocaust Begins in Europe

Without the slightest warning the whole character of the war in Europe changed in April 1940. Like a swarm of locusts the Nazis descended upon Denmark and Norway. Having already demilitarized themselves, the Danes surrendered without a blow; their government was allowed to remain in office, but henceforth it became the merest echo of Berlin. The Norwegians put up a desperate resistance, but neither their own efforts nor those of the British who came to their aid availed. Norway was simply overwhelmed, its leading ports were occupied simultaneously as far north as Narvik, its inland communications were smashed by Nazi bombs, its government was forced to flee, and an infamous puppet ruler, Vidkun Quisling, was set up in its place. Norway was the first demonstration of what treachery from within, when combined with perfect planning from without, could accomplish in the collapse of a whole nation.

One month later the Germans repeated the feat in Holland, Belgium, and Luxembourg. Costly preparations made by the Dutch and Belgians for their own defense counted for naught. The Germans had planned for a wholly new type of warfare; mechanized columns, paratroops wearing the Dutch and Belgian uniforms, the merciless destruction of cities from the air, and the successful advance plotting with traitors from within who had sold themselves to the Nazi idea paralyzed the people of the invaded countries. But the greatest shock of all was yet to come. The Allies had entered the war in the general belief that they could win by waiting: economic strangulation would prove the successful weapon, as it had in 1918. They did not intend to invade Germany, and they did not fear invasion of themselves. The great Maginot line would take care of that.

Never was there a more futile belief. The Nazis swept around the Maginot line from Belgium; having made no preparations to meet the new strategy, the French generals found their armies, theoretically the best-trained in Europe, cowed and bewildered before the German onrush. More than three hundred thousand British were cut off from their allies and crowded into a small place along the French-Belgian coast. From this perilous position they were miraculously rescued during the week of May 27 through the genius of the Royal Navy operating with the assistance of hundreds of small craft manned by volunteers from England. The British sacrificed practically all of their arms and equipment, however, and England itself was unprepared to resist invasion. It was at this point that the Germans had to make a choice. Either they could concentrate all their might in an effort to overwhelm the British, in which case they would leave the French on their flank; or they could turn inland toward Paris. They chose the latter course. France was subdued and forced to sign an armistice on June 22, but England was still safe and preparing with feverish haste for the invasion that she was sure would soon be attempted.

It would be hard to imagine a worse predicament for the British than that in which they found themselves in June 1940. Not even in the darkest days of the previous World War had there been a possibility of invasion; the enemy had never wrested control of the Channel ports. Now, however, he was master of the whole European coast from Spain to the Arctic Circle. More than a hundred years before Napoleon had held the same geographical advantages. The Germans held all of these, and in addition they had unquestioned superiority in the air. From a score of French, Belgian, Dutch, and Norwegian ports they could swarm in upon the English. Once they could defeat British air power over its own territory, the Royal Navy could be neutralized and the island itself made a direct prey to an invading force.

Isolationism at Rope's End

The possibility, which many informed persons for awhile thought a probability, of the downfall of Great Britain invoked questions for the United States which had never been asked in the nation's history. Fundamentally there was just one question: How would the elimination of Great Britain as a world power affect American security? The issue was so sudden, its implications suggested so many ramifications, that it was difficult to formulate a comprehensive answer.

One reply, of course, was that there was no connection—or at least there need not be—between Britain's integrity and the safety of the United States. Such a response had to assume either (a) that relations with Germany and her Axis partners would become as peaceful as they had been with Great Britain or (b) that the United States could trust exclusively to its own armed might in case of attack by the Axis. Most of those who wished to find this answer used a train of logic that was a blend of these two assumptions. They accepted Hitler's argument that he had no designs on the Western Hemisphere; they held that commerce with Europe could be resumed once the war was over, even though Germany dominated the Continent; and they rejected the notion that the United States was beholden for its safety to British sea power. In short, they concluded, there was no real reason why Germany should not be just as good a friend of the United States as Great Britain.

A compound of these opinions and others of a similar character was set forth repeatedly by the isolationists between the fall of France and the Japanese blow at Pearl Harbor. Among the most insistent of the isolationists were the former aviator, Charles A. Lindbergh, Senator Burton K. Wheeler of Montana, Senator Gerald P. Nye of North Dakota, and Representative Hamilton Fish of New York. The organization which backed them took the characteristic name of the America First Committee. This committee proceeded to mobilize the familiar tools of publicity in a fight to "keep the country out of war" and defeat the positive measures advocated by the Roosevelt administration. It built up a considerable following, especially in the Middle West, during the winter of 1940-41 and it succeeded in delaying, though not defeating, such important measures as the Lend-Lease Act and the Military Service Act of 1941. The latter passed the House of Representatives in August by only a single vote. Its failure would have meant the discharge from the army of selectees who had had their year's training and the necessity for military authorities virtually to start all over again in training a national army.

The America First Committee was the spearhead of a virulent isolationism which step by step fought to keep the United States neutral. It thought consistently in terms of the conclusions of the Senate Munitions Committee of 1934 and the Neutrality Laws of that decade. It enjoyed the parallel activity of many pacifist groups, and its chief asset was the widespread fear among the people of getting into the war. Nevertheless, there was now far less hesitation, as we shall see, and a much sharper evaluation of the issues, than in the period 1914–17. The isolationists had their largest following in the Middle West, the majority of whose votes in Congress were mustered against such key measures as the act repealing the arms embargo in October 1939 and the Lend-Lease Bill in March 1941. The section showed some distaste for the draft, for the lengthening of the term of compulsory service beyond the one year originally required, and for the giving of a free hand to the War Department in ordering troops to duty outside of the Western Hemisphere. In other sections of the country isolationism was pronouncedly weak.

Party politics had considerable influence; the Republicans were in the majority in the Middle West, and the Republican membership in Congress consistently opposed the Administration's wishes.

The great majority of the people, however, as measured repeatedly by the Gallup polls, were committed to steps in aid of Britain. In fact these polls showed that public opinion in this respect was consistently ahead of Congress. Most efficient in publicizing measures desired by the government was the Committee to Defend America by Aiding the Allies. This was a private organization whose leaders had through the years kept the faith with Wilsonian principles of collective security. The Committee was a direct outgrowth of the League of Nations Association, which with the help of the Carnegie Endowment had managed to weather the storm of isolationism that had swept over the country during the 1930's. The Nazi invasion of France and the resulting alarm in the United States afforded striking testimony to the soundness of the Association's past teachings. Under the chairmanship of the famous Kansas editor, William Allen White, the new organization carried on an energetic publicity campaign throughout the entire nation. It reached the smallest communities through local chapters, which in less than a year swelled to more than eight hundred in number. Reflecting the sectional differences in the country, these were most numerous in the Northeast, in the South, and on the Pacific Coast; relatively weak in the Middle Western states, the growing number of the Committee's chapters in that area, however, showed that isolationism was even there declining.

The directors of the Committee to Defend America were in close touch with the authorities in Washington, and it proved an extremely effective agency in cultivating public sentiment in advance for measures which the administration desired. Indeed the Committee scored practically one hundred per cent in the relation between the measures for which it fought and those which were later put into effect. A striking illustration was the destroyer deal of September 1940: The Committee began the campaign for this proceeding in July; it got advance information from the Administration of the number of destroyers the latter expected to transfer to the British, and the public was familiarized with the facts and the necessity well in advance of the event. The Committee had the endorsement of some of the best-known figures in American public life; General Pershing, Admiral Yarnell, Admiral Stirling, President Conant of Harvard, and scores of prominent persons representing a cross section of society supported it heartily. In general, it followed the opportunistic line of advocating aid "short of war." "War" the popular mind interpreted to mean the sending of an expeditionary force, as in 1917. It was shown beyond a doubt that the people did not care what they did to Germany; they wanted the Nazis beaten; and the popular conscience was not troubled by oft-heard warnings from the isolationist camp that the destroyer deal and other measures of assistance really constituted "acts of war." So they undoubtedly did in the eyes of formal international law. But only the most punctilious legalists clung to the fiction that the United States was a neutral nation. There was neither a political nor an ethical basis for neutrality in the great conflagration that was menacing every principle dear to American civilization. The American public was prepared to do anything short of sending its boys to fight. At length Pearl Harbor swept even this reservation into oblivion.

The traditional idea of American security was founded on the belief that distance was a permanent protection. Three thousand miles of ocean were the invariable justification for the policy of isolation from Europe. The freedom of action which the United States enjoyed during the nineteenth century fixed this belief as one of the great dogmas of American history. The debacle of 1940 forced a decisive reconsideration of this concept. Distance, of course, had been shrinking for some years, thanks to the speedier means of communication. The airship practically wiped it out. Even while France was being invaded, Mr. Roosevelt made telling use of this fact. A mere recital of flying schedules was enough to overthrow the popular confidence in geography; not even the Middle West would be safe from air raids, once an enemy gained the right positions. The immediate effect of the French collapse was to create a frenzied demand for national defense: Mr. Roosevelt asked for money to build fifty thousand planes. But that was only a start. Congress speedily adopted a program to create a two-ocean navy, one designed to maintain a fleet in the Atlantic equal to that already in the Pacific. It was tacit acknowledgement of the fact that the United States had hitherto trusted to British sea power to safeguard the Atlantic approaches. In other words, there had been a hidden factor in American security which was quickly appreciated once its existence was threatened. But the American people were far from satisfied with sea and air power alone. Before the summer of 1940 was over, the National Guard had been mustered into the regular Army for indefinite service and Congress had passed the Selective Service Act authorizing the conscription for a year's training of men between the ages of twenty-one and thirty-five. It took nearly three months to get the bill through Congress; furthermore, the distrust was keen lest this be the entering wedge for the dispatch of an expeditionary force. It was hard to overcome the thought-pattern of 1917, and the bill contained the proviso that the drafted men could not be used outside of the Western Hemisphere or the possessions of the United States. In spite of these limitations, however, the Selective Service Act was a revolutionary measure—it was the first time a draft of man power had ever been applied in advance of actual involvement in war.

Toward a Shooting War

These frenzied efforts to repair the military deficiencies of the country, it must be remembered, were set in motion only after the French Republic had fallen in pieces. Under the armistice of June 22 the French surrendered two-thirds of their country to the German and Italian enemy. The remnant, known henceforth as Unoccupied France, comprised a portion of the interior south of Paris and a part of the Mediterranean coastline, including the port of Marseille and the naval base at Toulon. Fearing trouble from Italy even before the Germans struck at Holland and Belgium, the Roosevelt administration had used its utmost persuasive powers to keep Mussolini out of the war. The Italian dictator was told that the United States had an important economic stake in the Mediterranean, that it had traditional and historical interests in that sea that could not be ignored, and that if the war were thus extended the United States would redouble its aid to the Allies. Furthermore, an attempt was made to detach Mussolini from his German alliance; if Italy would state her specific desires, he was told, they would be communicated to Great Britain and France, an effort would be made to reach an agreement, and the United States would obtain an assurance from the British and French that they would faithfully execute the agreement at the end of the war. It was an eleventh-hour adventure in appeasement in the hope of keeping the war out of the Mediterranean; but it failed to make an impression. Mussolini had already pleaded with the United States to accept the "new geography" of Europe, and on June 1 he told the President he had decided on war. By this time the Nazis were on the road to Paris, and the Italian jackal, having gambled at least since 1937 on the triumph of Germany, leaped for the few crumbs of French territory while yet there was time. Mr. Roosevelt only voiced a common thought in the United States when he publicly declared on the day Italy attacked that "the hand that held the dagger has struck it in the back of its neighbor."

The conversion of the Mediterranean into a theater of war, with the odds heavily in favor of the Axis, had far-reaching effects on the American position, just as had been feared. Vichy, the new capital of the French state, was in charge of men who displayed increasing tendencies to collaborate with the Germans. The immediate problem was to keep the French fleet, which in the Atlantic was second in size only to the British, from getting into German clutches. With a force of that size under their command, the Nazis might well roam the seas without hindrance. By directly warning the French authorities that if they gave up their navy they would "permanently lose the friendship and good-will" of the United States, Roosevelt extracted a pledge that it would not be surrendered. This did not end the peril, however. A powerful segment of the French fleet was in North Africa, and its commander, Admiral Darlan, refused to bow to the joint British and American efforts to immobilize it or get it to support the British Navy. In consequence the British fell on it at Oran, Algeria, in July; they sank part of it, but the remaining vessels took flight and escaped. From that time the British and the Vichy French were unofficially at war. A minority of French fighting forces, calling themselves the Free French, rallied in London, however, under the lead of General de Gaulle and remained steadfast to the Allied cause. The French colonial empire likewise split in twain; and as the war continued to spread and the contest for strategic positions between the Axis and their foes became fiercer, the allegiance chosen by the several French colonial governors became of the utmost importance.

Central in this strategy was French North and West Africa. If Algeria and Morocco passed into German hands, the British would be driven from the Mediterranean. Through Dakar French West Africa was an open bridge to South America, one thousand seven hundred miles distant; but for immediate operations Dakar's chief value to the enemy was its position as a submarine base for cutting the British shipping route to South Africa and the Indian Ocean. Alert to these possibilities, the American government hastily opened a consulate there. Meanwhile in September the Vichy government, which had rejected British and American efforts to persuade France to remain in the war, sent General Maxime Weygand to Algiers with viceregal authority over all North and West Africa. Not being a collaborationist, Weygand had no intention of admitting the Nazis to his jurisdiction; and as for the British, he took the position that he would help when they were ready to come in force. "If they come to North Africa with four divisions, I'll fire on them; if they come with twenty divisions, I will welcome them," he declared. Hitler, on the other hand, was eager to get both France and Spain in on his side. He could then capture Gibraltar and occupy the Canary Islands and the Azores. To achieve these prizes he journeyed all the way to Hendaye on the Franco-Spanish border to meet the Spanish dictator General Franco. But Franco, having no intention of letting a German army into Spain, asked a price which Hitler could not pay. Among other things, he demanded a generous slice of French North Africa, thus playing the Germans off against the French. So exasperated was Hitler with this meeting that he later told Mussolini: "Rather than go through it again, I would prefer to have three or four of my teeth out!" But Hitler could get no promises from the French either. He saw Marshal Pétain on his way back from the Spanish border, but Pétain, while resigned at this time to the prospect of Britain's downfall, meant to hedge as long as possible. "It will take six months to discuss this program and another six months to forget it," he remarked after the meeting.[9]

Not knowing of this stalemate in France, however, and fearing the worst, President Roosevelt dispatched a very stern warning to Pétain against joining Hitler. Roosevelt invoked the pledge he had already secured respecting the French fleet. If France now violated this pledge or otherwise helped her conqueror, her action "would constitute a flagrant and deliberate breach of faith with the United States Government." In December the President sent a trusted emissary, Admiral William D. Leahy, to Vichy with the express purpose of influencing Pétain and persuading him of the certainty of an Allied victory. The United States intended to support Britain, the Marshal was told; and if he performed no favors for Germany, France would be rewarded with food shipments for relief. Leahy arrived in Vichy in January 1941, during the coldest winter that France had endured for ninety years, and remained until April 1942. During this period the Lend-Lease Act was passed and the United States slipped into a "shooting war" with the Germans in the Atlantic and then, after Pearl Harbor, into full scale warfare on a global scale. At Vichy Leahy had two dangerous rivals in the contest for the support of Marshal Pétain. One was Pierre Laval—"Black Peter," he was called—who was the most outspoken adherent to the cause of Hitler. The other was Admiral Darlan, an unscrupulous opportunist who held the French Navy in the palm of his hand and whose every motive seemed to be dominated by a maniacal hatred of Britain. Darlan on May 28, 1941, signed protocols with the Germans in Paris, giving them operational bases in Tunis and Syria, the services of French ships in the Mediterranean, and the use of Dakar as a supply base for submarines and aircraft. This move was checkmated, it appears, through the intervention of Weygand, at a time when the tide of German victory in the Eastern Mediterranean was running high. Weygand held on until the following November, but being the arch foe of collaboration within the Vichy government, he was a natural target for the Nazis. American diplomacy had no real card to play at this time—the United States was not in the war— and the Germans finally forced his dismissal. "Black Peter" returned to power in April 1942, and Leahy was recalled forthwith. Whatever success his mission had had must be reckoned in terms of the personal relations between the American Ambassador and the Marshal of France. It was the sturdy opposition of Weygand that kept the Germans from the North African prize. With the withdrawal of Leahy, relations with Vichy all but stopped, but a door was kept open through North Africa. Here during the autumn months of 1942 the ground was carefully laid for the first great Anglo-American offensive against Hitler's "Fortress Europe," the invasion of North Africa.[10]

The Threat of a Two-Ocean Attack, and the Transfer of
Destroyers to Britain

Now to return to 1940. The prime problem in American security, as viewed by the government, was how to get enough aid to the British. Not only must Britain be helped to stand the Germans off, but she must eventually defeat them. In an immortal speech, delivered during the dark hours after Dunkerque, Winston Churchill, the British Prime Minister, breathed defiance. But the task seemed all but hopeless. England had sacrificed the best of her heavy equipment in Flanders, and was feared to be open to direct invasion. The Nazis had only twenty miles of water to cross, and they could get at the country by air from as many points on the Continent as they chose. It was doubted whether the English had sufficient air power to cover the movements of their fleet, and the usefulness of the heavy ships of the Navy in the emergency was doubted. Even though the Nazis failed to make a direct landing, the odds were still heavily in their favor. With the French ports in their grip and with aircraft scouting the seas against British ships, the enemy could wage a devastating submarine campaign.[11]

If Britain fell, the advantages in the entire Atlantic would alter heavily in favor of Germany; and if the Germans obtained control over any considerable portions of the British or French fleets, their superiority over the United States would soon be overwhelming. The latter country would immediately be outranked in the North Atlantic, and the Germans could now make easy prey of Dakar. The United States possessed only a weak force in the Atlantic; if it shifted its fleet to meet the German challenge, its Pacific flank would be dangerously exposed to the Japanese, and there could, of course, be hardly a doubt as to what the latter would do in any event in the region of the Dutch East Indies. The possibilities of a two-ocean attack on the Western Hemisphere indeed stirred the American imagination. Visions of superior enemy fleets on both oceans, built and maintained by slave labor in Europe and Asia, made these fears the more vivid. For the first time the disadvantages of the thousands of miles of undefended coastline of the two continents and the comparative helplessness of the other American nations began to be appraised realistically. It was questioned whether any aggregation of naval strength on the part of the United States could offset these natural handicaps. Then there was the new vulnerability to attack from the air. Flights to the New World by the North Polar route were entirely possible. Many years previously Captain Mahan had pointed out that the genius of British sea power rested fundamentally on the location of the island of Britain athwart the trade routes from western Europe. Now the United States was suddenly required to look upon Britain as a great bastion in the northeast Atlantic, a fortress which must be held at all costs against the Nazi torrent.

Thoroughly aware of the supreme crisis with which it was faced, the government of the United States found the means of effectively reinforcing Great Britain. Over night that country transformed herself into an arsenal; but for the moment she even lacked small arms. By means of trade-in agreements with private manufacturers, in which the latter contracted to make replacements, the American government freed large quantities of unused stocks of rifles, ammunition, machine guns, and so forth. This material had been left from the last war, and no one could say how effective it would prove against modern equipment. That it was considered worth shipping attests the extreme gravity of the crisis.

Far more important was the decision to transfer to the Royal Navy fifty of the one hundred-odd destroyers left over from the First World War. Unlike the trade-in agreements of June, this involved a direct transaction with the British government; the destroyers were destined for convoy duty, and they made up for the naval losses which the enemy had inflicted on the British during the summer. The agreement was effected on September 2, 1940, through an exchange of letters between the Secretary of State and the British Ambassador. As its part of the bargain the British government promised to turn over, on the basis of a ninety-nine-year, rent-free lease, the sites for six naval and air bases in British Guiana and the British West Indian islands. Having sounded public opinion in advance, Mr. Roosevelt confronted Congress with the accomplished fact, and by making the appropriation for the improvement of the said sites that body shortly after set the seal of its approval upon the whole transaction. Isolationists had a right to complain that the deal was a violation of American "neutrality"; it was an outright repudiation of the rules set up in 1871 at the instance of the United States itself respecting the transfer of vessels of war from a neutral to a belligerent. But the President shrewdly put the emphasis on the value of the rights acquired by the United States and the defensive nature of the proceeding; the public was indifferent to legal arguments over neutrality, and in voting for the money with which to develop the bases even the isolationists in Congress showed a practical disregard for consistency.[12]

The Second Re-election of Roosevelt Endorses Measures "Short of War"

These events took place in the midst of a heated campaign over the re-election of Mr. Roosevelt to a third term in the Presidency. Issues of foreign policy offered a golden opportunity to the President's opponents to throw the country into an uproar, had they so chosen. Nothing of the sort took place. So mild were the criticisms offered by Wendell Willkie, the Republican candidate, that they suggested the possibility of a pre-arrangement between the two men. Willkie censured the *method* of concluding the deal but approved the objective. It was a harmless criticism that caused little embarrassment to either party. After the campaign was over, Mr. Willkie showed by word and deed that he would have behaved in the same manner himself; much to the discomfiture of the isolationist Republicans in Congress he cast aside all restraint and became even more blunt than Roosevelt in demanding energetic steps to assist Great Britain. Henceforth Willkie filled a unique position: still a political opponent of the President, he nevertheless conferred frequently with Roosevelt, made a special trip to England on his own initiative, and on his return announced himself as advocating the establishment of American naval bases in Greenland, Iceland, and even Northern

Ireland. The occupation of the first two took place in the spring of 1941. While troops did not actually appear in Northern Ireland until after the declaration of war by Germany upon the United States, the preparation and installation of the necessary facilities for them were begun well in advance. Like the Committee to Defend America, Mr. Willkie more than once acted as a mouthpiece for the administration in priming public opinion for aggressive measures against the Axis.

The election campaign out of the way, a succession of vigorous acts aimed at the Axis was carried out. The list is so extensive as to make an exhaustive itemization here unfeasible. Flying Fortresses were transferred to the British government to aid in the long-range bombing of Germany and Italy, revenue cutters were dispatched to prosecute the war against the submarine under the British flag, the ships of the Danish merchant marine which had been immobilized in American ports were seized and put into service, German and Italian vessels were sequestered, German and Italian consulates were ordered closed and the banking credits of both countries frozen, a blacklist was enforced against Latin-American firms for having done business with the Axis, and convoying by American destroyers part way across the Atlantic was introduced. These were among the less important measures "short of war" taken between November 1940 and the following summer. Meanwhile the Germans were busy trying to cut the British Empire in two in the Mediterranean; in a spectacular winter campaign they overran Jugoslavia and Greece and got as far as Crete, from which island, however, they showed no ability to attack the main British base at Alexandria. They had, however, succeeded in conjunction with the Italians in making the Mediterranean too dangerous for British shipping; the garrisons in Egypt and the Middle East had to receive their supplies by means of the long haul around Africa. This was a fairly safe route, and when by April 1941 the Italians were forced out of Ethiopia and Somaliland, Mr. Roosevelt used his executive power to declare the Red Sea no longer a war zone. This enabled the United States to begin the building of a "bridge of ships" from its ports on both coasts in aid of the gigantic task of keeping the British forces supplied in the Middle East.

Meanwhile Mr. Roosevelt had realistically outlined the principles of American security, scoffed at the absurdity of a negotiated peace advocated by isolationists and pacifists, and pledged the United States to become the arsenal of democracy. "The experience of the past two years," he declared in a memorable radio address on December 29, 1940, "has proven beyond doubt that no nation can appease the Nazis. No man can tame a tiger into a kitten by stroking it." Five months later he followed this with the proclamation of an unlimited national emergency; he called attention to the dangerous rate of ship sinkings in the Atlantic, more than twice the combined output of British and American yards at that time; and he stressed the supreme importance of keeping the control of the seas out of Axis hands. All of this time the Gallup polls showed that the great majority of the people in the United States related their own individual fortunes to the cause of victory or defeat overseas; if Hitler won, it was agreed, each individual American would feel the effects. The President in his speech of May 27, 1941, only put into words the opinions most Americans had already formed. He declared:

The dictatorships would force the enslaved peoples of their Old World conquests into a system they were then organizing—to build a naval and air force intended to obtain mastery of the Atlantic and the Pacific; an economic stranglehold would be fastened upon the nations of the Western Hemisphere; the American laborer would have to compete with slave labor in the rest of the world, and trade unions would become "historical relics"; the American farmer would face obvious disaster and complete regimentation; the whole fabric of business, manufacturing, mining, and agriculture would be mangled and crippled; a permanent conscription of our manpower would be necessary, and our resources would be permanently poured into armaments. We did not accept and we would not accept this Nazi "shape of things to come."[13]

Lend-Lease for the Opponents of Nazi Germany

The keynote of American policy was, as the President declared, to make the United States the arsenal of democracy. We have already reviewed the progress the country was making in its own military preparations. But fully as important was the determination to keep the nations already at war with Hitler supplied with the planes, tanks, ships, and guns they so desperately needed. Down to the time of the President's radio address the British government had fully met these needs out of its own cash resources. To pay for the immense quantities of materials it had bought in the American market it had even sold the two billion dollars worth of American stocks and bonds held by British owners. It had commandeered these securities in exchange for its own bonds and then had sold them back to American buyers, thus accumulating dollars to spend in the United States. In many instances it had even financed the erection of new plants, especially aircraft factories, not to mention additions to older industrial plants in the United States, thereby relieving the private American manufacturer of anxiety over possible postwar losses.

~ There was a limit to this, of course, and the end was in sight by December 1940. The British Ambassador, Lord Lothian, threw out a warning, and Mr. Roosevelt in his annual message outlined his plan for meeting the situation. He said:

We cannot, and we will not tell them that they must surrender, merely because of present inability to pay for the weapons which we know they must have. I do not recommend that we make them a loan of dollars with which to pay for these weapons—a loan to be repaid in dollars.

I recommend that we make it possible for those nations to continue to obtain war materials in the United States, fitting their orders into our own program. Nearly all their material would, if the time ever came, be useful for our own defense.[14]

Such was the kernel of the Lend-Lease Bill, which the Administration introduced into Congress in January 1941. The purpose of the bill was "to further promote the defense of the United States." It authorized the President to manufacture in arsenals, factories, and shipyards belonging to the United States government, or to buy from any private corporation, "any defense article for the government of any country whose defense the President deems vital to the defense of the United States." The term "defense article" meant any weapon, munition, aircraft or boat, any machinery or tool essential for the manufacture or repair of any other "defense article," or "any other commodity or article for defense." It included food. Moreover, the President might "sell, transfer, exchange, lease, or otherwise dispose of, to any such government any defense article." He might repair or recondition any defense article belonging to any such government, and communicate to it any "defense information" (meaning secret plans or specifications regarding weapons or other implements). In return for the help thus granted, "the benefit to the United States may be payment in kind or property, *or any other direct or indirect benefit which the President deems satisfactory.*"[15]

The Lend-Lease Bill presented a challenge to Congress such as that body had not faced since 1861. In that year President Lincoln had used his Executive prerogatives to save the Union; he had actually made war without consulting Congress, and he had made preparations for conducting the conflict on a large scale before he appealed to the national legislature. Needless to say, the war thus already begun would have turned into a fiasco unless Congress had come to the President's support. Like Lincoln, President Roosevelt had instituted measures which committed the country to a certain objective. Those measures, furthermore, were sharply at variance with the spirit, though not the letter, of the only authoritative expression of the Congressional will—the Neutrality Act of 1939. But Mr. Roosevelt was in no better position to make the United States "the arsenal of democracy" than Lincoln had been in 1861 to "save the Union," unless Congress now agreed to underwrite his policies. Obviously the task of insuring a British victory was now too large for the Executive alone to cope with. The full weight of American economic resources had to be thrown into the struggle, and Congress alone could authorize that.

With the same brand of self-assurance exhibited by Lincoln, and confidence in the rightness of its position, the Roosevelt administration proceeded on the assumption that it was going to win Congress to its views. It told the British government to make its plans in expectation that the Lend-Lease Bill would pass. In the Administration's eyes, the crisis was fully comparable to that in 1861. Secretary Hull warned:

The most serious question today for this country is whether the control of the high seas shall pass into the hands of powers bent on a program of unlimited conquest. It is in this light, above all, that we should order our present-day thinking and action with respect to the amount of material assistance which our country is prepared to furnish Great Britain. . . . .

In the face of the forces of conquest now on the march across the earth, self-defense is and must be the compelling consideration in the determination of wise and prudent national policy. . . . .

The great problem of democracy is to organize and to use its strength with sufficient speed and completeness. The proposed legislation is an essential measure for that purpose.[16]

There was an abundance of evidence, as we have seen, that the majority of the people wanted drastic measures, though they were still insistent on "keeping out of war." They were ready to vote billions for defense, but they were not reconciled to doing the fighting themselves. This was really the only issue, paradoxical though it was: whether passing the bill would mean plunging the United States into war or whether it would help the country to stay out. No one, of course, knew the answer. Mr. Wendell Willkie undoubtedly expressed the most enlightened opinion on that score, and offered the sagest advice, in his testimony to the Senate Committee on Foreign Relations shortly after his return from England. He said:

No man can guarantee to you that the policy of aid to Britain will not involve the United States in war. It is my solemn opinion, however, that, providing the aid is effective, it offers the best clear chance for us to keep out of war. Hitler will make war on us, or on our friends and allies in this hemisphere, when, as, and if he chooses. That is his record. But he is far less apt to be aggressive while Britain stands, than if she were to fall.[17]

The Lend-Lease Bill was the occasion for a full-dress review of American foreign policy. The Foreign Affairs Committees of both houses held public hearings on the measure, and the bill was debated on the floor of both Senate and House. The isolationists had their chance, and they made the most of it. It was at this time that the America First Committee displayed its greatest activity. The House passed the Bill in less than three weeks; the Senate, the traditional critic of Executive foreign policies and the body where the isolationists were most vocal, consumed two months. The Bill became law on March 11, 1941, after the House had voted 317 to 71 and the Senate 60 to 31. A few days later both Houses, by an almost unanimous vote, appropriated seven billion dollars with which to carry out the Act; and eighteen months afterward, when the President issued his sixth report on the operations under the Act, the country was sending aid to foreign countries at the rate of eight billion dollars a year.

Lend-Lease led to a practical experiment in collective security on a scale undreamed of by the men of 1918. During the debates on the measure the frame of reference was chiefly aid to the nations of the British Commonwealth, with whose defense the United States was identified through the all-important problem of controlling the high seas. When they saw they were going to be defeated, the opposition tried to limit the benefits of the Bill to the British Commonwealth. The Administration, however, took the broader view that *any* nation fighting the Axis was contributing to the defense of the United States and was therefore entitled to assistance. This view prevailed, and the Act was subsequently administered accordingly. By September 1942, thirty-five foreign countries *in addition* to the British Commonwealth came under its provisions. The Soviet Union came second to the United Kingdom in the amount of assistance, and every European government which the Nazis had driven into exile, except Luxembourg, was a recipient. Besides these, the list included the Fighting French (whose leader, de Gaulle, did not enjoy diplomatic recognition by the United States), Ethiopia, Iraq, Iceland, and all of the twenty republics of Latin America.

More than that, the United States had taken the initiative in concluding Master Lend-Lease Agreements between itself and the United Kingdom, China, and the Soviet Union, respectively; under these agreements the resources, man power, and inventive genius of each and every member of the United Nations were thrown into a common pool. Thus, Mr. Roosevelt reported, British labor, paid by the British government, built bases for the American Army, British factories furnished American troops with "a formidable amount of munitions and supplies," while the peoples of Britain, Australia, and New Zealand, "already on short rations, are freely sharing what they have with our troops." The same sort of reciprocal assistance came from the Fighting French in Equatorial Africa and New Caledonia, while the Lend-Lease system "also has been applied to relations between other United Nations. The United Kingdom, for instance, is so supplying military stores to the Soviet Union." By this time, too, the distribution of American troops, a million and a half strong, among widely scattered but strategic locations around the world and the system of interchanging forces among nations where they could be used most efficiently (Canadian units in Alaska, for example) gave grim testimony to the completeness with which the United States and its allies could practice the principle of collective security.[18]

The Master Lend-Lease Agreements were a far cry from the blueprint of international co-operation made at Paris in 1918; but they were a faithful reflection of the principle there laid down that the safety of one nation is the safety of all. Indeed they went beyond that, for they recognized that the problems of Lend-Lease would not expire on the day the fighting should stop. No man could say in 1942 what form the conditions of repayment would take for the gigantic quantities of goods and services being supplied by the United States during the conflict. The Lend-Lease Act, let us remember, spoke of *benefits*, rather than dollars, and left the question of repayment to Executive discretion. Mindful of the fiasco of the war debts and of the ruinous tariffs that grew out of the fierce competition of the 1920's, the parties to the Master Agreements pledged themselves against the recurrence of such evils growing out of Lend-Lease. When the benefits to the United States should be finally determined, each Agreement provided, "the terms and conditions thereof shall be such as not to burden commerce between the two countries, but to promote mutually advantageous economic relations between them and the betterment of world-wide economic relations."[19] Lend-Lease made collective security the practicing creed of the American people in time of war; it remained to be seen whether the lessons thus applied could be carried out as loyally and intelligently in the peace to come later.

The Lend-Lease Act committed the United States to the defeat of Germany. Legal fiction and the absence of fighting, it is true, sustained the illusion that the two countries were still "at peace." They even kept open their respective embassies, each one no doubt perceiving the advantage of retaining a listening post on the soil of the other. The Germans were too busy in Greece and Crete to retaliate in the spring of 1941, and after that Russia absorbed their attention. The United States twice warned that country that she would be attacked; secret reports that this was Hitler's intention reached the State Department even before the enactment of the Lend-Lease Act. Hitler's most gigantic aggression, a battle line a thousand miles long, from the Baltic to the Black Sea, commenced on June 22, 1941.

As for the United States, the American people neither wanted to declare war nor to fight; the time was not ripe to do either, and there was still the possibility that, with the proper material support, Britain could fight the war through to a successful conclusion. Not idealism but cold calculation of self-interest was behind the Administration's policies and the enactment of the Lend-Lease Act. When Russia involuntarily entered the war, she became potentially an ally of the United States and actually so in the following November with the conclusion of a Lend-Lease Agreement. Having resolved to square the account with Germany, the United States was not disposed to risk the added danger of a Nazi triumph over the Soviet Union.

War's Outcome Hangs on the "Battle of the Atlantic"

Meanwhile the United States concentrated on the "Battle of the Atlantic," as the increasing onslaught by German submarines on shipping was commonly called. The submarine menace this time was far worse than it had been in 1917: then the area of infested waters was comparatively restricted to the region of the British Isles; in 1941 mechanical improvements had immensely extended the cruising range of submarines. In contrast to 1917 the greatest zone of danger was far out on the Atlantic, where long-range German scouting planes spotted enemy vessels and reported their location to lurking U-boats. Nearer home waters the British had been able to organize their convoys and use their aircraft to such effect as to beat off the submarine; on the other side of the ocean the Canadians were rendering yeoman service with a growing navy of destroyers, corvettes, and other pursuit ships. Still the combined British and Canadian strength was not sufficient to protect the fleets of merchant ships all the way across the ocean. According to Mr. Roosevelt, in May 1941 the Germans were sinking at the rate of two to every one produced in British and American yards together.

On the Battle of the Atlantic hung the outcome of the war. If the sea lanes to Britain were not kept open and made comparatively safe for shipping, the Lend-Lease Act, it is needless to point out, would prove futile. Two basic steps were essential: (1) American naval and air power had to be used to make the convoy system effective, and (2) the available tonnage had to be greatly increased. Both of these steps were logical corollaries of the Lend-Lease Act; but because they entailed what was coming to be called a "shooting war," from which public sentiment recoiled, the government resorted to some indirection in putting them into effect. The Gallup polls showed how hard it was for the public to face the logic of the situation. In April 1941, a month after the passage of the Lend-Lease Act, only 41 per cent favored convoying; by June the percentage had risen to 55; and in October 62 per cent advocated "shoot-at-sight," which as a practical measure was more drastic than merely convoying. By this time an American destroyer also, the "Greer," had been fired upon, and the President in a speech on September 11 had announced that, pursuant to a policy of active defense, the "rattlesnakes of the Atlantic" would be shot at sight. It was partly a matter of keeping the public abreast of the facts and the seriousness of the situation in the Atlantic, and then waiting until reason had overcome sentiment. Meanwhile the Germans had notified the United States that they had officially extended their war zone westward in the Atlantic so as to enclose the island of Iceland and approach near to the shores of Greenland. The move was, of course, intended to imperil the Iceland route now being used to the British Isles; but it was a striking illustration of Germany's ability to zone off large sections of the ocean and carry the war to America's doorstep. It was practical evidence of the myth that the Atlantic furnished natural protection, a myth which received its deathblow the next year when the Germans effectively operated against coastwise shipping along the Atlantic Coast.

"Patrols" Become "Convoys"—The U.S. Is Committed to Defend Freedom of the Seas

This growing warfare in the North Atlantic enabled the President to make use of the ancient slogan, "freedom of the seas," in order to justify a "shooting war." It was a case of appealing to a historical memory: the Nazis, said Mr. Roosevelt, were trying to abolish freedom of the seas, like the French in 1798 and the Barbary pirates in 1805. "Freedom of the seas" in 1941 was something of an anachronism, however, made so partly by the United States itself through its neutrality laws obliging the President to proclaim a war zone from which American shipping was to be barred. As a battle cry it had not the same power to excite anger as it had a hundred years before, or even in the preceding World War. And it certainly had scant relation to the facts. The stark truth of the issue in 1941 was, as the United States government itself had repeatedly asserted, whether or not the control of the Atlantic was to remain in British and American hands. If the high seas ever were converted into a Nazi lake, American security was a thing of the past; moreover, the United States could not make its policies effective unless the submarines were driven from the ocean.[20]

Preparations to make the Iceland route effective, as a matter of fact, had gone forward without delay shortly after the passage of the Lend-Lease Act. The government had had no intention of fatuously allowing the Germans a foothold in this area. On April 10 American forces planted a base near the southern tip of Greenland, thus guarding the flank of the route to Iceland and heading off a possible Nazi attempt to set up an air or submarine base from which to harass shipping in the rear. Three months later came an agreement with the Icelandic and British governments whereby American forces were gradually to replace British troops in the protection of that precious halfway station. By this time Russia also was in the war, and Iceland was to prove an equally important junction on the route to Murmansk and Archangel.

When on May 27 Mr. Roosevelt proclaimed the unlimited national emergency, he also made a veiled announcement of the intention to convoy. The American patrol (which had existed since the beginning of the war) had been extended and strengthened in North and South Atlantic waters. Its purpose was to "warn of the presence of attacking raiders, on the sea, under the sea, and above the sea." "Our patrols are helping now to insure delivery of the needed supplies in Britain," he added. *"All additional measures necessary to deliver the goods will be taken."*[21]

To Battle Stations—Repeal of the Neutrality Act

The precise date when the "patrol" became a "convoy" remains a naval secret. Considering the complex organization involved in the wartime convoy system, a real distinction between a patrol and a convoy is doubtful. Patrols are necessary to convoys in that they scout the seas and warn the convoying ships by radio of lurking danger. American patrols were doing scout duty and informing British and Canadian warships of the whereabouts of enemy U-boats some time before engaging in actual convoy themselves. Nevertheless, the government was loath to drop the use of the word "patrol." Its destroyer "Greer," which was "attacked" by a submarine, strictly speaking was on patrol duty; it was advised by a British plane of the presence of a submarine, the plane attacked the U-boat, and the "Greer" gave chase and was itself fired upon in return. It was a case of the pot calling the kettle black. The U.S.S. "Kearny," damaged by a torpedo on October 17, was on convoy duty, though the government at first announced it as on patrol: it went to the rescue of a convoy that had been attacked. When the U.S.S. "Reuben James" was sunk on October 30, she was on convoy duty in the literal sense of the word; she was with one convoy and went on call to the aid of another which the Germans had engaged. The incident of the "Kearny" forced the Administration to drop the mask, and on October 27, three days before the sinking of the "Reuben James," Mr. Roosevelt delivered a fighting speech in which he wound up with the words, "We Americans have cleared our decks and taken our battle stations!"[22]

Meanwhile there were a number of ways in which the question of securing adequate tonnage was tackled. Danish, Italian, and German ships were commandeered, as we have already noted, and put into service; many, perhaps most of them, in company with an unpublished number of American ships, were put under foreign registry, particularly Panamanian, so as to avoid embarrassments over the Neutrality Law. By this simple legal device the vessels could be used anywhere in the world regardless of the existence of war zones. The final hurdle, and the one which the Administration was most cautious in approaching, was the repeal of those parts of the anachronistic Neutrality Law which kept American flag ships out of war zones. Public opinion, according to Gallup, was more stubborn on this issue than it was on that of convoys; moreover, on this occasion legislative action was required, whereas in the ordering of naval ships and planes to duty the President had a clear field. After the incident of the "Greer" the time appeared ripe for repeal.

The isolationists made a last stand, and the debate consumed a month. Naturally the Administration desired and asked for the right to arm American ships, and it had a number of sinkings on the high seas with which to fortify its arguments. One of the most spectacular, the "Robin Moor," had occurred in the preceding May. This was an unescorted American ship bound from New York to Capetown with a general cargo; the cruelty inflicted on passengers and crew, who were turned loose in small boats far from shore, was wholly in keeping with the traditions of U-boat warfare but in view of the declared policy of the United States under Lend-Lease the attack occasioned only mild surprise. Compared to the emotions generated in 1917, the American public in 1941 remained objective and refused to be swept off its feet by wrath over such inhuman but none the less commonplace occurrences as the torpedoing of the "Robin Moor." The Neutrality Act was finally repealed, with respect to the sections relating to shipping, on November 13, but only after events had more than caught up with the law. The sinking of the "Reuben James" had reduced it to the hollowest mockery.[22a]

The Atlantic Charter, and a Consequence: The Japanese Decision in the Pacific

We are now at a point where we must draw together the various threads in the tangled world skein. We must pause here because, on August 9-12, 1941, occurred one of the great dramatic episodes of the war—the meeting of President Roosevelt and Prime Minister Churchill in Placentia Bay, Newfoundland. As this Atlantic Conference was about to begin, the Battle of the Atlantic was in full swing and the Americans were Britain's fighting allies in all but name. Iceland had been occupied on July 7, and, with suspicious glances fastened on Hitler and Franco and the possibility of a sudden assault on Gibraltar, Britain was poised for descent upon the Canaries, the United States for descent upon the Azores and Cape Verde Islands of Portugal. In the Eastern Mediterranean, with Greece, Crete, and Libya in their hands, the Germans were straining themselves to reach Egypt and Suez, while at the same time the Wehrmacht was biting deep into Russia. In the Pacific the Japanese had made their fatal move into southern Indo-China only to come face to face with the

American-British-Dutch embargo of July 26. Preliminary to the Atlantic Conference was the establishment of an Anglo-American-Russian entente, in the making of which Harry Hopkins, the President's special emissary to Moscow, was the key figure. Hopkins had two long conferences with Stalin on July 30 and 31—he had flown to Moscow from England—and he came away with a long bill of particulars on Soviet military needs. He returned to England sick and exhausted, but elated over the success of his journey and convinced of Russia's power to resist the Germans. The entente began to function in November, when the President formally added the Soviet Union to the list of Lend-Lease countries.[23]

Hopkins was no sooner back in England, "dead-beat from Russia," than he was off with Churchill on the "Prince of Wales" for the rendezvous with the President. On board ship the Prime Minister wrote the first draft of the document that was to be issued as the Atlantic Charter. The two countries, Churchill's draft declared, sought no aggrandizement, territorial or other; they desired no territorial changes contrary to the freely expressed wishes of the peoples concerned; they respected the right of all peoples to choose their own form of government; they would "strive to bring about a fair and equitable distribution of essential produce, not only within their territorial boundaries, but between the nations of the world"; and "they seek a peace which will not only cast down forever the Nazi tyranny, but by effective international organization will afford to all States and peoples the means of dwelling in security . . . . and of traversing the seas and oceans without fear of lawless assault or the need of maintaining burdensome armaments.[24] Somewhat expanded and with the phraseology partially modified, this document, published at the conclusion of the Conference, immediately became, like the meeting itself, a demonstration and a symbol of Anglo-American solidarity.

This then is the real importance of the Atlantic Conference. Its meaning is to be found in the context of events that were taking place all around it. The United States was already an ally of Britain and Canada in the Battle of the Atlantic, committed to take whatever action was necessary to win that battle. In challenging Britain, the Nazis had also challenged the United States, and on the outcome of the battle depended the question whether the Atlantic would remain an Anglo-American lake or become a German property. On this issue was forged the Anglo-American alliance. The occupation of Iceland in July, the correlative preparations for installing operating bases in Northern Ireland, the carefully laid plans for a quick descent upon the Azores and the Cape Verdes, and the diplomatic pressure on Vichy France—these are the real earmarks of the alliance. The Atlantic Conference was the symbolic nucleus around which these actions gathered. And within the month after Roosevelt and Churchill went their separate ways from Newfoundland, the American Navy broke into open combat with the Germans in the North Atlantic. Nor must the operation of the Anglo-American alliance in the Pacific be forgotten. In that area the combined embargo against Japan, proclaimed July 26, forced the issue: Would the Japanese bow to Anglo-American demands for a wholesale retreat from the South Pacific and even from China, or would they risk all in a single mighty blow that would cast out the Anglo-American powers from the region of East Asia? This was the question that the Japanese leaders were compelled to ponder in the four months during which the embargo pressed ever more heavily upon them. The quick, co-ordinated blows that rained suddenly on Pearl Harbor, the Philippines, Hong Kong, and Malaya in December registered their decision in this weighty matter. And with the blow at Pearl Harbor, December 7, the period of suspense abruptly came to an end. With a loud explosion the United States threw itself remorselessly into the great battle for the world.

World War II

More than three years of desperate war followed. General George C. Marshall, Chief of Staff of the United States Army, crowds the whole, vast nature of the struggle into one terse passage. "It has been declared axiomatic," he writes, "that a nation cannot successfully wage war on two fronts. With a full appreciation of the difficulties and hazards involved, we felt compelled to wage a war not only on two fronts, but on many fronts. Thus we arrived at the concept of global war in which the vast power of American democracy was to be deployed all over the earth."

The blackest days of the war fell between Pearl Harbor and the middle of the year 1942. In six months the Japanese enemy established an immense perimeter of conquest: he advanced more than halfway across the Pacific, where he was stopped by decisive American naval action at the Battle of Midway; southward he spread out until he almost brushed the northern coast of Australia; heroic resistance by outnumbered American and Australian vessels halted him there in the Battle of the Coral Sea; and driving to the west past Malaya the Jap reached the mountain barriers separating India from Burma. A rush into Burma succeeded in breaking all surface connections between China and her Western allies. Only a thin line of air supply, five hundred miles long, rising over the Himalayan Hump from Assam in India to the Yunnan plateau, kept China breathing.

Meanwhile the German Wehrmacht crashed its way onward toward the East. Two great German armies, one pushing through southern Russia to the Black Sea, the other marching eastward from Tripoli along the shores of North Africa toward the Nile and the Suez Canal, threatened to come together somewhere in the Middle East. Hitler was stalking the ghost of Napoleon on the road to India. The Russians balked him at Rostov near the Caucasus, and the British Eighth Army turned him back at El Alamein, only forty miles to the west of the Nile. The Nazis and the Japanese never closed the gap between them; they missed the control of the great seaway that holds the key to world mastery. Reviewing these crucial months, General Marshall writes:

> There can be no doubt that the greed and the mistakes of the warmaking nations as well as the heroic stands of the British and Soviet peoples saved the United States a war on her own soil. The crisis had come and passed at Stalingrad and El Alamein before this nation was able to gather sufficient resources to participate in the fight in a determining manner. Had the U.S.S.R. and the British Army of the Nile been defeated in 1942, as they well might if the Germans, Japanese, and Italians had better co-ordinated their plans and resources and successive operations, we should have stood today in the Western Hemisphere confronted by enemies who controlled a greater part of the world.[25]

Operations Torch, Avalanche, Anvil, and Overlord

A brilliant strategy aimed at a crushing defeat of the Axis powers began in the meantime to emerge from joint British and American councils. A conference in December 1941 of the President, the Prime Minister, and their respective chiefs of staff of the Army, Navy, and Air Forces laid the basic structure. "It was the most complete unification of military effort ever achieved by two Allied nations," remarks Marshall. "Strategic direction of all the forces of both nations, the allocation of manpower and munitions, the coordination of communications, the control of military intelligence, and the administration of captured areas all were accepted as joint responsibilities."[26]

Operation Torch—the Allied assault on North Africa—was the beginning of the great counter-offensive. It sucked the German armies into a pocket in Tunisia and provided a vast staging area for wresting the Mediterranean from the enemy and for making thrusts by way of Italy at the "soft under-belly of Europe."[27] In January 1943, midway through this campaign, Roosevelt and Churchill met again at Casablanca, Morocco, to mark out the next steps. It had been their intention from the very outset to strike first at Germany—the nearer and greater enemy—confining the operations in the Pacific to limited offensives and to the holding of the Hawaiian-Australian line. Then in May 1943 came another vital meeting of the heads of government and the combined chiefs. "This meeting [at Washington]," declares General Marshall, "may prove to be one of the most historic military conclaves of this war, for here the specific strategy to which the movements of the land, sea, and air forces of the Americans and British Allies conformed was translated into firm commitments." This conference, known by its code word Trident, decided upon forcing Italy out of the war and executing a daring raid by air on the German oil supply at Ploesti, Rumania, a feat that was accomplished with astounding success in the following August. The Trident Conference also planned the final blow —appropriately renamed Overlord—and set the target date for the spring of 1944; in the meantime it ordered unremitting pressure on the Japanese, an increase in the flow of matériel to the Chinese across the Himalayan Hump, and a series of assaults by American forces on the Aleutian Islands, the Marshalls, the Carolines, the Solomons, the Bismarck Archipelago, and the uncaptured portions of New Guinea.[28]

Nine months after the first Allied landings in North Africa, enemy forces were cleared out and Sicily captured. The Allies now had a bridge to Italy; and on September 8, 1943, that hapless country yielded unconditionally. Meanwhile two other offensive movements were planned: Operation Anvil, an assault on southern France with the object of effecting a lodgment in the Toulon-Marseilles area and working northward up the Rhone Valley; and Operation Avalanche, the invasion of the Italian mainland with the object of keeping the German divisions in Italy busy and of capturing bases from which shuttle bombing could be conducted against Germany and the Balkans.

But Operation Overlord was the supreme undertaking. "Victory in this global war depended on the successful execution of Overlord," writes Marshall. "That must not fail." He continues:

Yet the Japanese could not be permitted meanwhile to entrench in their stolen empire, and China must not be allowed to fall victim to further Japanese assaults. Allied resources were searched through again and again, and strategy reconsidered in the light of the deficiencies. These conclusions seemed inescapable: France must be invaded in 1944, to shorten the war by facilitating the advance westward of the Soviet forces. At the same time German technological advances such as the development of atomic explosives made it imperative that we attack before these terrible weapons could be turned against us. In addition, the pressure on the Japanese in the Pacific must not be relaxed. Communications with China must be reopened. Resources were allocated accordingly. The balance was extremely delicate but we had to go ahead.

Conferences at Cairo and at Tehran dealt with these problems. The first meeting, held in November 1943, was unique in that Chiang Kai-shek, the Chinese Generalissimo, sat for the first time with his Western allies. But the meeting at Tehran, the capital of Iran, was an even more extraordinary event because of the presence of Josef Stalin. Separate conferences were essential for appearances' sake: Russia was studiously neutral in the struggle with Japan. But the Tehran conclave followed immediately after the meeting at Cairo, public declarations summing up the results of the respective conferences were issued simultaneously, and the impression seems to have been intended that the Soviet Union would sooner or later identify itself openly with the war in the Far East. Said Stalin to Roosevelt: "We shall be able by our common front to beat Japan." Such an eventuality had been ardently desired by the American Army Chiefs ever since Pearl Harbor. Indeed, Russian participation in the war against Japan formed part of their basic strategic calculations.[29]

Meanwhile preparations for Overlord were pushed relentlessly. In August 1943 there was but a single American division on the soil of the United Kingdom, and the shipping of the two powers was strained almost to capacity by the demands of the Mediterranean operations. On D-Day, June 6, 1944, the United States Army had 1,533,000 men mobilized in Britain, an average of 150,000 per month having been transported thither during the interim. Bombs fell on Hitler's Fortress Europe now by day and by night. A shuttle system between bases in the United Kingdom and Italy started in mid-August 1943; in the following June a second such service was inaugurated between Italy and the Soviet Union. Then came the great day of the assault on the Normandy beaches, chosen "after long study of the strength of German coastal defenses and the disposition of German divisions." The beach areas totaled ten thousand yards in length. Every seventy-five yards a landing craft loaded with assault infantry touched down. "By the second morning it was clear that the beachhead was secure and that the greatest and longest step toward the destruction of the German armies of the west had been taken."

May 7, 1945: The German Surrender in Europe

From the beaches of Normandy to the banks of the Rhine the battle raged for nine months. To describe the complexities and difficulties of this dazzling campaign of American and British armies, supported to an increasing degree by Free French forces, is beyond the range of this book. The liberation of France was the immediate goal, and it was achieved swiftly, efficiently, and brilliantly, but at heavy cost in blood and equipment. Paris was entered on August 25; meanwhile the American Seventh Army had executed a landing in southern France (Operation Anvil), and started up the Rhone Valley; strong pockets of German resistance remained, to the very end of hostilities, in control of the critical French ports to prevent their use by the Allies; but in spite of the almost insuperable handicaps of transport and supply, the victorious armies had the defeated foe streaming back toward the Rhine by the first of September. British troops took the vital port of Antwerp twelve days later. More than two months were required to clear its ruined harbor, but at length this port proved to be a great asset in shortening the lines of supply. Beginning in late November it handled 25,000 tons of stores daily, in spite of the V-bombs the Germans expended on it in the desperate hope of keeping the port unusable. Pushed almost to the Rhine, the Wehrmacht dealt its last great blow in December: hoping to recover Antwerp, it drove a wedge fifty miles deep into the American line in Belgium. This German offensive held up the Allied advance six weeks but failed to achieve any important objective.

Meanwhile, Soviet armies were in Hungary and on their way up the Danube; other Russian armies were advancing through Poland into Germany itself. On March 7, 1945, American forces, probing the Rhine south of Cologne, found a bridge across the river that the Germans had failed to destroy. Their discovery was a windfall. Before the end of the month the British and Americans had built seven bridges across the river, and, with the Russians closing in on Berlin from the east, the Allies were at last ready for the kill. There was a rush across Germany to the Elbe, and another quick advance into the heart of Bavaria and the Harz Mountains. Under such punishing blows Germany literally disintegrated. "Surrounded on all fronts by chaos and overwhelming defeat," concluded General Marshall, "the emissaries of the German Government surrendered to the Allies at Reims on 7 May, 1945, all land, sea, and air forces of the Reich."

August 10, 1945: The Japanese Surrender in Asia

The defeat of Japan was near at hand too. The basic strategy against the Nipponese enemy had been laid down more than two years previously at Casablanca. Roosevelt had two objectives: to overwhelm Japan by sea and from the air, and to promote the cause of China, making secure at the end of the war her position as the leading power of the Far East. The first was an attainable objective, the second ended in ghastly failure. To keep China in the war and bring about a surrender of the Japanese armies operating within her borders, the air line over the Himalayan Hump was utilized to the full. From a thin trickle in January 1943 the monthly flow of cargo over this costly and hazardous route rose two years later to a capacity volume of 46,000 tons. This route was the life line to Chiang Kaishek, whose Nationalist armies were expected to bend all their efforts against Japan. Meanwhile a China-Burma-India theater of operations was created, with the intent of expelling the Japanese from Burma and of building a road that would open up China to invasion from the south. The road was completed across the most formidable mountain terrain on the face of the globe and the Japanese were expelled from Rangoon and the coastal areas of Burma, but the projected invasion of China by Allied forces never materialized.[30]

Combined operations in the Pacific led to the mastery of that ocean in less than a year. They began with the seizure of the Gilbert Islands in November 1943; two months later came an invasion of the Marshalls, and by July 1944 Operation Forager had resulted in the occupation of the key islands of Guam and Saipan in the Marianas. Meanwhile MacArthur had been advancing, leapfrog fashion, along the north coast of New Guinea in the direction of the Philippines. In this region, as in the island clusters to the north and east, scores of enemy-held islands were by-passed: "hundreds of thousands of Japanese troops were isolated in the jungles of the Pacific islands, dying on the vine, and of no further use to their Emperor." The Philippines campaign began on schedule in September 1944, and Manila Bay was open early in the following March. By this time, too, Iwo Jima in the Bonins had been taken in a desperate battle. On April 1, 1945, the first landing on Okinawa in the Ryukyus was made, and the day of final reckoning was at hand. American and British men-of-war were in Japanese home waters by the summer of

1945, the Island Empire's last communications with the mainland were cut; and bombs were rained incessantly on Japanese cities. Then on August 6, 1945, an event took place that startled the world: a single atomic bomb, a weapon for which the scientists of all the principal belligerents had been searching since the beginning of the war, was loosed on Hiroshima. The fatality list, according to Japanese reports, exceeded 100,000. Three days later the port of Nagasaki met a similar fate. Meanwhile Soviet armies, long poised on the Manchurian border, advanced aggressively into the province. Harbin fell. On August 10, 1945, the Emperor of Japan sued for peace.[81]

The Tally—The Troubled Accord with Russia

Thus ended in total victory the Second World War. Among the victors, Britain and the United States had together knocked out Italy; the United States, with some British help, vanquished Japan; but only the combination of Anglo-American and Soviet power broke the back of Nazi Germany. Invaluable to the Anglo-American cause was the steadfast support of the British dominions, notably of Canada in the North Atlantic, and of the numerous resistance movements and governments-in-exile that had found fair haven in London from the storm that had burst upon them. Among the latter was the Polish, whose legitimacy it soon suited the Soviets to deny. Thinly disguising their opinion that this government was an Anglo-American puppet, the Russians trained a group of Polish Communists and seated them at Lublin as the true provisional government of Poland. Tremors of disagreement over the Polish question had shaken the foundations of the alliance of the three great powers ever since December 1941; and the issue of the Lublin versus the London Poles, which reached a climax in February 1945, when the three powers met at Yalta in the Crimea, threatened a jolt severe enough then and there to bring down the edifice of Soviet friendship toward the West. Unity—its appearance at least—was restored at Yalta, and the three great allies marched on gloriously together to victory over the most formidable of their enemies.

The shadow of Soviet power over Europe, it will be remembered, had fallen first on Anthony Eden, the British Foreign Secretary. At Christmas 1941, Russian demands included: the incorporation of the Baltic States and also portions of Finland, Poland, and Rumania in the Soviet Union; the dismemberment of Germany and the payment of reparations in kind, though not in money; the restoration of Austria to independence; and various territorial changes in Eastern

Europe affecting Czechoslovakia, Jugoslavia, Albania, and Turkey. The issues of the Baltic States and of Poland aroused the opposition of the Western powers at once. Bound together by the Atlantic Charter, to which the Soviet Union had paid lip service but which clearly it did not take seriously, Britain and the United States refused their consent; and the Soviet effort to draw the British into a separate agreement met with failure. Henceforward Stalin kept his own counsel, until at Yalta the Polish question burst into the open; but Russian ambitions left an impression on Washington and London. Bent on keeping Russia at their side in the war against Germany, the Anglo-American powers knew that with victory they would come face to face with the Soviets.[32]

Over the treatment to be meted out to the Germans the Anglo-American powers and the Russians found little on which to disagree. Reacting instinctively to the famous phrase used by General Grant in 1865, Roosevelt publicly announced at Casablanca that nothing less than unconditional surrender would be required. Stalin's bill of particulars on Germany, already offered to Eden in December 1941, was the same thing in substance; and at a conference in Moscow in October 1943 the three powers agreed to undertake occupation of the enemy country, to wholly disarm Germany and impose a reparations program upon her, and to extirpate the Nazi party. At Tehran Roosevelt offered a plan for the separation of Germany into five autonomous states, to which Stalin took no serious exception; and at the close of the Yalta Conference the three great allies publicly pronounced the doom of Germany.[33] "It is our inflexible purpose," they declared, "to destroy German militarism and Nazism and to ensure that Germany will never again be able to disturb the peace of the world."

The United Nations—Four Policemen, or Three?

Locked in with the German question was Mr. Roosevelt's zeal for a permanent United Nations organization. Despite the misgivings over Russian ambitions aroused in December 1941—misgivings which the British government never was able to forget—the President's confidence in Russia appears steadily to have risen during the war years. The core of the United Nations, according to Roosevelt, would consist of the "Four Policemen"—the U.S.S.R., the U.S.A., the U.K., and China—and the countries which the "Policemen" would need to watch the most closely were Germany and Japan. With these enemy nations put in their proper places, the peace of the world was good for fifty years. All through 1942 and 1943 Roosevelt showed an eagerness to meet Stalin face to face. Moreover, we must remember, American ideas of waging war against Germany agreed with Russian more than with British ideas. The "Second Front" in France was the darling of the American Army as it was of the Soviet Union, a point of agreement which Molotov in his visit of May 1942 to Washington did not hesitate to exploit.

The President did not get his wish to meet Stalin until December 1943, when at Tehran he repeated with considerable elaboration the ideas respecting the "Four Policemen" that he had expounded to Molotov. The proposed organization was to consist of an assembly of nations, large and small, on a world-wide scale, an executive committee made up of the "Four Policemen" and certain other states, and a third body which was to be limited in membership to the Policemen. Stalin's reactions were very simple: three policemen were all that were needed to keep the peace; China could not qualify; and as for the world-wide assembly, the Soviet leader dismissed it with a shrug.[34] Roosevelt kept on with his plans, however; from a meeting of the four powers, which lasted two months through the autumn of 1944, emerged a formal set of Proposals for a United Nations organization; and at Yalta, the Americans being determined not to let the opportunity slip, the others acquiesced somewhat reluctantly on a definite date for the Charter meeting in San Francisco.

It was at Tehran and especially at Yalta that the three great powers compared notes on their respective attitudes toward the coming problems of peace. All three—Roosevelt, Churchill, Stalin—hoped they could take the same road, and all three tried to set up their positions at a common starting point. Roosevelt wanted two things of the Russians: support for the United Nations and participation in the war against Japan, to be followed by an equitable settlement in the Far East based upon recognition of China as a full partner in the quadripartite alliance. Relatively free of suspicion of Russia, he acted on the assumption that he could bind the Soviets permanently to the American side. He could do this, he believed, partly by argument and by giving them all-out support in the war against Germany, and partly by making concessions within the context of practical international politics to Russian national ambition and interest. Thus at Tehran he introduced his United Nations idea to Stalin in the homely but effective way that had served him so well on numerous occasions in the past. The United Nations were the Four Policemen, destined to keep order on the globe. Stalin caught this notion readily enough, rejecting only the fourth policeman—China. At Yalta, after the four powers had met at Dumbarton Oaks and had agreed upon the Proposals for the United Nations, American (and also British) concepts of what the new organization ought to be appeared to the Russians in a more elaborate but indubitably less realistic light: the lesser, and even the smallest, nations were to have a voice. Stalin immediately objected, singling out Albania for his special scorn. To which Churchill responded: "The eagle should permit the small birds to sing, and care not wherefor they sang."[35] To this the Russian made no answer. He was pleased with the two extra seats in the Assembly pledged to him, but his main thought remained fixed on the Three Policemen. The peace of the world, he hastened to explain, centered on the ability of the Three to avoid quarrels among themselves. Neither Roosevelt nor Churchill could find fault with this sentiment.

Russian and American Aims in Asia

If the American desire to enlist Russia in the cause of the United Nations is readily understandable, the eagerness with which Russian help against Japan was sought is less so. The matter cannot be discussed lucidly, because we lack a clear record of the inside pressures in Washington upon the Chief Executive to keep him on the track of a Russian alliance.[36] Those pressures came chiefly, if not exclusively, from the War Department, which soon after Pearl Harbor tried to get the Soviet Union to grant bases in Eastern Siberia for air operations against the Island Empire. To the very end of the conflict with Japan, it was axiomatic with the Army Chiefs that an invasion would be necessary. Operation Olympic—the proposed landing on southern Kyushu—was scheduled for November 1945, to be followed in the spring by Coronet, the main invasion. Viewing this operation with grave hesitancy, the Army wanted the Russians to invade Manchuria and keep the Japanese garrison there—the famed Kwantung Army—preoccupied. Even after the Potsdam Conference in July the Army Chiefs kept up their pressure to get Russia in the war. But since the Soviets had no motive of their own to join hands with the United States in crushing Japan, they remained unresponsive. They had their nonaggression pact of 1941 with Japan at which to point, and all through the war they maintained an elaborate and meticulously careful appearance of neutrality in the Far East. With canny shrewdness, Stalin volunteered to Hull at Moscow in October 1943 that, after the defeat of Germany, he would join in making war on Japan. This bait may, or may not have led President Roosevelt at Tehran to offer

Stalin the port of Dairen, subject only to its becoming a free port under international guaranty.[37]

"I only want to have returned to Russia what the Japanese have taken from my country," said Stalin to Roosevelt at Yalta. To which the President replied: "That seems like a very reasonable suggestion from our ally—they only want to get back that which has been taken from them."[38] And so a three-power agreement was concluded to the effect that "in two or three months after Germany has surrendered and the war in Europe has terminated," Russia would enter the war against Japan on condition that her position in Outer-Mongolia was preserved and her former rights, "violated by the treacherous attack of Japan in 1904," were restored. These rights included the southern part of Sakhalin and its adjacent islands, the restoration of Russia's "pre-eminent interests" in the commercial port of Dairen and of the lease of Port Arthur as a naval base, and the joint operation with the Chinese of the Chinese Eastern and South Manchurian railroads. The Kurile Islands were also to "be handed over" to the Soviets; and since these arrangements required the concurrence of Chiang Kai-shek, the President, it was agreed, would "take measures in order to obtain this concurrence on advice from Marshal Stalin." In return, the Soviet Union agreed to recognize the "full sovereignty" of China in Manchuria, and to conclude a "pact of friendship and alliance" with the National government of China "in order to render assistance to China with its armed forces for the purpose of liberating China from the Japanese yoke."[39] In "fulfillment" of these terms, the U.S.S.R. crossed the Manchurian border on August 8, 1945, two days after the American atomic attack on Hiroshima and two days before the Emperor surrendered!

The China Question

We have now looked at American war aims in terms of (1) the decisive defeat of Germany and Japan, (2) the firm establishment of a United Nations, and (3) a lasting friendship with the Soviet Union. The third objective was regarded as the linchpin for the first two. But there was a fourth aim that will not bear being overlooked. This was the unification of China under the National government, and the elevation of that country to the rank of a great power. China was the Fourth Policeman: her help in the war was needed against Japan, and in the peace the beaten enemy would be the principal object of her watch.[40] It had been Chiang Kai-shek whom, we remember, Japan had been told in November 1941 she must recognize if she were to have peace with the United States. And it was Chiang with whom

Roosevelt personally conferred at Cairo in November 1943, just prior to his meeting with Stalin at Tehran. We cannot doubt Mr. Roosevelt's great dreams for Nationalist China. To Stalin he stressed the importance of her future. From Churchill he expected eventual sacrifices of British interests, notably of Hong Kong, for China's benefit. He never seems to have doubted that he would get British co-operation. Of the Russians the State Department had asked a helping hand at least as early as 1942. Their moral influence with the Chinese Communists would be invaluable. "We did not put any specific proposal to Russia on this score during my period of service," writes Mr. Hull, "but we repeatedly talked with her. . . . ."[41] No doubt the Russians in this case made good listeners: the Secretary was unable to record any replies from them.

For its China policy the Roosevelt administration ever kept ready its rose-tinted glasses. If the fatal weakness of the National government was not visible at the time of the Cairo meeting, it began to be demonstrated by the spring of 1944. A violent altercation between Chiang and the peppery General Stilwell, who had promoted the idea of a Burma campaign, uncovered the gravity of Chiang's war with the Chinese Communists. Roosevelt made an effort to compose the struggle. The American embassy in Chungking argued with Chiang the possibilities of sharing his power with the Communist leaders. A special mission headed by Henry A. Wallace presented the same case to the Generalissimo, but got for an answer the advice to the United States to "show aloofness" toward the Chinese Communists. Wallace was followed immediately by a second mission headed by Brigadier General Hurley, chosen at the instance of Stimson and Marshall. Hurley paid a visit to Moscow in September 1944, and got from Stalin's own lips an expression of indifference toward the Chinese Communists. Hurley then ranged himself violently against the latter; and when the two Communist leaders, Mao Tsê-tung and Chou Ên-lai, secretly approached General Wedemeyer to arrange for them a personal interview with the President in Washington, Hurley intervened to foil the attempt. What might have came of this, we cannot say. But the President, who was by now out of touch with the Department of State, was deprived of his last opportunity to hear the case of Chiang's opponents. Roosevelt stuck by Chiang to the last. Meanwhile, the Soviet government continued to assert its lack of interest in the Chinese Communists and to express its readiness to recognize the National government. At Yalta, Stalin, having made provision for the restoration of Russia's rights in Manchuria, raised no objection to concluding a treaty with Nationalist

China. This, in fact, he did on August 14, 1945, six days after his army had started into Manchuria.[42]

Victory—Its Legacies

Now, to prepare ourselves for a comprehensive view of the unprecedented world situation at the close of hostilities, we must look briefly at the principal war aims of the other two great allies, Britain and the Soviet Union. Leaving aside the matter of unconditional surrender of the Axis enemies, on which there was substantial accord, let us consider the ideas for peace entertained respectively by the British and Soviet governments and the objects on which each of these governments intended to place emphasis. On the subject of the United Nations Britain, with some notable differences, co-operated fully with the American government.[43] Of the Russian attitude, no more need be said. Stalin confined his interest to the affairs of the Three Policemen; the elaborate organization which Roosevelt designed for the UN, and the dramatic Charter meeting at San Francisco for which the United States was so eager were, to the Russian mind, innocuous measures in which the American President could be safely indulged. The same may be said with respect to Roosevelt's China program. Neither the British nor the Russians could look seriously upon China as a great power. That was an American whim, toward which the two other allies could be skeptical, though polite. Nothing as yet has come to light to incriminate the Soviet government in a perfidious program during the war of promoting the Chinese Communists against the National government. Russia, to be sure, had definite objectives in China; but the road to those objectives was opened at Yalta in collaboration with the United States, and the easy way to get them was through the treaty with Chiang Kai-shek.

On the matter of the future relations of the Soviet Union with the two Western powers, both Churchill and Stalin thought more closely and less confidently than Roosevelt. Like Stalin, the President was content with the concept of the Big Three; and in the reservoir of good feeling created at Tehran and Yalta he dreamed of an ever-widening area of friendship and co-operation between Russia and the West. Neither Churchill nor Eden shared this faith. Great Britain, they saw, was not strong enough to hold Western Europe alone; and with them, as indeed with the President, it was axiomatic that the American Army would not long remain in Europe. Against Stalin's, and also at first Roosevelt's opposition, Britain made her key policy at Tehran and Yalta the restoration of France as a great power. The French must be given a share in the occupation of Germany and admitted to equal membership on the Allied Control Council. Stalin actively, and Roosevelt passively, opposed this policy. But at Yalta Harry Hopkins intervened effectively in support of the British. Hopkins won Roosevelt's support; and Stalin, having concluded a good bargain over Poland, graciously yielded to this Anglo-American front on France.[44] In April, two months after the Yalta meeting, Averill Harriman, the American Ambassador to Moscow, defined Soviet policy in these terms: collaboration with the Anglo-American powers in a world organization; creation of a security ring through the domination of the border countries; and penetration of other countries through their Communist parties. It was vital, Harriman pointed out, that the Western powers give the Soviets no opportunity to come between them.[45]

It was over the second of these policies that the Soviet Union locked horns with the West. At Yalta Churchill, backed by Roosevelt, made it clear that he wanted the London Poles to constitute the interim government of Poland, pending the holding of a general election in that country. Stalin on his part made it equally clear that he would support only the Lublin Poles. The London Poles, he declared, were enemies of Russia. To add point to this position, Russian armies had already overrun Poland and the Lublin government had actually been set up. Confronted with this fact, Roosevelt and Churchill agreed upon a formula whereby "The Provisional Government which is now functioning in Poland should therefore be reorganized on a broader democratic basis with the inclusion of democratic leaders from Poland itself and from Poles abroad." Roosevelt, and apparently Churchill too, left Yalta with the understanding that Stalin would permit a genuine reorganization, including one or more representatives from the London Poles, and that this would be followed by a free and unfettered election. But by April 1 it was clear that such was not to be. The Soviet government reopened its case against the London Poles and insisted upon hand-picking certain Poles with whom to *enlarge* the Lublin regime. It flatly refused to permit a reorganization of the Polish government as the Western powers had conceived it. A similar deadlock ensued over Rumania. The powers had subscribed to a "Declaration on Liberated Europe," which had stipulated that the peoples of liberated countries should be assisted to form interim governments "broadly representative of all democratic elements in the population" and pledged to holding free elections. But a bare two weeks after the adjournment from Yalta, the Soviet commissar, Vishinsky, arrived in Bucharest and forced upon the King a pro-Communist regime headed by Petru Groza. An American protest against this act was roughly rejected; and on April 29, 1945, Churchill sent a final, eloquent personal appeal to Stalin. "There is not much comfort," wrote the British Prime Minister, "in looking into a future where you and the countries you dominate plus the Communist parties in many other states are all drawn up on one side and those who rallied to the English-speaking nations . . . . are on the other. It is quite obvious that their quarrel would tear the world to pieces. . . . ."[46]

With this somber warning the Second World War drew rapidly to a close. On June 5, 1945, the supreme Allied commanders, joined by the French, issued from Berlin a declaration formally depriving Germany of her sovereignty and splitting that country into four distinct zones of occupation. Greater Berlin was constituted a fifth zone, subject to the occupation and joint control of all four armies. And in July the heads of the three great allies—Truman sitting in Roosevelt's place—had their final meeting at Potsdam, the ancient seat of Prussian militarism, where they confirmed the terms of the military declaration and where the Anglo-American powers—Russia still maintaining her neutrality—laid down the terms which Japan was to accept less than a month later.

III

New Worlds,
New Quarrels

1939: The Department of State Plans for the Peace—Beginnings of the UN Concept

GREAT HOPES and painstaking preparations distinguished American diplomacy in its quest for a better and safer world to be built from the wreckage of the Second World War. Eager to succeed where Wilson had failed, the American government set to work as early as September 1939 on plans for peace. The initiative came from the Department of State, which was painfully aware of the neglect it had suffered at the hands of the President in 1918. In December 1941 Mr. Hull was ready with a proposal for an Advisory Committee on Postwar Foreign Policy, to be led by the Department of State but its membership to be drawn in addition from the several other departments of the government, from the Senate and the House of Representatives, and from private life. Under the Advisory Committee a large staff of experts was created to plan for peace; and elaborate studies were undertaken bearing on the political reorganization and economic reconstruction of Europe, on the problems of the Middle and Far East, on the treatment of dependent peoples and areas, and on the matter of reconciling the conflicting postwar policies of the great powers and inducing them to co-operate together permanently. All the plans were harnessed to the great central concept of a permanent United Nations organization, which would stand or fall according to the respective attitudes that the three great allies would assume toward it. Under Churchill the British government early displayed a strong preference for a regional type of world organization in place of a general one like the League of Nations. In March 1943 Churchill publicly announced his desire for a Council of Europe and a Council of Asia, each operating somewhat independently under a world organ-

85

ization. Roosevelt's idea of the "Four Policemen" shows that he too inclined in this direction, though the sequel shows that neither he nor Churchill intended giving Russia the right to operate exclusively within her chosen sphere. In the end this issue was straddled, the Charter recognizing regional organizations subordinate at least nominally to the Security Council.[1]

1944: Dumbarton Oaks, and the Russian Insistence on the Veto

Meanwhile, relying on its initial success in 1942 in silencing Soviet demands for territory, the Department of State proceeded on the assumption that self-interest would induce the Russians to support the United Nations. An elaborate declaration issued at the instance of Mr. Hull by the three powers in October of the following year reinforced this assumption. But the Russian mind saw the United Nations in the very simple uniform of the "Three Policemen." When at Tehran in December 1943 Roosevelt attempted for Stalin's benefit to etch in a few of the details of the complicated organization being planned in Washington, the Russian leader displayed indifference. By May of 1944 the State Department was ready for a formal conference with the Allies. It had now perfected what it called a "possible plan" that it wanted to submit for their approval. By taking into its confidence a considerable number of Senators and Congressmen from both parties, the Department had protected its work against an attack from that direction. It was also assured of support from the United Kingdom and from nineteen smaller governments, mostly Latin-American, whom it had consulted unofficially. But Moscow at first neglected to reply and then, though acquiescing, obtained postponements until the end of August. On August 28, a week after the conference had started at Dumbarton Oaks, the Russians demanded that all sixteen of the Soviet republics be made charter members of the organization; and at the same time they revealed how literally they adhered to the theory of the "Four Policemen" by insisting upon the right of a great power to veto consideration by the Security Council of any question to which it was a party.

With this bucket of cold water emptied over its head, the American government calmly consented to adjourn the meeting and proceed with the second or Chinese phase from which, it had been understood, the Soviets would be absent. Accompanied by a vague announcement of a delay in reaching agreement on the question of voting in the Security Council, the Dumbarton Oaks Proposals were then published. A most serious dilemma confronted the administration. The Soviet attitude threatened its plans with total defeat: Andrei Gromyko, the Ambassador, declared flatly that his government would not even attend a general conference unless its conditions were accepted in advance. On the other hand, the administration remembered 1919: the cause of the League of Nations had been lost in the United States itself. Pitiless publicity, with its opportunity to play up doubts and disagreements, had undermined an otherwise well-disposed public opinion. With the fall elections approaching, the naked truth regarding the Soviet Union might, if uncovered at the moment, then and there have swept away the slender chances of the United Nations.

Other clouds were gathering fast: in Jugoslavia a civil war had already burst, with the pro-Communist partisans of Tito gaining the lead over the Chetniks and the government-in-exile; in Greece a similar conflict was about to begin; and as for Poland, the Soviet-sponsored Lublin group was pitted against the government-in-exile seated in London. President Roosevelt dared not leave the American public wholly unprepared. The task of creating a world order, he declared on October 21, "was one that now appeared to be increasing in complexity." And he added: "I am certain, for myself, that I do not know how all the unforeseeable difficulties can be met."[2]

The public eye was, however, already fixed upon the Proposals. Doubts about Russia were thrust into the background, and approximately a hundred public organizations, including churches, volunteered their services in spreading information and stimulating discussion. On its part, the State Department set up a special Office of Public Affairs, in charge of an Assistant Secretary, which, by furnishing speakers, organizing panel discussions, and arranging group meetings with high officials, threw itself vigorously into the campaign of education. Even the Republican presidential candidate, Governor Dewey, chimed his approval; and the Republican leader in the Senate, Arthur H. Vandenberg, seized the initiative in laying the ghost of senatorial obstructionism. The United States, he roundly declared, could co-operate militarily with the other powers during a crisis without the President's first getting the consent of Congress. "There should be no need to refer any such action back to Congress any more than Congress would expect to pass upon battle plans today. The Commander in Chief should have instant power to act, and he should act."[3] Thus was American public opinion primed well in advance on the subject of the Charter.

Yalta: Compromises to Save the UN

Meanwhile at Yalta Roosevelt, Hopkins, and Stettinius, who had followed Hull in the State Department, concluded what seemed like a

firm compromise with the Russians. Stalin received and accepted an
offer of two extra seats in the United Nations Assembly, one for the
Ukraine and one for Byelorussia. In the matter of voting on the
Security Council, Stettinius read a prepared statement endorsing the
principle of great power unanimity, but took care to emphasize the
importance of full and free discussion and the right of any member
state, even the smallest, to present its case. Molotov, the Soviet foreign minister, having declared the statement acceptable, the Americans emerged from the conference in an exultant mood. They had (so
they thought) surmounted the hurdles the Russians had laid across
the United Nations track, and they now had both the date (April 25)
and the place (San Francisco) for the conference pinned down. The
public at home had been taught to expect the conference and to believe that "world peace" would this time come forth from the bosom
of the new-born United Nations. Said Hopkins:

We really believed in our hearts that this was the dawn of the new day
we had all been praying for and talking about for so many years. . . . .
The Russians had proved that they could be reasonable and farseeing and
there wasn't any doubt in the minds of the President or any of us that we
could live with them and get along with them peacefully for as far into
the future as any of us could imagine. . . . .[4]

On the other hand, for Roosevelt to have departed from the Crimea
unable to promise the United Nations would have been a crushing
blow not only to himself and his immediate followers, but to the people
of the United States. Too much was at stake for the outcome to be
otherwise. And after the tension and uncertainty that the administration had had to bear since the deadlock at Dumbarton Oaks, it was
quite natural for it to rejoice over its apparent victory at Yalta.

But Marshal Stalin, it seems clear, did not share the faith. At
Yalta he was gracious to a degree not previously granted his allies because by this time they were doing so much for him. The lingering
Russian fear of a separate peace between Germany and the Anglo-
American powers evaporated with the punishing blows being dealt
the Germans in the west; in Poland and in Eastern Europe the Soviets
held all the advantages; and as for the Far East, Roosevelt's pledges
respecting China and Manchuria gave Russia a free hand in that vast
area. Stalin at Yalta had good reason to feel that his own idea of the
three policemen managing the world, each operating in his own sphere,
was at last on a working basis. The ponderous institutional machinery
which so fascinated the Americans in connection with the United Nations got scant respect. Dumbarton Oaks had impressed the Russian

leader so little that, before coming to Yalta, he had made no study of the Proposals. His attitude of tolerant indifference remained the same thereafter.

San Francisco: The United Nations Charter

While the other powers prepared to send their foreign ministers to San Francisco, the Russians let it be known they would send merely their Ambassador in Washington. A last-minute appeal from the American government brought a change of mind: Molotov, Stalin decided, would go. In San Francisco the Soviet foreign minister brought the conference to a standstill over the same question that had jeopardized Dumbarton Oaks: the right of a great power to silence discussion in the Security Council. Again the whole project trembled on the verge of futility, and again it was rescued in consequence of a special appeal to the Marshal. Harry Hopkins made his last journey to Moscow at the end of May. There in lengthy conversations with the Soviet leader he tried to repair the already badly damaged bridge in the relations between Russia and the two Western powers. Stalin had a catalogue of complaints and doubts: the manner in which Argentina had been maneuvered into representation at San Francisco; the admission of France to membership on the Reparations Commission on a par with Russia; the abrupt, unilateral termination by the Truman administration of Lend-Lease; the indisposition of the Western powers to share with Russia the surrendered German fleet and merchant marine; and above all, the question of Poland where, the Marshal believed, the United States was playing what he called "the British game" in promoting a government unfriendly to the Soviet Union. Stalin's mind never got far away from Poland: it was traditional in the West to favor a government in that country hostile to Russia; she had been an essential part of the one-time *cordon sanitaire*; and twice in a quarter century the Germans had used her as a corridor for the invasion of Russia. Hopkins insisted that the United States and Great Britain wanted Poland to be "friendly" to Russia— he even disavowed a special interest in the London Poles—but the term "friendly" was too ambiguous to satisfy the Russian mind. In Poland at least a "friendly" government had to be a controlled government.

All told, between May 26 and June 4 Hopkins had six conferences with Stalin. Only at the sixth and final one was the matter of the United Nations brought up. The Russian showed a keen distrust of small nations (this had been evident from his attitude on the Polish and other questions involving small powers); but he also evinced a desire to retain American friendship. Hopkins played on this desire: he emphasized the importance the American people attached to the United Nations and the mortal blow that would fall on Soviet-American friendship if Russia blocked the conference at San Francisco. As a gesture of friendship for the United States rather than as a concession to the principle of free discussion in the Security Council, Stalin decided that the impasse was over "an insignificant matter" and that the American position should be accepted. On the basis of this summary statement Hopkins gave Truman an all-clear signal, and the San Francisco Conference went on to a triumphant conclusion of the Charter.[5]

The Machinery of the UN

An organization chart of the United Nations shows three coequal organs: the International Court of Justice, resting on a new Statute but nevertheless closely resembling the old World Court created in 1920; the General Assembly; and the Security Council. The Security Council was intended to be the fountainhead of the organization, the member states being obligated to accept and carry out its decisions. The Council has eleven members: the five great powers who occupy the permanent seats and six other states chosen by the Assembly for terms of two years. Decisions were to be reached through "an affirmative vote of seven members including the concurring votes of the permanent members." Thus a negative vote by any one of the five permanent members or by five of the nonpermanent members acting together constitutes a veto. At San Francisco the great powers reiterated their determination to work together, each one pledging itself not to use the veto willfully to obstruct the operation of the Council. Of course, everything had to be left to the spirit shown by each of the five permanent members: if they co-operated reasonably together, the Council would come close to being an international government.[6] The Charter obligated all member states to conclude contracts with it, making available to it on call armed forces, assistance, and facilities, including rights of passage. These agreements "shall govern the numbers and types of forces, their degree of readiness and general location, and the nature of the facilities and assistance to be provided." Taking a leaf from the book of the Second World War, the Charter also provided for a Military Staff Committee to advise and assist the Council. This committee "shall consist of the Chiefs of Staff of the permanent members of the Security Council. . . . . The Military Staff Committee shall be responsible under the Security Council for the strategic direction of any armed forces placed at the disposal of the Security Council." Here, obviously, was an attempt to profit from the experience of the Anglo-American Combined Chiefs of Staff during the war. The Charter, moreover, envisioned an international army operating under the direction of the Security Council. But although the Military Staff Committee was duly constituted, it functioned in an atmosphere of increasing political warfare between the Soviet Union and the Western powers and in 1948 it was indefinitely suspended.

With this and other disappointments in connection with the Security Council, the Western powers turned to the General Assembly as an instrument for making a success out of the United Nations. The Assembly was designed, like its predecessor in the former League of Nations, to be the open forum of the small nations. There all members, large and small, meet on a common level. Originally it seems to have been intended principally as a safety valve. While it could debate freely, it was not permitted by the Charter to interfere with the Security Council when the latter was exercising its functions. On the other hand, any of the powers might submit to it any question affecting international peace; and by resorting to the device of an interim committee, the Assembly under American and British leadership managed from 1947 onward to remain in continuous session. The "Little Assembly," representative of all the member states but composed of smaller delegations, thus began to function as a sort of rival of the Security Council. Decisions could be reached by a two-thirds majority of the members present and voting; and though the Charter conferred upon the Council alone the power to undertake "enforcement actions" (sanctions), the Assembly under American urging assumed jurisdiction in the fall of 1950 over UN forces operating in the Korean war.[7]

UN Operations: Economic and Social Assistance, Trusteeship Versus Colonialism, Financial Reconstruction

The object of the conference at San Francisco was not merely to create a permanent alliance among the great powers, but to give birth to international government on a grand scale. The UN was planned as a vastly more complex organization than its predecessor, the League of Nations. The national state with its principle of separate sovereignty might be the necessary member unit in the new structure; but institution-building for the postwar world pointed in the direction of a closely knit global society that would gradually displace the historic system of independent national states. Thus the Economic and Social Council, comprising eighteen members of the UN and voting by simple majority, was charged with ambitious undertakings for the betterment of living conditions throughout the world. How remote from reality these aspirations were, may be judged from a brief glance at a single phase of the problem: the question of feeding and relocating the vast numbers of refugees torn from their homes by the war and by the political disturbances in Europe and Asia that followed in the wake of the war. An International Red Cross estimate in 1950 placed these numbers at somewhere between sixty and eighty million, fifteen million of whom were in Europe alone. Although the UN set up an International Refugee Organization to care for these wretched people, the actual burden fell on the local authorities. The majority of the membership on the Economic and Social Council came from "underdeveloped" nations—countries of scanty resources, crowded populations, and low productivity. Naturally these nations held out their hands to the more prosperous states for vast sums of money to be sunk into development enterprises in their territories. When in January 1949 the Truman administration volunteered a "bold new program" for "the improvement and growth of under-developed areas," hopes began to soar, only to fall swiftly when the American government made it plain before the Council that it did not regard itself as a cornucopia. Associated with the Economic and Social Council were a number of specialized agencies, such as the Food and Agriculture Organization, planned during the war to find ways of moving food surpluses to hungry populations; the World Health Organization, committed like its predecessor in the League to an international program of control of epidemics; and the United Nations Educational, Scientific, and Cultural Organization, assigned the task of preparing a program for evening up differentials in educational opportunity.

To the same end of building on the work of the League of Nations the Charter of the UN created an international trusteeship system. It was a fresh attempt to advance the principle of international accountability for dependent peoples as a substitute for the colonialism of the nineteenth century. A Trusteeship Council of twelve members, including the five permanent members of the Security Council, was put in charge of the trust territories; and the General Assembly, where, of course, the noncolonial powers greatly outnumbered those having colonial possessions, was given supervisory authority over the Trusteeship Council. During the war the British dragged their feet on this matter, while American diplomacy under Roosevelt pushed zealously forward. Suddenly, however, while the conference at San Francisco was laboring hard on the Charter, the United States awoke to the danger of seeing its hard-won island conquests in the Pacific pass into the hands of an international authority, and along with them the loss of control over the vast ocean which the victory over Japan had bestowed. A quick reaction in the Senate, carrying with it the threat of rejection of the Charter, made its influence felt in San Francisco, with the result that allowance was made for strategic areas to be exempted in whole or in part from the operation of the trusteeship system at the will of the administering power. All of the former Japanese Pacific islands were forthwith declared a strategic area, thus putting them under exclusive American domination. Two years later, however, the United States modified to a large extent this policy by concluding a trust agreement with the UN placing all but the atoll of Eniwetok under the supervision of the Trusteeship Council. All told, eight trust territories were created from the former mandates of the League of Nations; and the Trusteeship Council was distinguished by an equal division in numbers between the powers with direct administering responsibility and those without. Meanwhile the General Assembly displayed a disposition to use the trusteeship system as a peg on which to hang condemnation of the colonial powers. Objects of this fire in particular were the British, French, and Belgians, and with the Soviet Union joining eagerly in the affray the Americans played the role of mediator in the verbal clashes between the colonial powers and the delegations from the emergent, nationalist-minded peoples who demanded complete freedom and admission to the UN. With the cold war between Russia and the West fully under way, the issue of colonialism passed far beyond the modest limits of the trust territories: virile nationalist movements, as in Indonesia and Libya, had to be appeased but not to the extent of ripping away the foundations of the European states close to the frontier line of Soviet Russia.[8]

Equally experimental, though no less essential, were the plans developed during the war to deal on a collective basis with postwar problems of financial reconstruction. Insight into these problems was shown by the United States and British treasuries as early as 1942; and a continued exchange of views between them, the drafting of plans for international monetary stabilization, and the careful publicizing of the plans led in July 1944 to the United Nations Monetary and Financial Conference at Bretton Woods, New Hampshire. Prior consultations with financial experts from thirty other countries contributed no doubt to the success of this conference in reaching definite agreements at the end of a three-week session. The Bretton Woods Agreements provided for two new and significant international institutions: the International Monetary Fund and the International Bank for Reconstruction and Development. The Fund was designed to accomplish what gold had done once when, under conditions of a free international monetary market, national currencies were readily convertible into the precious commodity. Member states, short in the supply of the currencies of other countries with whom they traded, might buy from the Fund the amounts they needed. The Fund originated in payments made according to a quota by the various member states, partly in gold and partly in their respective currencies. Management is in the hands of a Board of Governors which, by itself engaging in the business of foreign exchange, aims at keeping national currencies at parity. Being the country contributing the largest quota to the Fund, the United States is the seat of the Board of Governors. The International Bank for Reconstruction and Development was intended to assist in getting the flow of international investment capital started. Thus while the Fund aims to open up the ordinary channels of trade between nations, the Bank is an instrument for the reconstruction of the basic economies of nations impoverished by the war.[9]

Britain's Dilemma, and Europe's

Hopeful and well grounded as these new institutions appeared to be, trained minds during the war realized they would hardly be equal to the colossal task of rebuilding shattered industries and helping stricken countries all around the globe to work their way out of hopeless poverty. The United Nations Relief and Rehabilitation Association (UNRRA) was created in 1943 as a temporary agency to take over from the Allied armies the job of civilian relief in countries to be freed from the foe. Its function was to meet immediate human wants in food, clothing, and medical assistance, but to be effective it found that it also had to spend money repairing railways, industries, and public utilities.[10] UNRRA was hastily promoted as an instrument of sheer mercy and as a stopgap against social collapse in desperately ravaged or famine-stricken lands like Italy, Greece, and India.

Far more formidable in the long run than these relief problems was the question of how to make good on the modest plans for world recovery initiated at Bretton Woods. Secretary Morgenthau and others believed this could best be done through a continuation of the flow of Lend-Lease funds; and the various mutual aid agreements drawn up during the war years, on the basis of which Lend-Lease was implemented, made no provision for automatic termination at the close of hostilities. On the contrary, they anticipated an extended period of assistance accompanying the process of postwar economic adjustment. Great Britain's future in particular was the cause of much anxiety. At one point in 1944 Morgenthau proposed a postwar credit of $6,500,000,000 to her alone, and President Roosevelt himself privately declared in September 1944: "The real nub of the situation is to keep Britain from going into complete bankruptcy at the end of the war."[11] But unfortunately no conclusion was reached. The subject aroused acrimonious disputes inside the administration, and few steps were taken to enlighten the public on its importance. Consequently Lend-Lease in the popular mind was limited to the cause of winning the war; and on May 8, 1945, the unseasoned new President, Harry S. Truman, without even an advance warning to Britain and Russia, abruptly announced the termination of Lend-Lease.[12]

Swift repentance followed this precipitate action. Hard-working men in the United States and British treasuries labored incessantly to avert what seemed to them an appalling financial crisis. Political considerations had to be taken into account: Truman's act was popular in the United States, a vivid revelation of the national instinct to cut loose from Europe at the earliest opportunity. On December 6, 1945, the two governments signed a Financial Agreement under which the United States opened a credit of $3,750,000,000. The declared purpose of the credit was "to facilitate purchases by the United Kingdom of goods and services in the United States, to assist the United Kingdom to meet transitional postwar deficits in its current balance of payments, to help the United Kingdom to maintain adequate reserves of gold and dollars, and to assist the Government of the United Kingdom to assume the obligations of multilateral trade. . . . ." Unlike Lend-Lease, the transaction bore the earmarks of a commercial loan, the administration fearing that otherwise it would fail in Congress. Repayment of dollar for dollar was required over a period of fifty years, commencing December 31, 1951, and an interest rate of 2 per cent, a rate slightly in excess of the cost of money at the time to the American government, was imposed. These terms signified a reversion to the unrealistic procedures of the debt-funding agreements which followed World War I, but even so the Agreement had a stormy passage lasting seven months through Congress. Said *The Economist* of London at the time when these dollar funds finally became available: "Western Europe is the typhoon centre, and the British ship of state seems to many individuals a mere cockleshell in atomic storms."[13] Barely two years later the entire line of credit was gone.

Britain's plight, fated to get worse rather than better during these two years in which she lived off the American and the even larger (proportionately considered) Canadian credit, was, indeed, also Europe's plight. In general, the British economy is merely an intensified version of the economic life of Western Europe. Europe is a workshop which draws its materials from all over the world, processes them into finished goods, and then sells the manufactured goods abroad at a profit. The earnings of its factories, their ability to compete in the markets of the world, constitute the bedrock of the Western European standard of living. The one time luxurious cushion of European comfort, the invisible exports, had been flattened out. Consequently there was but one road back, and it was a hard one: industry had to be revived and export markets regained. Progress along this road was made in 1946—Britain, France, Belgium, the Netherlands, and Norway, respectively, showed an index of production ranging from 81 per cent to 110 per cent of the 1937 level. But handicaps existed, their full strength being felt during the terrible winter of 1946–47 when all Europe shivered and went hungry. Prominent among these was the scarcity of coal, the fuel that alone could make an industrial revival succeed. Britain, Germany, and Poland, the three principal coal countries, each fell short of its average annual prewar production in 1946. Actually for two years Europe bought quantities of coal (on credit) from the United States.

European industry even showed an inability to satisfy the requirements of its home market, and this had disastrous effects upon agriculture. Since the farmer could get no fertilizers, machinery, clothing, or household goods from the cities, he reverted to a subsistence economy, raising enough for himself but leaving the urban populations to their fate. The Continent in 1947 was a vast poorhouse, with the signs visibly pointing toward the condition becoming permanent. The governments drew feverishly on their diminishing reserves and on their American credits for food and relief supplies rather than for fertilizers and industrial equipment indispensable for sparking a revival; and with the arrival of spring, accompanied by droughts and crop failures, American loans, grants, and private contributions made since 1945 totaled up to $11,000,000,000.

The Secretary of State Has a Plan

The government in Washington now grasped the dilemma in its true perspective. It was already committed to a costly military and relief program in Greece, where Communist incursions from the north threatened to overturn the government and, in behalf of the

Soviet Union, seize strategic control of the Eastern Mediterranean. The deepening misery of Europe, accompanied by alarming successes of Communist parties at the polls, was daily carrying the Continent in the direction of a social and political catastrophe from which it could never recover. Thoroughly aware of this gloomy forecast, the American Secretary of State, George C. Marshall, speaking publicly on June 5, 1947, at Harvard University, made a simple but convincing statement of the case destined to prove the starting point for an entirely fresh and co-ordinated attack on the problem of European recovery. Political stability and assured peace, declared Marshall, could not be had without a return to normal economic health. Europe's requirements of food and other essentials for the next three or four years would be far in excess of her ability to pay. American assistance would be forthcoming, but it must be conserved for Europe as a whole rather than parceled out on a piecemeal basis, country by country. It was the business of the Europeans to take the initiative in preparing a European program, agreed to by a number, if not all, of European nations. And it was the role of the United States to give friendly aid in the drafting of the program and later to support it so far as practical. The European Recovery Program, better known as the Marshall Plan, was the fruit of this address. To it we shall return, but it becomes necessary at this point to examine the diplomatic issues that developed between the two Western powers on the one hand and the Soviet Union on the other as they faced each other in 1945 inside the borders of their ruined foe.

Germany's Fate—Dismemberment or Occupation?

Superficially the Big Three powers were agreed on how to cope with Germany, once that country had been brought to surrender. They would disarm her completely, demilitarize her, and *dismember* her. This was their declared attitude at Yalta. Actually, behind the scenes, confusion and dissension prevailed. It was easy to subscribe to the formula; it proved impossible to draw up a plan. Soon after the meeting in December 1943 at Tehran the three powers had constituted the European Advisory Commission with the ostensible object of preparing a concerted plan. The British Foreign Office wanted the commission clothed with authority for this purpose, but it soon developed that each government held a veto over both the speech and the action of its representative. The free use of the veto, not merely by the Russians but by all three, brought the commission to a standstill repeatedly, and it ended its work in August 1945 in a complete stalemate.

In the first place, no agreement was reached over the wisdom or the practicability of dismemberment. Inside each government opinion divided on this vital question. President Roosevelt himself shifted his position at least three times. At Tehran he declared himself in favor of creating five autonomous German states. At the second Quebec conference, September 1944, he with Churchill endorsed an extreme plan drawn up inside the Treasury Department and eagerly pushed by Secretary Morgenthau for destroying German industry and pastoralizing the country. Shortly thereafter, Secretaries Hull and Stimson convinced him of the errors of this plan, and he attempted to shrug off the whole matter. An offhand statement to Hull on October 20 to the effect that he disliked "making detailed plans for a country which we do not yet occupy" put a stop to the work of the American representative on the Advisory Commission. Again, however, when pressed by Stalin at Yalta for a decision, Roosevelt agreed to dismemberment and to the Advisory Commission's working out the procedures. Nothing happened, however.

Meanwhile the President was at loggerheads with the British government over the location of occupation zones. A British memorandum of January 1944 had proposed giving Russia for occupation purposes East Germany, comprising 40 per cent of the territory. Britain was to occupy the northwest ports and the main industrial area, and the United States was to control the southwest sector bordering on France. This proposal brought acceptance from Moscow but rejection from Washington. The President wanted the northwest, especially the ports. This dispute was eventually quieted through a compromise giving the Americans an enclave in the British zone which included Bremen; but in the meantime, it having been decided that Berlin would be occupied jointly by the three powers (with the later addition of France), the vitally important question of creating a corridor through the Russian zone so as to give the Western powers direct access to Berlin was neglected. John G. Winant, the American Ambassador in London and representative on the Advisory Commission, urged this point very strongly; and he had it from his Russian colleague, Mr. Gusev, that "of course" Russia would give the Americans and British the necessary facilities through her zone. But Winant was blocked in Washington by the civil affairs division of the War Department which represented the latter on an interdepartmental committee empowered by the President to determine policy for the United States. Each of the three departments—State, War, and Navy—represented on this committee exercised a free veto, the practical effect of which was to make Winant's position in London untenable. The War Department insisted that the surrender and occupation of Germany was "a military matter," and it refused to the bitter end to conclude any advance agreements on occupation zones.[14]

To review in brief this wilderness of discord that dominated the scene not only among the three allies, but also within the inner councils of each government: President Roosevelt displayed a fairly consistent desire to dismember Germany permanently. The Department of State and the American members of the European Advisory Commission regarded this as unwise and calculated to lead to bitter international rivalry over the control of Germany. For the same reasons the Department tried to conclude a definite agreement in advance with Britain and Russia over the boundaries of the occupation zones, but was thwarted by the War Department and by Roosevelt himself. On the part of the British government, Churchill favored dismemberment or at least made no strong stand against it. The Foreign Office, like the Department of State, was definitely opposed.[15] As for Stalin, he, like Roosevelt, appears to have shifted his position on dismemberment, though occupation was to him more important. Roosevelt told the Russian leader that American military occupation would probably not last more than two years. Stalin volunteered no opinion as to the length of Russian occupation. At Yalta Stalin endorsed dismemberment, but in May he publicly announced himself against it, thus leaving the Anglo-American powers to swallow the dilemma into which they had got. Roosevelt staked his all on good relations with the Soviets and on the United Nations, but did not give to the State Department the needed support for concluding binding agreements over Germany. Dismemberment and occupation were theoretically two different things, but with the disintegration of the Third Reich in May they became for practical purposes one and the same.

The Potsdam Decisions

The military directives that followed and the protocol signed by the Big Three at Potsdam, August 2, 1945, succeeded for the time being in keeping up the appearances of Allied unity. Germany was now split into five military zones, Poland having been brought into the case by Russia. The supreme authority was the military government—in theory the Allied Control Council acting for Germany as a whole, in practice each commander functioning in his respective zone. References to dismemberment were studiously omitted, the powers simply stating that for the time being no central German government would be permitted. Over Berlin all four powers (Poland not included) presided, each taking a zone but committed to govern the city jointly with the others through the *kommandatura*, composed of the four commandants acting under the control council. The Allies declared they would extirpate German militarism and Nazism, and to this end would take measures to destroy industry that could be used for military production, dissolve the Nazi party, and control education so as to make possible the growth of democratic ideas. They would restrict the production of the metallurgical and chemical industries to minimum peacetime needs, and reorganize the German economy with the view to emphasizing agriculture and small domestic industries; yet they would also treat the country as a single economic unit. Partly to effectuate demilitarization and partly to collect reparations, they would dismantle and remove from the country factories and equipment, the Soviet Union to remove whatever it pleased from its zone and, because of the heavy concentration of industry in the western zones, to get 15 per cent of the usable and complete capital equipment in the other zones in exchange for food, coal, potash, and other commodities. Finally the German populations still living in Poland, Czechoslovakia, and Hungary were to be transferred to Germany, and the Allied Control Council was to see to it that these people were distributed equitably through the several occupation zones.[16]

The contradictions and cross-purposes inherent in this Agreement were not slow in coming to the surface. The Potsdam powers wanted to impose a long period of penal servitude on the Germans. They would dismantle and ruin the Ruhr, the historic arsenal of German militarism, try to convert it into second-rate agricultural land, and yet squeeze 66,000,000 or more people into a country about the size of Great Britain. Germany was to be allowed to keep sufficient industrial plant and equipment to support a standard of living not better than the average of the European Continental countries. The remainder were to be judged surplus and subject to removal as reparations. On this principle the powers concluded in March 1946 a Level of Industry Agreement which permitted Germany a productive capacity equivalent to roughly half of her capacity in 1936. A collision, however, occurred over the reparations issue. At Potsdam, realizing that the Germans would have to import certain raw materials, the Western powers had got the Soviets to agree to recognize that whatever exports the Germans were able to make out of current production would go first to pay for imports. Thus reparations were not to obstruct the normal economic balance of the defeated country. Theoretically too the Western powers would be saved the pain of supporting a pauper.

But having originally set their bill at ten billion dollars, the Russians proceeded to dismantle plant and equipment and, in addition, to take from the Germans in their zone food and goods produced currently. Since these commodities furnished payment for imported supplies from the West, their diversion into Russia caused a void which the Western powers were forced to fill. When, moreover, the Russians discovered their inability to set up and operate the dismantled German equipment in their own country, their desire to collect reparations out of current output naturally increased. But the Western powers were in effect paying the Russian bill; and since the Russians insisted on managing their zone without reference to the economy of Germany as a whole, the British and French, led by the American commander, General Clay, suspended further deliveries from their zone. Thus occurred the first open breach with the Soviets in the attempted joint management of Germany.[17]

Meanwhile stagnation in the Ruhr coal and iron industries, whose actual output in 1946 was far below the Allied Level of Industry Agreement, brought Western Europe face to face with economic destitution and political chaos. Britain and the United States, moreover, found themselves saddled with occupation costs in excess of $500,000,000 per year. Nor was even the military outlook promising. In numbers and in efficiency the American occupation troops had shrunk alarmingly. Discontented soldiers in Berlin publicly demonstrated their desire to go home. Worse still, a great tidal wave of popular sentiment for "bringing the boys back home" had rolled up after V-J Day; and with Congress giving little heed to the problem of replacement, it became a serious question whether the United States could long continue to participate effectively in the occupation of Germany. Given the pace of demobilization in the winter of 1945–46, the country would soon become militarily impotent. In April 1946 Secretary of State James F. Byrnes tried to reassure the British and French with an offer to conclude a four-power treaty pledging each party to the occupation and control of Germany for a period of twenty-five years. The proposal got a rebuff from the Soviets, but whether Byrnes could have fulfilled it satisfactorily, if it had passed, was at the time a question.

Potsdam was the kind of an agreement that either Russia or the Western powers could quote against the other. At a meeting of the Council of Foreign Ministers in Paris in July, Molotov used it against the West. He demanded a share in the control of the Ruhr, thereby exploiting the French desire for internationalization of that district, and he expressed vehement opposition to "agrarianizing" Germany.

Byrnes, for the United States, resolved on a direct approach to the German people. At Stuttgart on September 6, 1946, he virtually repudiated the punitive provisions of Potsdam. Germany, he declared, should not "become a pawn or a partner in a military struggle for power between the East and the West." The barriers between the four zones were "far more difficult to surmount than those between normal independent states." Payment of reparations was "wholly incompatible" with a program of deindustrialization. Germany was a part of Europe, she must have a balanced economy, and the German people "should now be given the primary responsibility for the running of their own affairs."[18] The speech was the signal for the renewal of political activities on the part of the Germans. Furthermore, it announced the decision of the British and American governments to fuse their zones, a step which was consummated in the following January. Long overdue—General Eisenhower had urged it earnestly even before Potsdam but, for political reasons, had been rebuffed—this merger threw down the barrier between the two zones which economically depended on each other. Furthermore, political autonomy for the Germans in the combined zone was not far behind. A self-governing state, known as Bizonia, subject to the supervision of the occupying authorities, made its appearance in May 1947. Bizonia survived for two years, to be graduated and expanded through the addition of the French zone into the West German Federal State.

The Iron Curtain

Meanwhile, from the Baltic to the Adriatic, an iron curtain had descended across Europe.[19] East of the Iron Curtain—in Poland, in Hungary, in Rumania, and in Bulgaria—the invading Russian armies had enabled local Communist parties to secure a stranglehold over the governments. Czechoslovakia was to remain free until February 1948, but in Jugoslavia the pro-Communist partisans of Tito had seized power even before Nazi Germany had collapsed. Potsdam had authorized the Council of Foreign Ministers to negotiate peace with Italy, Rumania, Bulgaria, Hungary, and Finland, and to propose settlements of European territorial questions. But the Council, starting its sessions in London in September 1945, had deadlocked at once. Molotov seized his chance in the Italian negotiation to take a long leap over the heads of the Western powers and plant Russian influence in the Eastern Mediterranean. A trusteeship in Tripolitania, a crushing levy on Italy for reparations and a transfer of Trieste to Jugoslavia were the means to this end. The Western powers countered with demands for free elections in the Balkan countries and for renewal of their one-time right to free use of the Danube River. The Russians did not get their trusteeship or their reparations from Italy, and the Western powers were shut out of political influence in the Balkans and barred commercially from the Danube Valley. At Paris in July 1946, however, the two sides compromised over Trieste by agreeing to make it an international Free Territory with a governor responsible to the United Nations. But the Russian idea of administering the "Free Territory" was to merge it for practical purposes with Jugoslavia; while the Western powers, mindful of Hitler's easy victory in the Free City of Danzig in 1939, insisted upon a governor with absolute powers and an international police force at his back.

In the meantime Tito, who then openly boasted of his connections with Moscow, threw himself into the fray by shooting down two American transport planes flying over his territory. This incident pointed at a Jugoslav invasion of Trieste, and the United States made an issue out of it and forced the Jugoslav dictator to make redress. Eventually, in December 1946, the Council of Foreign Ministers agreed on the terms of peace with Italy and the former German satellite states, including reparations and the principle of free trade and free navigation of the Danube. The five peace treaties were duly signed in Paris in the following February; but Italy, pauperized by the war and supported by funds from the United States and Britain, yielded no reparations, while the Danubian states, securely behind the Iron Curtain, made no move toward restoring free commercial intercourse with the West.[20]

The Instability of Western Europe

Side by side with these solemn mockeries of peace negotiations were the grim realities of destitution and despair seizing hold of Western Europe from Italy to Germany. The real play put on by the Council of Foreign Ministers lay, not in the motions of agreeing to paper treaties which no one took seriously, but in the acts of the ministers themselves in dramatizing the political warfare under full swing between the forces of communism and the institutions of Western civilization. Sprouting from the misery of Europe during the winter of 1946–47, Communist parties pushed formidably forward. In Italy the king abdicated and the republican government of De Gasperi which followed kept an uneasy seat through the elections of November 1946. In France the Communists ran a close second among the parties and forced the government to seek their co-operation in every decision that it made. In Britain the Labor government ably and honestly set forth its dilemma in a White Paper, but continued to cling to the policy of Mr. Micawber. Russia, warned *The Economist* in May 1947, might win a great victory by default. Time was working on her side; an economic slump in the United States was now all that she needed. The great dollar shortage, it declared, overshadowed the whole of European life. The margin between recovery and collapse depended on massive imports from the United States, but Europe had little left in either cash or credit and was ready for bankruptcy.

From this abyss sixteen nations, answering the call of Secretary George C. Marshall in June, undertook an organized effort to save themselves. They instituted in Paris a Committee of European Economic Co-operation, which brought in a report in the following September outlining a co-operative European production program in food and agriculture, fuel and power, steel and machinery, timber and transport. Europe had to have working capital: food, feedstuffs, and fertilizers; some coal and large stocks of petroleum; capital equipment of every conceivable variety—tractors, freight cars, steel plate, and steel rails; dock installations and traveling cranes; electrical goods; heavy machinery for mines and factories; building materials to replace wrecked homes and plants; specialized machinery to re-equip canneries, small foundries, glass factories, pottery works, chemical industries, stone quarries, and countless other small industries. Given a continuous flow of these materials from the American continent through the year 1951, concluded the report, Europe could recover and even surpass its prewar productive capacity. This forecast seemed convincing, but whether, with the production targets gained, markets would open for the sale of the goods produced, and thus lead to the correction of the fundamental imbalance of trade of which the dollar shortage was the symptom, remained uncertain; the committee could only hope. The long-range cure had to be left for the future. The immediate catastrophe could not long be averted. Concluded the committee:

If too little is done and if it is done too late, it will be impossible to provide the momentum to get the programme under way. Life in Europe will become increasingly unstable and uncertain; industries will grind to a gradual halt for lack of materials and fuel, and the food supply of Europe will diminish and begin to disappear.[21]

Would Communism Triumph Where Fascism Failed?—The
    European Recovery Program

Investigations meanwhile undertaken in the United States under the direction of the government reached conclusions favorable to the wisdom and the necessity of proceeding with a large-scale program of aid calculated to "take Europe off the dole." Particularly influential was the report of the Committee on Foreign Aid, a group of private citizens got together by the Secretary of Commerce, Averill Harriman. The Harriman committee underwrote the report of the sixteen nations, emphasized the vital interest of the United States in helping Western Europe to regain its strength, and estimated the cost at five and three-quarter billion dollars for the first year and a grand total of twelve to seventeen billion dollars for the four years.[22] Acting on this report, the administration in December 1947 introduced into Congress the Economic Co-operation Act, which provided for an expenditure of seventeen billion over the four-and-a-half-year period. Evidence which some two hundred congressmen had collected for themselves on visits paid to Europe during the preceding summer was to come in handy in getting this bill enacted. Passage proved difficult, for while the measure appealed to a number of economic groups—the farm organizations, the National Association of Manufacturers, and organized labor—for what it would do for continued prosperity in the United States, it met with resistance from those who, like Senator Taft, emphasized the cost and the additional strain on the American economy in the form of higher taxes, a rising national debt, and an inflationary price curve.

Accelerated Communist aggressions in Europe, especially a bold coup d'état in Prague in February 1948 which put a Communist government in power in that bastion of democratic government east of the Iron Curtain, kept the political atmosphere tense. Czechoslovakia's fate ten years before at the hands of Hitler could not be forgotten, and if Europe were now abandoned the Iron Curtain would soon be moved west to the English Channel. Communist Russia would have the triumph of which Hitler had been deprived at terrible cost, and the United States forced eventually to face siege conditions in its continental homeland. Much the same pressures that won the battle for aiding the Allies in 1940–41 focused on the European scene in 1948. The Marshall Plan revived the concepts of Lend-Lease, and paralleling its program for economic assistance to Europe the Truman administration began a campaign for strengthening the armed forces. Meanwhile strikes and civil disorders in France and Italy made of those countries the crucial ideological battleground; and with the elections in Italy scheduled for April, Moscow and Washington each bent its efforts to win over the Italian voter. Each appealed to the nationalism of the Italians against the imperialism of the other, with the Catholic Church doing ideological battle on the side of the West. Washington scored a thrust when, with the support of Britain and

France, it suddenly announced its desire to see Trieste returned to Italy. But the European Recovery Program, with its assurance of substantial succor, clinched the matter. It became law on April 3, 1948, and gained its first psychological victory fifteen days later when the Communists lost their campaign for the control of Italy. On both sides of the Atlantic the Marshall Plan was accepted as an irrevocable commitment by the United States to stand behind the free institutions of Western Europe in their otherwise hopelessly unequal battle with the forces of Soviet communism.[23]

Western Europe now had grounds for confidence. Five powers—Belgium, France, Luxembourg, the Netherlands, and the United Kingdom—joined hands at Brussels in March to lay the foundations for permanent union. They agreed to co-ordinate their economic activities to the end of making a common effort at recovery and to form a defensive alliance. A consultative council was created to implement the pact.[24] Important decisions to merge Western Germany into the Recovery Program and to create a West German Federal Republic were reached about the same time. The Western powers had made their last effort in December 1947 to induce the Russians to treat Germany, economically at least, as a single unit. Reluctant to permit the re-creation of a German government, the French nevertheless made a virtue of necessity and on June 1, 1948, signed a report along with Britain, the United States, and the Benelux countries authorizing the military governors to summon the local German minister presidents in their three zones and prepare for a German constitutional assembly. Provision was made, furthermore, for constituting an International Authority to administer the Ruhr, prevent it from being exploited by the Germans for rearmament, and provide access to its supplies of coal, coke, and steel for those European countries dependent upon it. Steps to carry out this report were taken during the summer of 1948, and on September 1 the eleven German *laender* situated within the occupation zones of the three Western powers convened a constituent assembly.[25]

Berlin: Marshall Plan Versus Cominform

Soviet warfare against the West meanwhile concentrated on an all-out effort to drive the Western powers from Berlin. Here, we remember, the advantages lay heavily with the Russians: occupied Berlin was an enclave in the Russian zone, and the American, British, and French garrisons had no corridor to connect them with Western Germany. If the power of the Cominform (Communist Information Bureau) was not equal to thwarting the Marshall Plan for Western

Europe—it had been organized in September 1947 expressly for this purpose—the Soviets might win an easy victory at least in Berlin. The instrument chosen for the purpose was the blockade, a stoppage of all rail, highway, and water shipments from the western zones to the Prussian capital. The threat of starvation to 2,500,000 people under the charge of the three Western powers would generate the pressure needed to induce the latter to withdraw from the city. Of this the government in Moscow seems to have felt certain. There is no doubt of the Russian alarm at the prospect of a German revival under Western auspices: Ambassador Walter Bedell Smith was so informed by Stalin personally. The blockade was instituted in March as a deterrent to the Western allies from going further with their plans for Western Germany. A full blockade was imposed on June 24 in the expectation that the Western powers would be beaten and the Germans intimidated from holding the constitutional assembly scheduled for September. An evacuation of Berlin on the part of the West or a retreat from the announced intention to set up the West German Republic would be equally rewarding to Soviet policy: the Western powers would have so lost in prestige that the road to Russian domination of Germany would be reopened. Indirectly a grievous injury would be inflicted on the European Recovery Program.[26]

Fully aware that Berlin was to be the test of their whole position in Europe, the Western allies united to maintain themselves at all costs in the former German capital. The airlift succored the beleaguered population. By April 1949 it had achieved a daily average of eight thousand tons, a volume of cargo equal to the rail and water shipments from the west into Berlin before the blockade. Furthermore, the Russians had overlooked an important weapon available to the West for retaliation: the counterblockade on coal, steel, and manufactured goods moving from the western zones into Eastern Germany. The American and British military authorities used this weapon at once, and Russia and her satellites were deprived of all trade with the West. Russia not being able to meet the privations inflicted on Eastern Germany by the counterblockade, the Soviet zone actually suffered more grievously in the struggle that followed than did Berlin. By April Moscow realized that the jig was up, and on May 4, 1949, the four powers reached an agreement in New York leading to a lifting of the restrictions early in June. The contest had been severe, but the position of the Western powers was definitely stronger than it had been the year previously. The airlift was a remarkable demonstration of power in a way that Moscow could understand, and through it the Western allies not only saved Berlin and quickened the enthusiastic support of the German people for their side, but were able to complete without further interference the plan for the West German State.[27]

Toward European Unity—Britain the Balance Against Germany

Four related movements centering in Western Europe and directed or encouraged by American diplomacy must now be examined. These are: (1) the attempt on the part of Western Europe, stemming from the Brussels Pact of March 1948, to achieve permanent union; (2) the modification of occupation policy and the establishment of West Germany as a virtually independent state; (3) the creation of a North Atlantic security system; and (4) the substantial progress of European recovery under the direction of the Marshall Plan.

The intangible ideal of European union, long planted in the intellectual soil of the Continent, was given a trial run in 1949 when the five Brussels Pact powers, joined by Italy, the Irish Republic, and the three Scandinavian countries, subscribed to a Statute of the Council of Europe. The machinery of the Council follows the pattern of the United Nations: a Committee of Ministers from the member governments, a Consultative Assembly consisting of delegates chosen by the member governments, and a Secretariat. Functions and powers, however, are imprecisely defined. The Statute is silent respecting a veto, but since the Committee of Ministers meets in secret, the veto, it may be assumed, is there in disguise. At its first meeting in Strasbourg in August 1949 the Assembly displayed a genuine European spirit: it preached intensive cultural interchange at the popular level, for instance, and it urged a tariff union and freely convertible currencies. But the British government, which had inspired the movement the year previously, paradoxically fought shy of making any economic commitments and otherwise proved its waywardness by suddenly and drastically devaluating the pound. The Strasbourg meetings disclosed the Council of Europe gazing in two opposite directions: through the eyes of the Committee of Ministers it looked backward to the unilateral practices of separate national sovereignties, while through the Assembly, the mouthpiece of private individuals, it cast glances into a dim future when Europeans would have a common nationality and a federated governmental system. But with the pronounced separatism of Great Britain on the one hand and the reappearance of Germany on the European political stage on the other, European union under the Statute seemed as unreal as ever. Whether Germany joined the union or not, she would, because of her greater size and strength, dominate it, a condition not likely to be welcomed by the other European nations. Paul-Henri Spaak of Belgium, the Assembly's president, vented this attitude when he frankly admitted that the movement would come to nought without British backing. Britain was needed as a balance against Germany.[28]

The West German State

Meanwhile the crosscurrents of political warfare between Russia and the West continued to surge through Germany. Both sides reiterated their intentions of promoting German unity, with the Western powers, while embattled for the control of Berlin, boldly seizing the initiative by authorizing the Germans in their zones to perfect a constitution for a federal republic. Eight months of deliberation by the elected leaders of West Germany at Bonn on the Rhine resulted in a fundamental law creating a federal government with a titular president, a chancellor and cabinet, and a two-house legislature. The Allies in the meantime redefined their own position through an Occupation Statute, issued April 8, 1949. The West German Federal Republic was proclaimed the following September, and with it an Allied High Commission replaced military rule. Eager to capitalize their victory in Berlin and to bind the Germans to their cause, the Allies encouraged the new government to assume power in the western zones. Certain areas, however, were reserved for the High Commission—disarmament and the deconcentration of industry; foreign affairs; jurisdiction over displaced persons; foreign trade; and control of funds, food, and other supplies which still burdened the occupation costs.

The Soviet Union immediately countered the West German Republic by proclaiming in October the East German Democratic Republic; and each regime then engaged the other in ideological warfare for the ultimate control and reunification of all Germany. The unremitting stream of refugees from East Germany into the western zones at the rate of a thousand per day was mute testimony to the superior attractions of the West; but at the same time it thwarted the hopes of the Allies of being relieved of the burden of support without in the least strengthening their claim on the political gratitude of West Germany. Having made denazification one of their cardinal aims in the occupation, the Allies were confronted with the disquieting fact at the end of the year 1949 that from 40 to 80 per cent of the officials in the various branches of the Bonn Republic were reinstated Nazis. Out of the 950,000 trials conducted since the surrender only about 45,000 persons had been declared ineligible for public office. Nor, except in a few cases, were even these persons prevented from regaining their status in German private industry.[29]

Headed by the septuagenarian Dr. Conrad Adenauer, the new German government lost no time in exploiting its opportunities. Without Western Germany Europe stood no chance of economic recovery. Participation in the Organization for European Economic Co-operation (OEEC), admission to the Council of Europe, and membership in the International Authority of the Ruhr followed virtually as a matter of course. Dismantling operations, a convenient object on which German nationalists could agitate, were halted in November. Industries basic to German military potential—synthetic oil and rubber plants and the mammoth I. G. Farben chemical organization—were thus given a breathing spell. By the end of 1949 the Potsdam policy of imposing penal servitude on the Germans was dead in everything but name; and the Western powers, the United States conspicuously taking the lead, were publicly affirming their eagerness to unify Germany and make her a partner in the free community of Western Europe. The now serious strife with Russia forced this pace.

In the North Atlantic Treaty Organization, created this same year, the Western powers were developing a coalition for the defense of Western Europe. But it was painfully evident before the close of the year that without German support Western Europe could not be made secure against a Soviet invasion. Committed to giving military assistance to its allies, the United States in particular showed an enthusiasm for mobilizing German manpower and for putting German armament industries to work. This quick somersault from demilitarization to remilitarization within the course of a few months—the Americans insistently pushing forward, the French hesitantly accepting the logic of the situation—was completed in September 1950. The three Western powers announced formally: (1) that they would each terminate the state of war with Germany; (2) that they would strengthen their occupation forces and "treat any attack against the Federal Republic or Berlin from any quarter as an attack upon themselves"; (3) that they were hopeful of "German participation in an integrated force for the defense of European freedom"; (4) that they would rescind the restrictions on shipbuilding and steel production; and (5) that they would amend the Occupation Statute and prepare to receive Germany as a full and equal partner. The powers also declared themselves against the re-creation of a German national army, but at the same time they urged the Germans to establish a mobile police capable of enforcing internal security.[30] The Soviets, they asserted, had already created and equipped "outright military units" in their zone. Pursuant to this agreement among themselves, the powers in March 1951 handed to the Bonn government a fresh grant of authority in the field of foreign diplomatic and commercial relations and of internal legislation. One vital safeguard, however, was retained in the hands of the Allied High Commission. This was the right to intervene in any international negotiation and the right to demand information concerning any international discussions undertaken by the Bonn Foreign Office. This reservation reflected the fear that, once freed of control, the West Germans would make up with their Communist brethren to the east of the Elbe and play upon the mutual fears of the West and the Soviet Union.[31]

The U.S. Proposes a North Atlantic Pact

Meanwhile the American government followed up the economic alliance it had formed with Western Europe in 1948 with proposals for a military alliance. The five Brussels powers, it will be recalled, had with American encouragement bound themselves to a mutual defense pact. But the whole of Western Europe was no match for the great bulk of Russia in the military any more than in the economic sphere. Without the United States the Brussels Pact was like a carriage without a horse—or an automobile without an engine. Furthermore, the United States, not Britain and France, was on trial in the Berlin blockade. Surrender by it of its position in the German capital would have left the British and French helpless. Resistance to the Berlin blockade was paralleled by negotiations in Washington for a collective defense system that would take in the Atlantic area. The resulting North Atlantic Treaty, signed in Washington April 4, 1949, included twelve states: the United States and Canada, Italy and Portugal, Iceland and Norway, Britain, France, and the three Benelux countries. The parties agreed "that an armed attack against one or more of them in Europe or North America [would be] considered an attack against them all"; and if such an armed attack did occur, each of them would "assist the Party or Parties, so attacked by taking forthwith, individually and in concert with the other Parties, such action as it deem[ed] necessary, including the use of armed force, to restore and maintain the security of the North Atlantic area." A council, on which each was to be represented, was to be set up immediately; and the council was to establish whatever subsidiary bodies it thought necessary, but in particular a defense committee to recommend measures for implementing the Treaty. Moreover, the parties might, by unanimous agreement, invite any other European state "in a position to further the principles of this Treaty and to contribute to the security of the North Atlantic area" to accede to the alliance.[32]

Just as in the case of the Marshall Plan and other measures designed to strengthen Western Europe, the North Atlantic Treaty encountered a stormy passage through the Senate. The voices of Senator Lodge and his fellow Irreconcilables of 1919 spoke out again in 1949 when Taft of Ohio, Wherry of Nebraska, Flanders of Vermont and others of a small band proposed reservations that would take the meaning out of the Treaty. The United States had no duty to furnish arms or to use armed force; Congress, with its war-declaring power, was to be the judge of whether to aid in repelling an armed attack; and the Monroe Doctrine was to be extended to Western Europe in lieu of the Treaty, thus freeing the United States from an "entangling alliance" in its problem of containing Soviet Russia. But this time the Irreconcilables were routed from the field: the Senate voted down their reservations and gave the Treaty its approval by a majority of eighty-two to thirteen. Nor was the Treaty meant to be mere rhetoric. With the exception of Iceland and Portugal, the other signatories needed military aid and so stated formally. On July 25, the day of ratification, the administration introduced a Mutual Defense Assistance Bill appropriating approximately $1,450,000,000 for financing the requirements of both the North Atlantic countries and those, such as Greece and Turkey, whose defense had already been underwritten. Again the isolationists fought a running battle, and again they were beaten when at the end of September the bill passed both houses of Congress by substantial majorities.[33]

With this assurance of support, the Treaty powers set about creating the North Atlantic Treaty Organization with the object of developing a common strategic plan and of integrating their several forces. Rather than try the hopeless task of each nation duplicating what every other nation was doing, the Organization proceeded on the principle of building a balanced collective force, each member contributing that for which it was best fitted. Thus the United States, it was agreed, should specialize among other things in air power. Expansion of its land forces in Europe, however, proved unavoidable: the Soviet Union in 1950 held a lead of more than a hundred divisions over the combined armies of the North Atlantic powers stationed in Europe. National jealousies, furthermore, were obstacles to be taken into account; but in the hope of overcoming them and of building a genuine European army, the Organization appointed as its supreme commander the leader who had in 1945 led the victorious Allied armies into the heart of Germany, General Dwight D. Eisenhower.

There still remained the unsolved riddle of how to integrate West Germany into the security system, for without German reinforcement the Atlantic powers, particularly the United States, would be compelled to mobilize on a scale they had not intended if the declared object of defending Europe from a possible Soviet invasion was to be fulfilled. Although the Atlantic powers in 1951 had by no means achieved a balance against the Soviet Union, the latter nevertheless reacted nervously by showing a desire to revive the Council of Foreign Ministers for the purpose of reuniting on a program of keeping Germany disarmed. Fear of an armed West German Republic, encouraged by the Western powers to attempt unification by an invasion of the Russian zone east of the Elbe, thus emerged as a prime factor in the high policy considerations of Moscow. The North Atlantic Alliance, it was feared, might eventually change into a tool to be used by the Germans to recover their position in central Europe and menace once more the security of Soviet Russia.[34]

Achievements of the Marshall Plan

From bankruptcy and despair in 1947 Western Europe improved in 1949–51 to a point where economic recovery and political self-assurance were tentatively secure. The immediate objective of the Marshall Plan—the rehabilitation of the European economy—had been realized. Europe's farms and factories reached in 1950 a production level 24 per cent higher than in 1936–38, with the annual rate of increase in production being maintained at 7 to 9 per cent. So great was the improvement in 1950 that it was thought, contrary to previous expectations, that further dollar grants from the United States after 1951 would become unnecessary.[35] On the other hand, the magnitude of the remilitarization program adopted late in 1949, including the grants of military equipment and supplies by the United States to its European allies, indicated that aid in another form would continue for several years to come. An important shift in emphasis took place in 1950 from aid to a peacetime civilian economy to aid to a war economy. Against this must be balanced the industrial recovery of Western Germany, capable in the future of contributing heavily to European rearmament. During the same years the economy of Eastern Germany and the Communist satellites was firmly tied to the Soviet Union, thus rending Europe in twain economically as well as politically. What effect all these arrangements would have toward bringing about the desired goal of a long peace only the future could tell.[36]

Along the Iron Curtain: Greece as a Case Study of the West Versus Communism

We turn back once more to the meeting of the Big Three in February 1945 at Yalta. Yalta was a confession of faith, a catechism of good will between Russia and the West. The draft charter of the United Nations and the Declaration on Liberated Europe formed the book of rules. President Roosevelt championed them both, and Premier Stalin autographed them. The Declaration prescribed the behavior of the powers toward the smaller countries of the Continent. The Great Allies would "jointly assist" the peoples freed from the Nazi tyranny "to form interim governmental authorities broadly representative of all democratic elements in the population and pledged to the earliest possible establishment, through free elections of governments responsive to the will of the people." The Declaration applied to Greece as well as to her Balkan neighbors to the north. But in her case, as in theirs, suiting the action to the word was contingent upon practical politics. The British government was already committed to the Greek government-in-exile, headed by the King and resident in London. The King was to be restored to his throne, and *then* a general election was to be held. But the Greek guerrilla forces that had waged war constantly on the Nazis were split on this issue, and the strongest of the factions, the leftist EAM (National Liberation Front), was hostile to the King and insistent upon a plebiscite being held before his return. Over this issue a civil war broke out in Greece in December 1944, with a British garrison of three thousand men bolstering the minority party of Greek conservatives.

On his part, Roosevelt had committed himself at the Quebec Conference (August 1943) to the return of the King, and the following June had waded in deeper still by giving Churchill a free hand to conclude an arrangement with Russia giving the Soviets primacy in Rumania and Bulgaria and keeping primacy for Britain in Greece. When, however, the British intervention in behalf of the Greek conservatives did come, the President recoiled on the ground that he had intended giving the British and Russians, respectively, a free hand for military purposes only. And the new Secretary of State, Edward R. Stettinius, threw a brick at Churchill by announcing publicly that the American government expected liberated peoples to be left free to "work out their problems of government along democratic lines without influence from outside."[37] It was not long, however, before Washington began to assume a more understanding attitude. Reports that the EAM forces operating in Macedonia were allied with Bulgarian Communists and working to detach Macedonia from Greece brought the alarming thought that Bulgaria, under the heel of a Moscow-trained Communist named Dimitrov, might suddenly emerge as a Russian satellite with a frontage on the Aegean Sea. And so when, on the next to the last day of the Yalta Conference, Molotov introduced an innocent-looking amendment to the Declaration to the effect that "support should be given to the political leaders of these countries who took an active part in the struggle against the German invaders," Stettinius took the lead in opposing it.[38]

Meanwhile on January 11, 1945, a truce was patched up in Athens and a regency created. But the truce was made good because of the continued presence of British troops: the insurgents, reinforced from Jugoslavia, Albania, and Bulgaria, carried on an incessant war in the north along the Macedonian frontier. Internally the regency succeeded in stabilizing the country, but subsisted on grants and loans from UNRRA and from the British Treasury. Preparations were made for a general election, including a plebiscite to pass on the issue of the return of the King. (The British government had agreed at the time of the truce to keep the latter in London pending the outcome of the plebiscite.) An Anglo-French-American commission supervised the preparations, and when the plebiscite was finally held in September 1946, a veritable army of 692 American observers was on the ground. The plebiscite, it was agreed, was conducted fairly, and the outcome went in favor of the King. The latter's unpopularity had originated in the prewar days when he had supported the Metaxas dictatorship; but in 1946, with the line drawn against Communist domination from the north, there seemed to be no alternative.

Political warfare between the Soviet Union and the Anglo-American powers in the meantime opened up at Lake Success and at the sessions of the Council of Foreign Ministers, paralleling the quarrels over Germany. In March 1946 President Truman gave an important signal by accompanying Churchill to Fulton, Missouri, and sitting on the platform while the former British Prime Minister drew a candid picture of the chasm that had opened in Europe and of the need for a British-American partnership against Russia. Complaints from London and Washington against the new police states east of the Iron Curtain were countered by charges from Moscow of British domination in Greece. But the official American view in September, as set forth at Lake Success, was that the British garrison was a stabilizing factor; and the appearance in the Eastern Mediterranean of an American task force, coupled with the frank announcement from the Navy Department of its purpose, revealed the existence of an alliance far stronger than words. The United States was just concluding at this time its particular troubles with Tito over Trieste; and Tito, it was believed, had also taken over from the Bulgarian Communists the principal reinforcement of the Greek insurgents.

We have already noted how in the winter of 1946–47 the entire economic and social structure of Western Europe began to sag dangerously. The poverty of Greece, her naked dependence upon Britain for armed support and financial aid, and the enhanced pressure from the guerrillas who made free use of Jugoslav and Bulgarian soil from which to launch their attacks, indicated that she would be the first country to collapse. By March 1947 she was known to have funds sufficient only to pay for one month's supply of food brought in from abroad. Preparations for meeting this tragedy had begun in the preceding October when the Greek government started begging for American help. An American economic commission departed for Athens in January, and the Security Council dispatched a commission to investigate the charges of aggression leveled at Greece's northern neighbors. And on February 24, 1947, Britain, overwhelmed by anxieties for her own survival, suddenly announced that the aid she had been rendering Greece and also Turkey would terminate at the end of one month.

The specter of total collapse of a country accepted as the strategic corner of the Eastern Mediterranean, with its probable sequel of a Communist regime drawing Greece inside the Iron Curtain, was too much for the government in Washington to face. Without waiting for the reports from its own mission or that of the United Nations, the Truman administration determined upon a stand that would make of the United States a full-fledged substitute for Britain as the historic guardian of the Eastern Mediterranean. On March 12, after a series of conferences with key members of Congress connected with finance and foreign affairs, the President appeared personally before that body to ask for authorization of a loan of $300,000,000 to Greece and $100,000,000 to Turkey. The message was a forerunner of Marshall's proposals for European recovery, soon to follow: it stressed the importance of maintaining the flow of imports into Greece in order to head off revolution and give the country a chance to recuperate. But more than this, it openly linked Greece and Turkey with the military security of the United States. Turkey's needs lay not in food imports or industrial equipment—the war had left her unscathed—but in equipment and matériel for the use of an army able to absorb the shock of an attack from the Soviet Union. "I am fully aware," said Truman, "of the broad implications involved if the United States extends assistance to Greece and Turkey. . . . . I believe that we must assist free peoples to work out their own destinies in their own way. . . . . Should we fail to aid Greece and Turkey in this fateful hour, the effect will be far reaching to the West as well as to the East. We must take immediate and resolute action. . . . ." Intelligence subsequently released by the State Department that one half of the Greek loan and all of the Turkish loan would be used for military purposes left no room for doubt as to where the emphasis was intended to be put. After a month of debate Congress bowed to the emergency and approved the loan without reservation.[39]

The Lesson of Greece in the Near and the Middle East

The Greek crisis furnished the United States the opportunity to inject itself dramatically into the region of the Eastern Mediterranean and the Middle East as the leading rival of Russia. Various symptoms had been building up to this end. Thus on April 6, 1946, Army Day, President Truman had issued a forecast. The area, he declared

contains vast natural resources. It lies across the most convenient routes of land, air and water communications. It is consequently an area of great economic and strategic importance, the nations of which are not strong enough individually or collectively, to withstand powerful aggression. It is easy to see, therefore, how the Near and Middle East might become an area of intense rivalry between outside powers, and how such rivalry might suddenly erupt into conflict.

Iran had been the cause of this pronouncement. The Big Three, who had jointly occupied her during the war and who had developed her as a corridor for the shipment of supplies through to Russia, subscribed at the Tehran Conference in December 1943 to the principle of her territorial integrity and political independence. But Anglo-American efforts at Yalta to translate this sentiment into a concrete undertaking to evacuate after the war were parried; and with Russia in control of northern Iran, including the important strategic province of Azerbaijan adjoining Turkey, the Iranian government submitted a complaint to the Security Council at the latter's very first meeting in January 1946. A curiously obscure situation then developed. The Soviets had been openly sponsoring a revolutionary party in Iran. Falling short of their hope of seating a puppet regime in the country, they nevertheless remained in Azerbaijan until May, when that province was made securely "autonomous" under the insurgents. On the twenty-first the Iranian government reported that evacuation had been completed, and yet it acknowledged its own inability to penetrate Azerbaijan and verify the fact! The Security Council, having established its right under American leadership to discuss the question, then washed its hands of the matter. Clearly the two Western powers emerged from this brush with only a barren victory.[40]

Truman's veiled warning of April 1946 meanwhile did not deter the Russians from levying demands upon the Turks. Turkey's two northeastern provinces of Kars and Ardahan, adjacent to Azerbaijan, offered tempting prey for infiltration from across the Georgian border. Kars and Ardahan had been Russian from 1878 to 1921. Their repossession, covertly demanded by the Soviets in August 1946, would, side by side with a new agreement respecting the control of the Turkish Straits, make putty of Turkey in Russian hands. At Yalta and again at Potsdam Stalin had put the Western powers on their guard by asking for revision of the Montreux Convention of 1936, which neutralized the Straits under Turkish control. Turkey under that convention had been given the right to close the Straits to the passage of warships in either direction; and by implication she also had the right to fortify the banks. Russia had been a party, along with Britain and France, to the Montreux Convention, which at the time served her interests well: it protected her Black Sea flank against possible British aggression from the Eastern Mediterranean.

But the Russians gave the Western powers a jolt early in 1946 when they demanded a trusteeship over Tripolitania; and with the Iron Curtain down on the Balkans, the Soviets twice in the late summer and fall of that year put it squarely up to the Turks to tear up the Montreux Convention. Turkey, they demanded, should admit them to partnership in organizing "joint means of defense of the Straits for the prevention of the utilization of the Straits by other countries for aims hostile to the Black Sea Powers." If Turkey submitted, Russia could drive the final rivet in the Iron Curtain: she could bar the way to the Black Sea even to ordinary commerce. But more than that, with military privileges on Turkish soil, the Soviets would be poised for adventures in the Eastern Mediterranean and the Middle East. To head off this bland attempt to tuck Turkey under the Russian wing, the British and American governments both announced to Moscow their willingness to review the Montreux Convention, but only if Turkey were left in sole custody of the Straits. After this stalemate the Soviets made no further move in the open; but President Truman in March 1947, we remember, used the Greek crisis to identify Turkey with American national defense. Soviet fingers, we may surmise, were secretly probing Turkey's throat, and the government in Washington had knowledge of the fact which, for reasons of state, it chose not to divulge.[41]

The Lesson Demonstrated: The U.S. Rewards Jugoslavia

Meanwhile the Greek civil war continued on its way. The number of guerrillas active in the north increased from thirteen thousand to twenty thousand by the end of 1947, and the American Mission for Aid to Greece, dispatched to supervise the expenditures under the loan, fell in with the Greek government's desire to win the war before undertaking reconstruction. American military advisers took to the field, and before the close of 1948 the Greeks had an army American trained and equipped. The original loan having been exhausted at the end of the first year, Congress granted a fresh loan of $275,000,-000 to Greece and Turkey, all of which went for military expenditures. Funds for civilian purposes in Greece were charged thereafter against the European Recovery Program. Rumania in the meantime added her help to that of her three Balkan neighbors in encouraging the Greek insurgents to make free use of her territory. With these doors ever open to the rear, the insurgents eluded their pursuers, reformed on "neutral" soil, and returned to the fray when ready. They could keep up the fight indefinitely. But one door began in the early spring of 1949 to swing shut. That door was Jugoslavia, whose Communist ruler, Tito, had broken loose from Moscow's grip the preceding summer. We have no means of going behind the scenes. But in July 1949 Tito closed the Jugoslav border to the Greek rebels. This act was the next thing to putting out the fire: the insurgent ranks broke, and thousands fled across the borders to escape being caught by the new Greek army advancing from the south. Bulgaria and Rumania, Russia's satellites, meekly refrained from meeting this potential challenge; and left to their own devices, the ringleaders of Greek communism held a dejected meeting in Albania, where they decided to quit.

This remarkable chain of events points to the extraordinary importance of Jugoslavia in the international balance. Only two years previously, we remember, Tito had been Moscow's man. His defection in 1948 was Washington's opportunity. Once harnessed to the West, Jugoslav nationalism presented attractive possibilities for building a strong bastion on Europe's southeast frontier. Whatever Washington's secret moves may have been, Tito's repudiation in July 1949 of the Greek Communists was rewarded the very next month by the first open proffer of American friendship—permission to buy in the United States equipment for a steel mill. A second demonstration followed in September with the extension of a $20,000,000 loan, accompanied by further evidences of interest in investing in Jugoslavia's economic future. Meanwhile Moscow, enraged by the sudden loss of one of its most important satellites, turned savagely on Tito and compelled the other states behind the Iron Curtain to join in an economic blockade. By the spring of 1951

Soviet necessities progressed to the point of threatening Tito with invasion. Moscow, it was believed, had successfully Russified and equipped the armies of Rumania, Bulgaria, Hungary, and Albania. An attack on Jugoslavia by these states, acting under hidden orders from Moscow, would raise a formidable issue for the Western powers to meet.

The Middle East: American Power in the Arab World

We have now traversed the second great zone of friction between the Soviet Union and the West, a zone extending from Jugoslavia on the Adriatic to Iran on the Persian Gulf. South of this zone lies the ancient crossroads of the world, the Arab Middle East. Various forces during the last quarter of a century have been steadily drawing the United States deeper and deeper into the affairs of this region. The movement began in 1920 as a quest for oil, but though to the present day petroleum development continues to keynote American activity therein, other issues have pushed their way to the fore. Between 1940 and 1946 the Middle East was one of the principal theaters of war. The repulse of Hitler from the shores of North Africa was the outcome of operations started in 1940 by Great Britain in Egypt. It was here that the Middle East Supply Center was established and painfully built up with vast stores shipped by way of the long route around the Cape of Good Hope. Soon after the passage of the Lend-Lease Act in March 1941 Roosevelt began reinforcing the British, and before a year had passed the Middle East Supply Center had expanded into a huge Anglo-American base. The safety of these operations, however, was heavily mortgaged to the good will of the peoples of the area. Political friendships and alliances, their roots extending deep into the annals of British diplomacy, constituted sound insurance in this respect; and coincidental with its war effort in the Middle East, the United States underwrote these relationships. Lend-Lease was the main instrument, and before the end of 1942 the defense of Turkey, Iran, Iraq, and Egypt was officially declared vital to the defense of the United States. Saudi Arabia was added to the list shortly thereafter, and by the close of the war stood second only to Turkey among the countries of the Middle East which had received Lend-Lease supplies. Saudi Arabia's patriarchal king, Abdul Aziz ibn-Saud, kept his country faithful to the Anglo-American cause through the critical period of 1941–42, at a time when the Germans were trying to exploit an inspired revolt in the neighboring state of Iraq for obtaining a foothold from which to launch a flank attack on Suez.

Ibn-Saud's choice, decisive for the security of the Middle East, rested in part on a firm foundation of good relations with certain American oil and mining companies. The Bahrein Petroleum Company and the Arabian-American Oil Company, each owned jointly by the Standard Oil Company of California and the Texas Company, had grown out of a concession originally granted by the King in 1930. To Mr. Karl S. Twitchell, the mining engineer who had in 1933 convinced Standard of California that a vast wealth in oil lay beneath the sands of Arabia, the King in 1940 made known his wants for engineering and financial assistance in expanding the water supply and agricultural output of his country. These ambitions called for more money than the private companies were willing to put up; but the outcome of a visit by Mr. Twitchell to the United States was a decision by the Roosevelt administration early in 1942 to offer its help to the King through a special mission.[42] Security considerations thus drew the American government in collaboration with the oil companies into the affairs of the Arabian Peninsula, and by 1943 a ranking American minister was in residence at Jidda on the Red Sea. It would appear that Ibn-Saud shrewdly and tactfully chose the time for making his desires known to the appropriate parties in the United States.

At the same time the war marked the United States as an oil-hungry power. Inroads by 1942 upon its domestic fuel reserves were too great to permit political indifference toward an area already established as one of the greatest oil-producing centers of the world. The proved reserves of the Middle East as a whole total more than twenty-seven billion barrels, approximately six billion more than the proved reserves of the continental United States. The small principality of Kuwayt, wedged in between Saudi Arabia, Iraq, and Iran at the head of the Persian Gulf, has reserves estimated to equal one-half those of the United States. Iran comes second with six to seven billion, and Iraq and Saudi Arabia about the same with at least five billion each. But other countries as far west as Cyprus are known to contain oil, and only a very small part of the Middle East has yet been explored. The estimates are constantly being raised. Partly competitive with, and partly corollary to, British oil interests, which obtained during World War I a long head start, American interests have a stake in all of the great concession areas with the exception of Iran. As noted, the Arabian-American Oil Company and its smaller, but older affiliate, the Bahrein Petroleum Company, have Saudi Arabia to themselves. By 1946 Arabian-American's holdings covered roughly 250,000 square miles, with preferential rights to a further 200,000 square miles. All told, this is an area exceeding the combined areas of California, Oregon, Washington, and Arizona. Arabian-American now ranked second only to the Anglo-Iranian Oil Company among the great oil concerns of the Middle East. Its average daily production was 200,000 barrels, almost a fourfold increase in a single year, and it employed approximately one thousand Americans and eight thousand Arabs. The next year, with Standard of New Jersey and Socony Vacuum buying into the company and thereby furnishing the needed extra capital, plans were completed for building a thirty-inch pipe line 1,050 miles long from the Persian Gulf to the shores of the Eastern Mediterranean. Royalties paid by the company at the rate of 22 cents a barrel (changed in 1950 to an equal profit-sharing basis) constituted Saudi Arabia's principal source of income. But figures tell hardly half the story. Technical guidance and aid in improving the water resources of the kingdom, in extending the irrigation systems and promoting the agriculture of the country, and in surveys of the frontier, not to mention the effect of its constantly expanding wages bill on Arab standards of living, give to Arabian-American a unique importance in the Middle East.

Official American diplomatic contacts have tended to catch up with, but as yet do not equal, the intimacy of the relationship between the company and the government of the king. The pro-Zionist attitude of the American government in the heated international crisis that arose over the Palestine question aroused bitter indignation among the Arabs, of whom the House of Saud regarded itself as rightful champion. Despite the stinging defeat suffered by the Arab cause with the establishment of the State of Israel, however, Saudi Arabia did not break relations nor did it object to the United States continuing to maintain its air base at Dahran, the oil port on the Persian Gulf. Its political stability and conservatism stand out in sharp contrast to the corruption and ever-present threat of anarchy characteristic of Iran, the neighbor to the north. And its comparatively secure location, well south of the Soviet frontier and protected by Anglo-American sea and air power from both east and west, make of Saudi Arabia the natural hub of the Middle East.[43]

Palestine Becomes Israel

Meanwhile the explosive Palestine question drew the United States into the Middle East along quite a different tangent. Unlike British petroleum interests, American oil companies had succeeded remarkably well in winning the friendship of the Arab peoples.

But the American government found itself compelled to serve more than one master in the Middle East. On the one hand, it readily followed the trail blazed by the oil companies, but, on the other, it submitted to Zionist pressures determined to convert Palestine—a British mandate under the League of Nations since 1920—into an independent Jewish state. Jewish nationalism had clashed with Arab nationalism ever since the mandate had been constituted; and the efforts of Great Britain, as the mandatory power, to reconcile these rival forces had been utterly in vain. The mandate had been conceived in 1917 as "a national home for the Jewish people"—the cryptic phrase written into the celebrated Balfour Declaration which was obtained by English Zionists from their government on the eve of the liberation of Palestine from the Ottoman Turks. American Zionists, notably Louis D. Brandeis, were only a shade less urgent than their English brethren, and they got President Wilson to associate himself publicly with the Balfour Declaration.[44] No one cared to venture publicly a precise definition of the phrase "national home," though the Zionist leadership was believed even then to have had in mind the eventual establishment of an independent Jewish state.[45] At any rate the native population of Palestine, nearly nine-tenths of it Arab, refused to be placated by the assurance contained in the Balfour Declaration that their civil and religious rights would be protected; and they greeted the new regime in 1920 with a rebellion.

Under the leadership of Sir Herbert Samuel, a liberal English Jew, the British administration set itself the task of winning Arab confidence and creating a fusionist type of society whose achievements would arouse the pride of the Jewish people everywhere. But the olive branch was rejected. Not merely the Palestine Arabs, but the entire Middle East chose to regard the advent of the Jews as a new wave of Western imperialism, a "creeping conquest" that would eventually strangle the Arab and his simpler way of life. A great Arab rebellion in Palestine in 1936, supported openly by the independent Arab states, was merely climactic to many lesser disturbances during the intervening years; and although it was suppressed, it brought from the British a confession that the mandate had failed. After exhaustive investigation, an eminent royal commission recommended partition into two independent states accompanied by compulsory transfer of populations. This plan being rejected by both sides, the British government in 1939, a few months before the outbreak of the war, announced its intention of terminating the mandate at the end of ten years, during which time Jewish immigration would be limited to 100,000. This was equivalent to saying that at the end of the period Palestine would be handed over to the Arabs, whose numbers vastly exceeded those of the Jews.[46]

Since the Zionists were turned away by the British, they began to look to the United States for succor. Hitlerism meanwhile, with its murderous attacks on the Jews in Germany and in Central Europe, had given to their cause an urgency that it had not possessed in the more tolerant atmosphere of the 1920's. With thousands of Jews fleeing from the vengeance of Hitler, the phrase "national home" quickly became the rallying cry of embattled Zionism, and Jewish immigration into the Holy Land developed into a mass movement. A Jewish population estimated in 1925 not to exceed 108,000 increased nearly sixfold within ten years, most of the increase due to immigration after 1933. This was the movement that the British government, climaxing a succession of hopeless attempts at appeasement of the Arabs, tried to stem by its new policy laid down in 1939. In opposition the Zionist Conference, meeting in New York in 1942, demanded unlimited immigration and the creation of a Jewish state supported by a Jewish army. Two years later these demands found their way almost word for word into the Democratic party platform, and President Roosevelt himself publicly supported the Zionist aspirations. But it is doubtful whether the President grasped the implications of the Arab-Zionist feud. He came face to face with them for the first time in February 1945 in a personal encounter with King Ibn-Saud, arranged upon his own initiative immediately after the Yalta Conference. From the King he got a flat negative to his plea for the Jews and a warning of impending civil war in Palestine.[47]

The end of the war in Europe brought all these complications to a head: displaced and homeless Jews, computed to number 250,000, surging into the concentration camps of Germany and Austria in the hope of somehow reaching the Promised Land; a fiercely aroused Zionism in the United States bent on prying open the doors of Palestine and realizing at long last the Jewish state; angry, uncompromising Arabs from Saudi Arabia to Egypt who talked recklessly of waging holy war; a baffled and stubborn English government trying vainly to enforce the immigration restrictions of 1939 and drawing down upon its head the recriminations of both Arabs and Jews; and a swelling Zionist resistance movement in Palestine which a British garrison of eighty thousand men was powerless to control. The United States was now forced down from its one-time observation perch into the thick of Palestine politics. Succumbing to political pressures, President Truman took up the plea for the immediate admission of one hundred thousand Jewish refugees. A joint Anglo-

American Committee of Inquiry, sent to Palestine in 1946, endorsed this proposal but otherwise contented itself with a pious hope for an end of the feud.

Britain now refused to prolong the agony of a twenty-five-year-old failure. Abruptly in April 1947 she dumped the Palestine question into the lap of the United Nations with notice that she would withdraw her forces by May 15, 1948. Acting through a special committee, the Assembly of the United Nations attempted to step into the breach, and in November 1947 it committed itself in favor of partition, Jerusalem to be separated and governed by an international authority under the auspices of the Trusteeship Council. At first the American government supported this proposal, and the Zionists accepted it because, though it gave them only half a loaf, it granted the principle of unlimited Jewish immigration. The Arab attitude, however, showed that no peaceful solution was possible. Joined together in a league which they had formed in 1945, the Arab states prepared to invade the country and overpower the Jews. But the latter outmatched them in every way. Illegal Zionist armies, operating under the local Jewish agency and fighting with crusading zeal, fell on the local Arab population while British troops, preparing to withdraw, stood aside. A massacre in April 1948 at the hands of the Irgun Zvai Leumi, a terrorist society, led to a sudden mass flight of Arabs, the number of exiles being reported as high as 600,000.

On May 14, the Jewish Agency in Tel Aviv proclaimed the State of Israel, and the Truman administration in Washington, without even a glance in the direction of the United Nations, gave speedy recognition. Disorder continued to reign in the Holy Land, although the grandiose plans of the Arab League for invasion collapsed at the border. The mass exodus of the Palestine Arabs in the meantime gave the Zionists their opportunity to bring practically the whole country, except a portion of Jerusalem, under their control. Gradually the situation relaxed into an armed truce, the Arab states sullenly refusing to recognize the accomplished fact but divided among themselves and unable to retaliate. American recognition of Israel was soon followed by a large loan from the Export-Import Bank and the establishment of full diplomatic relations; and a year later the British, too, having overcome their distaste for Zionist ambitions, put their relations with the new state on a regular footing.

The Far East: The Iron Curtain at the 38th Parallel

In the Far East plans for the peace to follow the capitulation of Japan rested upon a triangular system of co-operation among the

United States, the Soviet Union, and the National government of China. The Sino-Soviet Treaty of Friendship and Alliance of August 14, 1945, the outlines of which, we remember, had been drawn at Yalta, provided the organic law for this proposed system. Nationalist China and Russia agreed "to work together in close and friendly collaboration . . . . and to act according to the principles of mutual respect for their sovereignty and territorial integrity and of noninterference in the internal affairs of the other contracting party." The testing ground of this treaty was Manchuria. Separate agreements, signed on the same day, set forth the details governing the relations of the two parties in that vast region. The U.S.S.R. admitted the Three Eastern Provinces to be part of China and recognized their territorial and administrative integrity. Dairen, it declared, would be "a free port open to the commerce and shipping of all nations." The administration of the city would be in the hands of China, but goods in transit from or to Soviet territory would be free of duty and China would lease to the U.S.S.R. free of charge one-half of all port installations and equipment. Port Arthur would be used jointly and exclusively by the two parties as a naval base, but its defense was to be entrusted solely to the Soviet Union. On the other hand, the civil administration of the whole area was to be Chinese, though the leading posts in the administration were to be filled only in agreement with the Soviet military command. At the end of hostilities with Japan the Chinese Eastern and South Manchurian railways would be consolidated as the Chinese Changchun Railway and placed under joint ownership and management. The railway guards were to be organized and supervised by China, in whom was vested responsibility for protecting the railway. Soviet troops were not to use it except during the war with Japan, an undertaking made the more convincing by an oral pledge from Stalin himself that Manchuria would be evacuated of Soviet troops within three months after the capitulation of Japan.[48]

Superficially the dream of a strong, independent China—the "Policeman" of the Far East—seemed about to come true. Once the Three Eastern Provinces were within her grasp, China's position would be assured. From Manchuria's rich and varied economy she could nourish strength. Corollary to the Sino-Soviet agreements was the entente that endured until September 1945, and perhaps longer, between Washington and Moscow. The United States was pleased with the agreements, the more so since Stalin personally pledged to the American Ambassador his disavowal of the Chinese Communists and his intention to respect the Open Door in Manchuria. An informal accord over Korea, reached meanwhile at Potsdam, formed part of the entente. Temporarily Korea would be administered as a trusteeship by the four allies, a governing commission to be constituted upon the model of the Allied Control Council for Germany. As a first step in the direction of the trusteeship, it was agreed that Soviet forces entering Korea from Manchuria and American forces entering from Okinawa would stop at the thirty-eighth parallel. This line, midway between the Yalu River in the north and the Korean Straits in the south, was a military line selected by the American and Russian chiefs of staff for their mutual convenience in taking over the country from Japan. From the personal contacts of the American and Soviet field commanders would come theoretically the beginnings of a trusteeship. Rebuffs administered by the local Soviet command to the friendly advances made by Lieutenant General John R. Hodge of the American occupation force constituted the first breach in the entente; and the first folds of the Iron Curtain became visible by the middle of September along the line of the thirty-eighth parallel.

The Emergency in Korea: A Case Study

The stage darkened during the ensuing months. North of the line "provisional people's committees" emerged to form a cluster around a central committee sitting at Pyongyang. In the south clamorous Korean nationalists, headed by the former exile, Syngman Rhee, denounced trusteeship and insisted upon independence at once. Lacking faith in the Korean nationalists, the American command was nevertheless forced to identify itself with them. And so by the end of the year two opposing Korean regimes, one in the north, bearing the hallmark of a Soviet puppet, and one in the south, which to the Russian mind bore the brand of an American proprietary interest, had begun to crystallize. Because the facts are only partially known, it is impossible to fix responsibility for the continuing schism. Through the Council of Foreign Ministers at its meeting in Moscow, December 1945, the American government recovered at least the appearances of Soviet co-operation. The two field commanders were ordered to "co-ordinate" the administration of their respective zones and to permit trade across the line. A fresh gesture was made in the direction of a unified provisional government to act under the supervision of the four powers. But when it came to the details, the two commands could agree on nothing, and the Korean nationalists muddied the waters by renewing their clamor for complete independence. Both of the occupying powers insisted they wanted an all-Korean government chosen by the Koreans; but the Russians throughout 1946 identified themselves more and more openly with the "people's government" of the north, and the Americans, while striving to maintain the appearances of impartiality among the local factions, were driven in the end to make the cause of Syngman Rhee their own.

Being the leader only of the extreme right wing, Syngman Rhee could not justly claim to speak the voice of a united Korea; yet in December 1946 he obtained at least the tacit support of General MacArthur in Tokyo and went to the United States to propose publicly the establishment of a separate South Korean Republic and its admission to the United Nations. This was not what the State Department or the American occupation authorities or the Koreans themselves wanted— Rhee and his faction were distrusted by the moderate nationalists, but being repatriates from the United States they had the advantage of language in their dealings with the Americans.[49]

Meanwhile Korea went through the winter and spring of 1947 in deeper misery and discontent, with American anxiety engrossed in the troubles of Greece and Western Europe. When in the fall of that year the American government was again able to give its attention to Korea, the Soviet Union, through clever manipulation of Korean sentiment and shrewd exploitation of the agreement made in 1945 by the United States to promote a trusteeship, succeeded in driving the United States, and along with it the United Nations, into the invidious position of advocating a separate South Korean Republic. Nothing would induce the Russians to permit interference of any kind north of the forbidden parallel. Not even a UN commission could get past the barrier. Thoroughly frustrated, the commission proposed separate elections in the southern half, and the United States with thirty-one other nations accepted the proposal. Thirteen nations, including Canada and Australia, however, either dissented or abstained from voting. The upshot was an election in South Korea in May 1948, boycotted by the leftist and also by some of the moderate factions. Syngman Rhee and his party were set up in Seoul as the government of the Korean Republic, but on the other side of the barrier at Pyongyang was the "Democratic People's Republic" likewise claiming to speak for all Korea. Unfortunately South Korea was far from being as well established as Greece; and economically, militarily, and even spiritually it was weaker than its opponent. Syngman Rhee had too many enemies, who withdrew and joined the rival regime. The United States terminated its military occupation in June 1949, but South Korea was nonetheless a helpless waif surviving on American grants and facing a formidable enemy, with vastly superior forces, on the other side of an artificial boundary. A UN commission, inquiring into the situation in September 1949, dismally reported that Korea was no better off than it had been in the beginning, but that on the contrary it was merely a pawn in the world-wide rivalry between the United States and the Soviet Union.[50]

China Communized—The Wedemeyer Report

Meanwhile, upon the surrender of Japan in August 1945, the Russians had quickly overrun Manchuria and the Liaotung Peninsula. At best the Sino-Soviet agreements had never meant anything more than that Chinese officials in Manchuria would function under Russian influence. Furthermore, working through the Communist party, Chinese Communist forces and North Korean Communists were associated with the Russians in taking over from the Japanese, so that actually the Soviet Union and its satellites were by September in complete possession of the entire area. The great seaport of Dairen was sealed tight; and pillaging, confiscation of food stocks, and systematic stripping of Manchurian industries threw the country into chaos and wrecked the slim chances of the Chinese Nationalists for turning Manchuria to their account.[51]

Inside China in the meantime the confused civil war continued on its course, with the Nationalists and the Communists both trying to reap the rewards of the Japanese collapse. The Nationalists, we remember, had always been favored by the Americans; and they got help now on a big scale in a dash for the northern ports in the hope of outflanking the Communists. United States Marines seized Tsingtao, Tientsin, and Peiping; and Nationalist armies, transported on United States vessels, invaded Formosa, the lower Yangtze basin, and Peiping and its vicinity. In this manner Chiang Kai-shek was able to seize control of Jehol Province, the southern gateway to Manchuria. But the Chinese Communists were still far from being defeated; and in November both Chiang and the government in Washington were warned by General Albert C. Wedemeyer, who had taken over Stilwell's command in China, against venturing into Manchuria. Peace with Chiang's enemies, honest government, and internal reform, asserted Wedemeyer, were prerequisites to an expedition that would otherwise tax the Nationalist government beyond its capacity.[52]

These warnings were disregarded, however. Chiang lunged ahead, and got his troops transported to Manchuria on American vessels. The object now was to get control of Manchuria ahead of the Chinese Communists, and hold the Russians to the pledge of withdrawal given by Stalin at the time of the August agreements. Shrewdly the Soviets played out the game. By barring entry to the port of Dairen they deprived their "ally" of the invaluable facilities of the South Manchurian Railway and forced him to use the inferior ports of Yingkow and Hulutao. Soviet evacuation was delayed four months, probably to allow time for the completion of the program of dismantling Manchurian industries; and then in April 1946 it was carried out rapidly and in a manner to enable the Chinese Communists to rush into the places left vacant. Quantities of Japanese stores and equipment, including tanks, were left for the convenience of the Communists. In spite of their handicaps, however, the armies of the Central government made impressive gains not only in Manchuria but also in the northern provinces of China proper, where, as in Shantung and Shansi, the Communists had long held sway. When in May 1946 his forces took Changchun, the key to North Manchuria, Chiang Kai-shek was sure he could overpower his enemies. Vainly his American advisers warned of the perils of venturing deep into a country without proper communications with the central base at Peiping. Out at the end of a thousand-mile-long supply line, the Nationalist armies in Manchuria early in 1947 found themselves exposed to piecemeal destruction. All of North Manchuria, including the rail junction of Changchun, was recovered during this year by the Communists; and by December 1948 Manchuria was a total loss to the Central government, together with great quantities of stores and equipment furnished by the United States.[53]

At this point we must turn back two years to December 1945 and observe the efforts of the Truman administration to bring about a reconciliation of the factions in China. Wedemeyer's thoughtful statement of the weakness of the Central government, on the one hand, and Hurley's angry charges leveled at the State Department and the professional diplomatic service, on the other hand, forced the administration to try something decisive. It sent General Marshall to Chungking with instructions to persuade the Central government to call a conference of all the major factions and to stop the hostilities, particularly in North China. Marshall reached Chungking early in January 1946, and lost no time in making himself chairman of a Committee of Three, the other two members being General Chang Chun for the Nationalists and General Chou Ên-lai for the Communists. From the start the American envoy worked in an atmosphere of distrust between the two Chinese parties, with the extreme reactionary wing of the Kuomintang, known as the CC Clique, obtaining the upper hand and refusing any compromise with the Communists.[54] Nevertheless on the tenth of January the Committee of Three agreed on issuing a cease-fire order, and plans were also laid for reorganizing the armies to the end of an eventual merger of the two forces. When it came to executing the cease-fire agreement, however, Marshall struck a snag. Chiang Kai-shek refused to permit interference with his ambitions for Manchuria and vetoed Marshall's proposal to send a field team to that country to stop the fighting. Elsewhere in China proper, Nationalist commanders gave the Communists good reason to complain of their bad faith. No peace having been reached, but on the contrary with Nationalist armies conducting offensive operations against them everywhere, the Chinese Communists in July launched a bitter manifesto against the United States for abetting their enemies. General Marshall's position as mediator now became untenable. Repeated warnings to the Generalissimo of the impending collapse, and admonitions to reform the Kuomintang and practice good faith toward the Communist leadership met with no encouragement. In a final exchange of views in December Chiang Kai-shek boasted he would destroy the Communists. Marshall's reply was that the National government could not destroy the Communists, but that rather it would destroy itself. His mission came to a formal and futile end on January 6, 1947.

Peace between the Kuomintang and the Communists and verbal efforts to persuade Chiang Kai-shek to introduce reforms continued to be the cornerstones of American policy throughout 1947. Thus the new Ambassador John Leighton Stuart, who had been appointed at Marshall's request because of his long experience in China, remarked:

Actually much of the apparent strength of Chinese Communism is due chiefly to the inefficiency and corruption of the Kuomintang and—with an alarming acceleration—to popular loss of faith in the Government. One can be reasonably certain that with sufficient evidence of competent statesmanship and determined moral reforms the Government could recover its hold alike on the intellectuals and the masses.[55]

But in spite of its announced intention, the American government dared not be neutral in China's civil war. Assistance in various forms continued to go to the Nationalists. Moreover, ever watchful for a chance to make a telling stroke against the administration, its Republican critics were not slow to apply to China the Truman doctrine, with its pledge of aid to "free peoples everywhere." Apparently hopeful of extricating itself from its embarrassment, the administration in July dispatched General Wedemeyer to make a fresh survey and to try to convince the Chinese Nationalists that it really meant what it said. Wedemeyer pulled no punches. A stinging rebuke delivered personally to the leaders of the Central government was followed by a public statement containing the flat declaration that "promises [of reform] will no longer suffice," if China was to get more help. This was accompanied by a masterly report analyzing in detail the abuses within the Nationalist regime. China, concluded Wedemeyer, had but one recourse: she must publicly acknowledge her predicament, request the United Nations to establish a five-power trusteeship over Manchuria, and submit to responsible American direction of her internal affairs.[56]

But the government in Washington quailed at making this report public. It did not want to take over Nationalist China and run it as a dependency. Its world-wide quarrels with the Soviet Union were now too bitter to make a trusteeship for Manchuria practicable. Moreover, it feared the growing power of the Chinese Communists and their entente with the Soviet Union—of these dangers Wedemeyer himself had spared no words of warning. What the administration would have done if left free to take its own course, we are unable to say. But its Republican opponents dogmatically espoused the cause of Chiang Kai-shek and made more aid to China the price of their support for the Marshall Plan for Europe. They even doctored a report of the Senate Committee on Foreign Relations in March 1948 by replacing, prior to publication, a passage critical of the Nationalists with a statement of fulsome praise of Chiang Kai-shek. The China Aid Act, with its appropriation of $463,000,000, committed the country to continued intervention in the Chinese civil war.[57]

Meanwhile the long-predicted Communist triumph was rapidly coming true. Even while Congress was voting more money for Chiang Kai-shek, the armies of Mao Tsê-tung were expelling him from Manchuria and regaining their strongholds in China proper. Remarked an American economic mission in July:

> The Mission was really startled by the facts about the military situation in China and to find such an enormous gap between what they had supposed to be the case and the actual truth. We were surprised at the wide gulf between the combined opinion of our own competent military in China supported by the Ambassador and the present military and related policy of the Chinese Government in Nanking. . . . .[58]

By March 1949 the Chinese Communists were in substantial control north of the Yangtze. Nanking, Shanghai, and Hankow were then taken, and Chiang Kai-shek took flight first to Canton and then to Chungking. By December no place on the mainland remained safe for him, and on the island of Formosa he found ultimate retreat where he could still boast of being the Central government of China. In the meantime his enemies proclaimed the Chinese People's Republic, and in February 1950 signed at Moscow a treaty of friendship and alliance with the Soviet Union. The published text of this treaty contained an agreement that, should one of the contracting parties be the object of attack by Japan *or any other state allied with Japan,* the other contracting party would "immediately render military or other aid with all means at its disposal."[59]

Japan Americanized?

To appreciate the full force of this Sino-Russian alliance we must pursue now the course of American relations with Japan during the five years since Nippon, like Germany, lay helpless in defeat. Here in the Orient the United States enjoyed a free hand, unhampered except in theory by the advice of its allies. Bearing the sonorous title of Supreme Commander Allied Powers (SCAP), General Douglas MacArthur entered Tokyo on September 8, 1945, at the head of an American army. Pointed comments by the Australians and remonstrances by both the British and the Russians subsequently covered with a veneer of international co-operation this position of dominance won for itself by the occupying power. As a result of an agreement reached by the Council of Foreign Ministers at its meeting in Moscow in December, two bodies with advisory functions were created, one sitting in Washington, the other in Tokyo. The first of these was the Far Eastern Commission, made up of representatives from eleven nations having interests in the Pacific and empowered to review directives issued to the Supreme Commander and also actions taken by him. The directives, however, emanated from the American government; and since the United States, in common with the United Kingdom, the U.S.S.R., and China, exercised a veto, the position of the Commission was hardly a strong one. The other body was an advisory council on which sat members from the United States, the British Commonwealth, the U.S.S.R., and China. Its chairman was the Supreme Commander himself, or his deputy; and at best it could do no more than criticize his policies. Furthermore, the position of the Supreme Commander rested not on the will of the Allied powers, but on the sole authority of the American government. From the outset General MacArthur showed a determination to exercise a free hand, uncontrolled either by Washington or by the Allied powers. Barely a week passed after his landing in Japan in September before he publicly defined his own attitude toward the occupation; and later, after the State Department had agreed with the powers on the establishment of the advisory councils, the General was not backward in letting his displeasure be known.

Unlike Germany, Japan at the time of surrender retained the outward attributes of sovereignty. But the Emperor and his government were now subject to the orders of the Supreme Commander; and the occupation policies evolved by the United States bore a strong resemblance to the Potsdam policies for Germany. Disarmament and demilitarization, including the dismantling of basic industries, and the Japanese equivalent of denazification were the stated goals under the basic postsurrender directive issued to MacArthur, November 1, 1945.[60] The political and economic structure of the Far East, we must remember, was supposed in the future to hinge on China and not on Japan. China was to get the resources and industries of Manchuria; Korea was to be rendered independent, economically as well as politically, of its former overlord; and the Japanese were expected to fit into this new and strange situation as best they could.

Historically Japan had been the workshop of Asia, exchanging her manufactures for the raw materials and foodstuffs of Manchuria, Korea, China, and Formosa. Loss of her trade with these and other countries dealt her a mortal blow. Considering this basic economic fact, formal declarations of intention to destroy her industrial system would seem superfluous. Nevertheless, as in the case of Germany, a level of industry was prescribed, and all plant and equipment in excess of that level were adjudged "surplus" and subject to removal as reparations. China principally, but also Britain, the Netherlands, and the Philippine Islands were to be the beneficiaries. Actually little or no removal of industrial plants was attempted, but the factories lay idle just the same. Japan was now a nation of 83,000,000 people, but the level of industry set for her corresponded with her productive capacity of 1930, when the population approximated 64,000,000. Ignoring this discrepancy in population and the greatly aggravated problems of labor that it entailed, the directive of November 1945 decreed that the Japanese be kept fully employed and made self-sufficient—they were even expected to meet the needs of the occupation forces. Actually the defeated country cost the United States $200,000,000 over and above the occupation costs in the first year after the war. As in Western Europe, Japanese agriculture was unequal to sustaining the population; and with Manchuria and other normal sources of supply cut off, Japan limped through 1946 on 830,-000 tons of food imported from the United States, an amount that doubled for the first nine months alone during 1947. The situation was so plainly disillusioning, especially when coupled with the troubles of China and the growing rivalry with the Soviet Union, that in words at least the United States executed an about-face. According to Secretary Acheson in May 1947 Japan was again to be made the workshop of Asia—the ultimate economic recovery of the mainland would, he declared, depend on this. But with Manchuria in hostile hands, Korea poorer than ever, and China in the travail of a civil war, little could be done toward putting this pleasant sentiment to work.

Meanwhile the abolition of militarism and the advancement of democratic government in Japan were undertaken in 1946 through a great purge of officials and businessmen from the top ranks down and through the promulgation of a new constitution with a bill of rights and a parliamentary form of government. Certain categories of persons—ex-officers of the army and navy, career members of the old bureaucracy, etc.—were automatically proscribed. Others, including teachers, doctors, and judges, were subjected to screening. An ordinance issued in January 1947 extended the proscription to relatives by blood, marriage, or adoption; and the number of persons either purged or exposed to being purged was estimated at one million.[61]

Contemporaneous with these blows at old feudal Japan went sundry efforts to "teach democracy" to the Japanese masses. To this end the new constitution was drafted in the general headquarters of the Supreme Commander and a free general election, embracing suffrage for women, was carried through. Parliament was now in form supreme over the Emperor, the cabinet, and the bureaucracy. After some pressure the premier apologetically presented the constitution to the legislative body, at the same time eulogizing the old constitution and chiding the Western powers for their "mistaken conception" of Nippon's ancient polity. When in April 1947 the time arrived to hold the elections, SCAP dispatched "observation teams" to the prefectures with the object of helping the local officials "understand" the reforms and keep the wrong persons from winning the elections. So convincing were the testimonials of Japanese compliance with the reforming zeal of SCAP that General MacArthur felt moved to publish an affirmation of faith in the "spiritual revolution" that had swept over Japan. "To a race long stunted by ancient concepts of mythological teaching," he declared, the occupation had brought "the refreshing uplift of enlightenment and truth and reality with practical demonstrations of Christian ideals . . . ."[62] More specifically, MacArthur showed an eagerness for concluding a treaty of peace and bringing the occupation to an end.

But the government in Washington was inclined to be cautious. It was ready enough to give credit for good conduct, and unmistakably Japan grew in the favor of Washington during the ensuing three years. Moreover, her recuperative powers came into play: her industrial production had risen by the middle of 1949 to 90 per cent of the level for 1930–34. But she was heavily dependent upon the United States for food and supplies, for which no means of payment existed. Fundamental sources of revenue, such as the merchant marine and the trade in raw silk had vanished. Her Asiatic markets were gone too, and the sentiment of Secretary Acheson to the contrary, United States policy did not look with favor upon Japan's reopening her workshop for the benefit of the masses on the continent. The sentiment, however sound, could not be squared with the implacable enmity generated in the United States against the Communist masters of China.

Cross-Purposes in Asia

At this point we must turn our attention again to the mainland of Asia. Under Mao Tsê-tung the Chinese Communists swept on in 1949 to total victory. Their rival, Chiang Kai-shek, still wore the "Policeman's" uniform which President Roosevelt had tailored over six years before: he was still head of the Central government with a permanent seat on the Security Council of the United Nations. But the "Policeman" was now an exile on the small island of Formosa, secured for him by the conquering forces of the United States. There his fellow "Policeman" chose to leave him for the time being. President Truman was willing to continue with the subsidies for economic support. But having no mind to pursue a course that would lead to involvement with the Chinese Communists, the President declared he would "not provide military aid or advice to Chinese forces on Formosa." In effect the Chinese Nationalists were a bankrupt government-in-exile, the United States in 1950 committing itself to keeping them on the pension list but otherwise telling them to mind their own defenses.[63] India, the United Kingdom, and several other countries had meanwhile bowed to realities in offering recognition to the People's Republic of Mao Tsê-tung. To the south in Indo-China and to the north in Korea at the same time there were two rival regimes, each pretending to jurisdiction over the whole country. In Vietnam (formerly French Indo-China) the Emperor Bao Dai functioned in the southern portion as a French puppet; the remainder of the country was in open rebellion led by the Communist-minded Ho Chi Minh. In Korea, as we remember, an artificial boundary separated the regime sponsored by America and the United Nations, in the south, from the Communist "Democratic People's Republic" of Kim Il Sung, in the north. Overshadowing the whole of East Asia in 1950 was the demonstrated military power of Communist China in alliance with Soviet Russia. Facing this enormous revolutionary mass the Western bloc of nations held, either through direct control or through weak puppet regimes, a string of disconnected bases which extended from Indo-China through Hong Kong and Formosa to South Korea. At the moment of the Sino-Soviet alliance of February 1950 France was waging war in Indo-China with the declared objective of defeating the Communists; Britain was relying on a diplomatic rapprochement with Communist China to protect the vulnerable Crown Colony of Hong Kong; and the United States was trusting to endless grants-in-aid to sustain its two puppets, Chiang Kai-shek and Syngman Rhee, in Formosa and South Korea respectively.

Korea: From Subversion to Direct Attack

Trouble between the two regimes in Korea had never abated. Kim Il Sung in the north had a Russian-trained army, superior in numbers at least to the American-trained force of South Korea. Reporting in September 1949, the UN Commission expressed its foreboding of the "military posturing" on both sides. Guerrilla incursions from the north ensued during the winter, but were eventually repelled by the South Koreans. Meanwhile Kim Il Sung kept up a running attack of abuse against the southern republic and its United Nations sponsors, just as in China the Communist leadership never ceased its denunciation of Chiang Kai-shek as "the running dog of American imperialism." An election in South Korea in May, supervised by the UN Commission, returned a majority of moderate nationalists out of sympathy with Syngman Rhee; and the North Koreans immediately accelerated their radio propaganda demanding unification. The new South Korean National Assembly showing no disposition to heed these calls, Kim Il Sung on June 25, 1950, launched a sudden invasion across the thirty-eighth parallel in such force as to leave no doubt of his intention to rid himself of the southern government. The Security Council, Russia being absent, at once voted this move a breach of the peace and called upon North Korea to withdraw. Furthermore, it asked all members to aid the UN and to refrain from giving assistance to North Korea.

The American government, which had prompted this resolution, took a more advanced position. Declared President Truman on June 27: "The attack upon Korea makes it plain beyond all doubt that Communism has passed beyond the use of subversion to conquer independent nations and will now use armed invasion and war." This was tantamount to accusing Russia and Communist China of starting the war, especially since it was followed by a commitment to defend Formosa and to furnish fresh military assistance to the French in Indo-China.[64] Thus the Korean war had the immediate effect of inducing the Truman administration to abandon its attitude of studied indifference toward Formosa and to announce a policy of resistance to "Communism everywhere" in the region of East Asia. But at the same time it hastened to put a damper on the ambitions of Chiang Kai-shek. The latter showed a desire to jump into the war with three divisions of troops and some naval and air support. He was told distinctly, however, to stay out and to cease all air and sea operations against the Chinese Communists on the mainland. And the administration still avoided a commitment on the future status of Formosa. That, it declared, "must await the restoration of security in the Pacific, a peace settlement with Japan, or consideration by the United Nations."

Both the United States and the United Nations were now committed to a full-scale war for the defense of South Korea. At first the North Korean armies drove all before them, but their short-lived triumph turned into defeat in September when General MacArthur, striking at their rear through the port of Inchon, recovered Seoul and captured Pyongyang, the North Korean capital. Kim Il Sung took flight at the end of October, and the war appeared to be over. Complex issues emerged in the meantime, however. President Syngman Rhee, MacArthur's protégé, attempted to shake off the United Nations and proclaim himself the ruler of all Korea. This ill-considered move was blocked at Lake Success. But no easy answer was forthcoming to the riddle of how to dispose of North Korea. The General Assembly, which had taken over the responsibility for the war from the veto-ridden Security Council, put it in charge of General MacArthur, but at the same time voted its desire to evacuate all UN forces as soon as possible. Considering the weakness of Korea, however, this seemed like a dim prospect. Both Lake Success and the government in Washington devoted themselves to confining the war to Korea. They feared to incite the Russians or the Chinese Communists to intervene, and in November a neutral zone near the Manchurian border was proposed. From the start, however, MacArthur had shown himself eager to enlist the Chinese Nationalists and carry the war into China. He had openly visited Chiang Kai-shek in August for this purpose, and certain elements in the United States displayed their zeal for backing him in a crusade against communism in Asia.

On their part, the Chinese Communists were restive over the Korean war and eager to supplant the Nationalists in the United Nations. Preparations for armed intervention in the war paralleled the dispatch of a special mission from Peiping to Lake Success. The reception of this mission underlined the deep divisions in the United Nations over the question of according recognition to Communist China and at the same time relieving the organization of its embarrassing commitment to uphold the independence and freedom of South Korea. France, the United Kingdom, India, Jugoslavia, and Norway voted with Russia to admit Communist China. The United States opposed and succeeded in keeping the door closed by a majority of only one vote. The rebuff apparently caused the Chinese Communists to resort to arms, and in December 1950, just after MacArthur had complacently announced the end of the Korean war, they began it all over again by a sudden mass invasion from Manchuria.

The second phase of the war followed much the same pattern as the first, with MacArthur at first retreating south of the thirty-eighth parallel and evacuating Seoul in late December and then retrieving most of his lost ground by April of 1951. Again displaying his zeal for a crusade against communism and his belief that he could settle the matter if only he were allowed to bomb their rear in Manchuria, the General openly allied himself with the leaders of the Republican party in Congress who had been untiring in their efforts to embarrass the government. A letter to this effect addressed to Representative Martin, the Republican floor leader in the House, was so flagrant a challenge to the authority of the President that it could not be ignored. On April 12 MacArthur was relieved of his command in both Korea and Japan. The emotional explosion that followed among the people, quickly capitalized by the Republican politicians, shook the country to its foundations.

Meanwhile by the summer of 1951 the Korean war settled down to a stalemate, with the opposing forces deadlocked in bloody but indecisive conflict in the vicinity of the thirty-eighth parallel. Both sides showed themselves tired of the war and ready to compromise on the basis of some kind of an armed frontier along this parallel. But truce negotiations, begun in the summer, dragged on through the autumn and winter months, and the end of the year arrived with no surety of a stoppage in the fighting. The Truman administration had kept the war localized to Korea; it had never committed the United States to the defense of that war-torn country north of the thirty-eighth parallel; and it had successfully checked the zeal of those who, following the lead of MacArthur, would embark on adventures that might lead to a great war with Communist China and Soviet Russia. But when it came to making terms that would offer some hope of even a breathing spell, it found itself facing discouraging obstacles. The Chinese Communists seemed willing to agree on a boundary line corresponding roughly to the thirty-eighth parallel, but unless they would also concede the reciprocal right of the two sides to inspect each other's forces in Korea, there could be no assurance of protection against a sudden blow calculated to drive all United Nations forces into the sea. Even should a truce be finally arranged, the conclusion seems unavoidable that the United States, leading a reluctant United Nations, is committed to maintaining indefinitely an armed frontier along the thirty-eighth parallel against a powerful foe.

Preparations in the meantime for a formal peace with Japan met with success in September when forty-nine nations joined together at San Francisco to sign a treaty previously negotiated by John Foster Dulles with the government in Tokyo. While this treaty restores to Japan her formal position as an independent state, it actually does little more than register the fact that she is a protégé of the United States. The United States is made the sole authority (under the guise of a trusteeship) in the Ryukyus, the Bonins, and other strategic islands of the western Pacific. A separate defense pact gives to the United States the right to station armed forces in the Japanese homeland and to use whatever facilities it chooses for safeguarding its own interests in the Far East. And while Japan is charged by this pact with assuming responsibility for her own defense, it remains an open question as to just what this means. Neither the treaty nor the defense pact make of Japan an ally of the United States in keeping the peace of the Pacific area. Defense pacts signed contemporaneously with Australia, New Zealand, and the Philippine Republic, on the other hand, do make allies of those three countries and obligate the United States to aid in their defense. Taken as a single piece, this security system is formal recognition that the future of the entire Pacific area hinges upon the primacy of American sea and air power.

In conclusion, the dilemma of American diplomacy in the Far East may be put as follows:

1. How is the Korean war to be brought to a close? In spite of the lip service paid to the "independence" of that country, Korea is only a pawn in the rivalries of the three great powers, the United States, Soviet Russia, and Communist China. The United States has filled the power vacuum created by the collapse of Japan. But its foothold in Korea is far less secure than was Japan's before the war, nor does it have the same advantages of position relative to China and Russia that Japan possessed. The Chinese Communists are strongly entrenched in North Korea and mean to stay. Any truce or peace in Korea will have to be made with them, but in addition the durability of any Korean peace will depend upon sheer military power mobilized and kept alerted by the United States in South Korea into the indefinite future.

2. What is to be done about Chiang Kai-shek and his government-in-exile in Formosa? In the making of the Japanese peace treaty the Chinese Nationalists were studiously ignored. Probably British and Japanese influence kept them away from the conference at San Francisco. To treat them as the government of China is sheer pretense. Yet the United States holds to this attitude (there seems to be no alternative) and is committed to their defense on the island of Formosa. Moreover, the Japanese treaty has yet to be ratified. Veiled hints arising from the visit of Winston Churchill to Washington in January 1952 disclose that Chiang may still be made a party to the treaty. This step may satisfy the American friends of Chiang and bring speedy ratification of the treaty, but it does not make the situation in the Far East any less precarious.

3. How far should we go toward giving Japan a free hand in the Orient? Or, what is equally to the point, how far can she go by herself? Is it possible for her to develop to the point where she can play the role of a mediator between the United States and Communist China? Given a free hand, she might show a surprising ability for ameliorating the ideological warfare between the Americans and the Communist Chinese. Japan's economic recovery depends in the long run upon peace and the reopening of her markets on the mainland. She has every incentive to play the role of a peacemaker. But she cannot perform this function if she is kept in leading strings by the United States. As things stand now, the United States is committed to maintain a vast armed frontier thousands of miles from its continental homeland, a frontier that absorbs more and more of its wealth and its energies. Is this a frontier that can be held forever? Is it not a better risk to make a real partner and ally of Japan and to encourage her to open a road for peace with Communist China?

These queries lead to the conclusion that, in the long run, the peace of Asia is properly in the hands of the Asians, notably the Japanese and the Chinese, and that it is wise American policy to help shape things to this end. The peace treaty with Japan is a signpost pointing in this direction. Certain elements, however, would like to ignore this and erect another signpost pointing at a *Pax Americana* to be extended into the heart of Asia. In the names of democracy and the Christian religion they preach a crusade against communism and apparently propose to make a start by expanding the war in China. A good deal of history lies behind this idea. Somehow or other, the conviction that it is the American mission to save China (even from the Chinese) has become lodged in certain corners of the American mind. Certainly American policy could turn in this direction, but it then must face the prospect of a third world war with only the most vaguely defined objectives in view.

Similar queries can be raised for Europe, where the prospects, in spite of the formidable obstacles, seem more clear-cut than in East Asia. One of the objectives of the North Atlantic Treaty Organization is to bring about European unity and independence as speedily as possible, *so that* the United States may withdraw. In Asia the aims of American foreign policy are equivocal. This is basically because it is long-standing tradition and practice to intermeddle in the affairs of China. Contrariwise, the American tradition toward Europe is to have as little as possible to do with the politics of that Continent. Toward Asia the tradition is imperialistic; toward Europe it is isolationist. Put in the simplest form, American foreign policy faces the paradox of two dangers: In Asia the danger is that it will meddle too much, in Europe that it will not meddle enough. The people who are trying to push us deeper into Asia are the same people who are trying to push us out of Europe. But in terms of sound policy, the idea of withdrawal from either area means something only in a relative sense. In Europe's case it spells out to the extent that the European countries regain their self-confidence and follow the long and hard road in the direction of economic and political unity. But to dwell on such possible outcomes is to look beyond the horizon and see nothing of the issues immediately ahead. Better to stay on the job which, avoiding gusts of passion and fanatical zeal for "destroying" communism, means continuation of the work for European recovery and of encouragement to Japan to resume her position as the principal stabilizing force of East Asia. Without stability there is no balance, and without a balance there is no peace.

Notes

I. The Pacific Becomes a Crisis Area, 1918–1941

[1] This paragraph is paraphrased from Benson's memorandum to Wilson, quoted in Ray Stannard Baker, *Woodrow Wilson and World Settlement* (3 vols.; New York, 1922), III, 214–16.

[2] *The Memoirs of Cordell Hull* (2 vols.; New York, 1948), I, 281–85.

[3] Hull, *op. cit.*, I, 717–30. The text of the Japanese note of September 5, 1939, to the powers and the American official comments on it are to be found in *Papers Relating to the Foreign Relations of the United States. Japan: 1931–1941* (2 vols.; Washington, D.C., 1943), II, 9–15.

[4] *Ibid.*, I, 896–98. The Australian minister, Richard G. Casey, was an active participant in these and subsequent Anglo-American conversations.

[5] *Foreign Relations. Japan: 1931–1941*, II, 86–95.

[6] *Ibid.*, II, 165. Italics inserted.

[7] The documentary record of Ribbentrop's overtures to Russia is to be found in *Nazi-Soviet Relations, 1939–1941* (Washington, D.C., Department of State, 1948), a publication in translation of captured German Foreign Office documents. See also Winston S. Churchill, *Their Finest Hour* (Vol. II of *The Second World War* [Boston, Mass., 1949]), pp. 576–93; and *The Ciano Diaries, 1939–1943*, ed. Hugh Gibson (New York, 1946), pp. 292–95.

[8] *The Memoirs of Prince Konoye*. This is an interesting historical document. The former premier himself delivered it to the United States Strategic Bombing Survey after Japan's surrender, and stated that he had prepared it after his resignation in October 1941. Naturally it presents the Prince in a favorable light, and there is the possibility of its being spurious. Since it checks with the *Memoirs of Cordell Hull* and with the selection of documents published in 1943 by the Department of State, however, the presumption is in its favor. The document is printed in translation in *Pearl Harbor Attack, Joint Committee on the Investigation of, 79th Cong., 2d sess.* (Washington, D.C., 1946), Part 20 (Exhibit No. 173), 3985–4029.

[9] Hull, *op. cit.*, II, 982–1015. *Pearl Harbor Attack, Report*, pp. 169 ff.

[10] Herbert Feis, *The Road to Pearl Harbor. The Coming of the War between the United States and Japan* (Princeton, N.J., 1950), pp. 227–29.

[11] *Foreign Relations. Japan: 1931–1941*, II, 501.

[12] *Ibid.*, pp. 529–30.

[13] *The Road to Pearl Harbor*, pp. 142–44. But there was strong opposition to this move, notably from Admiral Stark, Chief of Naval Operations. See "Letters of Admiral Stark to Admiral Kimmel," *Pearl Harbor Attack*, Part 16, Exhibit No. 106, p. 2173.

[14] *Ibid.*, pp. 227–48, gives details respecting the freezing order and its history.

[15] *Foreign Relations. Japan: 1931–1941*, II, 549–50.

[16] *Ibid.*, II, 556–57; *Pearl Harbor Attack*, Part 4, pp. 1784–92, memoranda by Sumner Welles; Winston S. Churchill, *The Grand Alliance* (Vol. III of *The Second World War* [Boston, Mass., 1950]), pp. 439–40; Hull, *Memoirs*, II, 1018–19.

[17] *The Memoirs of Prince Konoye*, pp. 3999–4003; Hull, *Memoirs*, II, 1016–27; *Foreign Relations. Japan: 1931–1941*, II, 550–65, 570–79.

[18] *Foreign Relations. Japan: 1931–1941*, II, 756–57.

[19] For the *modus vivendi* and accompanying documents, see Hull, *op. cit.*, II, 1072–73 and *Pearl Harbor Attack*, Part 14, Exhibit 18, pp. 1084–1200. For the text of the ten-point settlement, see *Foreign Relations. Japan: 1931–1941*, II, 768–70.

[20] Kurusu expressed this viewpoint to Hull on November 26. The Secretary dismissed it as "specious and unconvincing," confirming thereby how irreconcilable

were the two viewpoints on the fundamental matter of China and the future leadership of the Far East. *Foreign Relations. Japan: 1931–1941*, II, 764–66. Hull, *op. cit.*, II, 1083–86.

²¹ Churchill, *The Grand Alliance*, p. 593; Hull, *op. cit.*, II, 1090.

²² *Foreign Relations. Japan: 1931–1941*, II, 784–86.

²³ Intensive students of American diplomacy in 1941 will need to be conversant with the following works: Walter Millis, *This Is Pearl!* (New York, 1947); George Morgensterne, *Pearl Harbor. The Story of the Secret War* (New York, 1947); Charles A. Beard, *President Roosevelt and the Coming of the War, 1941* (New Haven, Conn., 1948); and Basil Rauch, *Roosevelt from Munich to Pearl Harbor. A Study in the Creation of a Foreign Policy* (New York, 1950). All four of these writers draw heavily on the documents in Joint Committee on the Investigation of the Pearl Harbor Attack, *Hearings* (79th Cong., 2 sess., Sen. Doc. No. 244), Parts 1–39, already cited. Millis' small volume is an interesting and fair-minded, but superficial, narrative of the diplomatic crisis of 1940–41, into which much pertinent material descriptive of the American domestic scene is woven. Morgensterne and Beard, like the two Republicans who wrote the Minority Report of the Joint Congressional Committee, prejudged their case. Devoted to a guilt thesis, with particular respects paid to President Roosevelt, their books are examples of badly warped history. Rauch, on the other hand, wants to refute Morgensterne and Beard. This end he accomplishes, but in consequence his book reads like an apology for Roosevelt and Hull. Herbert Feis, *The Road to Pearl Harbor*, already cited, is better than any of the others: it uses Japanese as well as American sources, and is able to show how governmental decisions made in Tokyo affected decisions in Washington, and vice versa. But Feis too fails to grasp the long perspective, and there is an unmistakable administration flavor about his book.

II. THE HOLOCAUST OF 1939–1945

¹ Quoted by D. F. Fleming, *The United States and World Organization, 1920–1933* (New York, 1938), p. 300.

² There appear to have been two factors which influenced the Western Powers to ignore Russia: (1) the dread of Communism, which was strong in capitalistic countries, especially during the years of economic depression; (2) the memory that it had been the quarrel between Slav and Teuton over mastery of the Balkans that had precipitated the war in 1914. The underlying meaning of the appeasement policy was the granting to Germany of a free hand in the East. Munich was the climax, and its sequel showed the perils to which Britain and France had exposed themselves. The British then sharply reversed themselves and tardily set to work to organize a "Stop Hitler" coalition.

³ The Japanese seized Canton in October 1938, thereby putting British and American interests in China virtually at their mercy.

⁴ The best study of Russian policy during this period is Max Beloff, *The Foreign Policy of Soviet Russia, 1929–1941* (2 vols.; New York, 1947, 1948). See also L. B. Namier, *Diplomatic Prelude, 1938–1939* (London, 1948) and R. J. Sontag and J. S. Beddie, eds., *Nazi-Soviet Relations, 1939–1941* (Washington, D.C., 1948). The latter is a collection of captured German Foreign Office documents, translated and published by the Department of State, throwing light on Russo-German diplomacy from the Treaty of August 23, 1939, to Hitler's attack on the Soviet Union, June 22, 1941.

At least twice before the outbreak of the war the Soviet Union offered to join the two Western powers against the Nazis. Maxim Litvinoff, the foreign minister, publicly offered support to the Franco-Czechoslovakian Alliance at the time of the Munich crisis; and again on April 16, 1939, when Hitler was making it clear that Poland was to be his next victim, Litvinoff proposed a triple alliance of Britain, France, and Russia. This second offer was rejected apparently as a result of protest of Poland and the other small states bordering on Russia, who feared Soviet aggression as much as they did German. The Germans used certain unfulfilled contracts which the Russian government had with the Skoda works, now under German control, as the entering wedge for a political agreement with Russia. Winston S. Churchill, *The Gathering Storm* (Boston, Mass., 1948), pp. 304–5, 362–68.

⁵ This and the succeeding extracts are from the volume issued by the Department of State in January 1943 entitled *Peace and War—United States Foreign Policy, 1931–1941.* This volume is "an introduction to a collection of documents" concerning American policies in foreign relations during the period, and was reprinted in full in the *New York Times,* January 6, 1943.

⁶ As a dispassionate historical analysis of the situation in 1914–17 and the reasons for American participation, the Committee's report was practically worthless.

⁷ Senator Burton K. Wheeler of Montana, one of the President's bitterest enemies and later a leading firebrand in the notorious America First Committee, privately expressed his approval of Germany's "right" to be dictator of all Europe (*Ambassador Dodd's Diary,* edited by William E. Dodd, Jr., and Martha Dodd, New York, 1941, p. 342). The pattern of thought developed by some of the most vocal isolationists is unmistakable.

⁸ Quoted from *The United States in World Affairs, 1938,* p. 128.

⁹ William L. Langer, *Our Vichy Gamble* (New York, 1947), pp. 84–96.

¹⁰ Langer, *op. cit.,* pp. 97–304; Hull, *Memoirs,* II, 948–66, 1038–45; Fleet Admiral William D. Leahy, *I Was There. The Personal Story of the Chief of Staff to Presidents Roosevelt and Truman Based on His Notes and Diaries Made at the Time* (New York, 1950), pp. 6–94.

The importance of the Free French movement under the leadership of General Charles de Gaulle greatly complicated this diplomacy. Popularly Vichy was assumed to be the tool of Hitler, though, as Professor Langer has shown, this was a distorted picture. De Gaulle maintained headquarters in London, and the Churchill government was constantly embarrassed by his insistence on being treated as the French government-in-exile, on a par with the refugee governments of the Netherlands, Czechoslovakia, Norway, and Poland. Britain, to be sure, could not deal with Vichy, but the United States and also Canada could. Churchill favored de Gaulle, but knew the value of American relations with Vichy. Moreover, he encouraged Canada to keep her contacts with Vichy even after Leahy had been recalled. A tempest in a teapot blew up in January 1942, after de Gaulle had seized the French islands, St. Pierre and Miquelon, in spite of a promise to the contrary. Hull lost his temper over this incident and, threatening to resign, without warrant charged Churchill with conniving with de Gaulle. Roosevelt pacified the outraged Secretary of State, but to Churchill shrugged his shoulders over what was really a trivial incident. Sherwood, *Roosevelt and Hopkins: An Intimate History* (rev. ed.; New York, 1950), pp. 479–86; Churchill, *The Grand Alliance,* pp. 666–67; Hull, *op. cit.,* II, 1127–38.

¹¹ For a graphic description of Britain's predicament and of German invasion plans (Operation Sea Lion) see Churchill, *Their Finest Hour,* pp. 161–76, 255–316.

¹² The destroyer deal made a profound impression in Europe, especially in Spain whose alliance Hitler was even then courting. Berlin talked of breaking diplomatic relations with the United States, and the German Navy wanted to retaliate by sending submarines at once into American waters. Hitler, however, turned down both of these proposals. Then and later he shrank from giving the United States cause for entering the war. Winston S. Churchill, *Their Finest Hour,* pp. 398–416; Samuel Eliot Morison, *The Battle of the Atlantic, September 1939–May 1943* (Vol. I of *History of United States Naval Operations in World War II* [Boston, Mass., 1947]), pp. 33–36. The violation of neutrality refers back to the successful American complaint against Great Britain for allowing the escape of the "Alabama" in 1862. A discussion of this may be found in the Introduction to Part III, pp. 692–94.

The destroyer deal was an executive agreement, not a treaty; it therefore did not require approval of the Senate. By a hair-splitting process the Attorney-General reconciled the President's right to dispose of the destroyers with domestic law.

[13] Quoted from the paraphrase of the President's address in *Peace and War— United States Foreign Policy, 1931–1941.*

[14] *The Public Papers and Addresses of Franklin D. Roosevelt* (1940 volume, New York, 1941), p. 669. Behind the scenes a vivid human drama was being enacted. Ceaseless conversation went on inside the Treasury at Washington on this formidable financial problem. At Lord Lothian's urging, Churchill prepared in the middle of November a long personal letter to Roosevelt, laying the whole British case before him and outlining Britain's prospects and needs for winning the war. The letter—"one of the most important I ever wrote," says Churchill—was finally sent on December 8; and the President "read and re-read" it as he cruised on a warship in the Caribbean. For two days "he was plunged in intense thought, and brooded silently." Oscar S. Cox of Maine, an attorney in the Treasury Department, hit on the idea of "leasing" public property for the public good after raking up an old statute of 1892; and the President at a press conference on December 16 used the homely analogy of lending a garden hose to a neighbor for putting out a fire as a means to attract the imagination of the people. "What I am trying to do," he declared, "is to eliminate the dollar sign." With this episode began the remarkable wartime career of Harry Hopkins. Churchill, *Their Finest Hour*, pp. 552–75; Sherwood, *op. cit.*, pp. 221–74; Hull, *op. cit.*, II, 919–34.

[15] Text of the Act in Jones and Myers, *Documents on American Foreign Relations*, III (1940–41), 712–15. Italics are inserted.

[16] Quoted from the Secretary's statement to the House Committee on Foreign Affairs on January 16, 1941, *New York Times*, January 16, 1941.

[17] *New York Times*, February 12, 1941.

[18] The quotations in this paragraph are extracts from the President's "Sixth Report on Lend-Lease Operations," *New York Times*, September 15, 1942. The number of American troops serving overseas was revealed by the President in his annual message, here quoted from the *New York Times*, January 8, 1943.

[19] *Department of State Bulletin*, Vol. VI, No. 140, February 28, 1942.

[20] The President's speech was broadcast from the White House on September 11, 1941. *Department of State Bulletin*, V (No. 116), 193–97.

[21] *Department of State Bulletin*, IV (No. 101), 647–54. Italics inserted.

[22] *Department of State Bulletin*, V (No. 123), 341–44. The *de facto* naval war with Germany began on September 4, 1941, when the Germans fired on the "Greer." (Morison, *op. cit.*, pp. 79–81). But this incident must be viewed in context with the plans and events of the previous twelve months. The Germans had planned since September 1940, partly as a result of the destroyer deal, to seize Iceland and the Azores. In preparation for these moves, Hitler tried to argue Franco, the Spanish *Caudillo*, into joining him and giving him leave to attack Gibraltar; but, while heaping compliments upon Hitler, the Spanish dictator maintained a stony neutrality. Franco wanted to have no part in the war, but his refusal, a major blow to Hitler, was made the bolder by the American support of Britain. Churchill, *Their Finest Hour*, pp. 520–24.

The American plans for occupying Iceland and for extending naval control over the Atlantic east as far as longitude 26° W. were accompanied by plans for seizing the Azores. The Azores came into view with reports of the German intentions toward Spain and the Canaries; and on May 22, 1941, Admiral Stark was ordered to assemble an expedition of twenty-five thousand men to set sail for the Azores within thirty days. The Portuguese minister in Washington got wind of this plan and protested, but he was told his suspicions "were entirely without foundation." Hull, *op. cit.*, II, 940–41. The State Department hoped that Brazil would join in the operation, thus softening the blow against Portugal. Because the Germans failed in Spain, the expedition against the Azores never materialized (although a subsequent "voluntary" arrangement was made with Portugal for their use as bases); but the occupation of

Iceland was completed on schedule. Right after this Admiral Stark advised the President to come out in the open for convoying at once: the two steps were inextricably connected; and the American desire to help Russia, attacked by Hitler on June 22, 1941, made the task of convoying the more urgent. *Pearl Harbor Attack,* Part 16, Exhibit No. 106 (Admiral Stark's letters to Admiral Kimmel), pp. 2168, 2175; Winston S. Churchill, *The Grand Alliance,* pp. 139–43; Robert E. Sherwood, *op. cit.,* pp. 290–96. The voyage in May of the great German capital ship "Bismarck," with the purpose of destroying shipping in the western Atlantic, supplied an additional incentive to these moves.

The American decision to establish bases in Northern Ireland was reached before April 4, 1941, and preparations for this move were well under way by the time Iceland was occupied. *Pearl Harbor Attack,* p. 2161; Sherwood, *op. cit.,* p. 309. The one country with important bases in the Atlantic area, where both Churchill and Roosevelt feared to tread, was Eire. The two Southern Irish ports, Cobh and Berehaven, had demonstrated their value in British hands during World War I: they were indispensable for the protection of shipping entering the Irish Sea from the south. The British government renounced all rights to them in 1938, and their loss proved a grievous handicap in World War II. After the fall of France the southern approach to British ports became unusable, and convoys had to be diverted to the north. Polite advances by President Roosevelt to de Valera in 1943–44 to induce the Irish president to make the ports available met with an adamant refusal. Hull, *op. cit.,* II, 1351–60.

[22a] Strangely the vote was close in both Houses, in marked contrast to the resounding majorities for Lend-Lease. There was an irritating labor issue at this time and a strong desire, particularly in the House, to "punish" the President for his favoritism toward labor.

The sections of the Neutrality Law relating to loans to belligerents and travel by American citizens on belligerent ships remained technically in force. In view of the Lend-Lease Act, these in company with the Johnson Act can be indulgently regarded as legislative curiosities. The prohibition against loans was finally amended by joint resolution in February 1942 so as to make it inoperative when the United States itself was at war.

[23] Sherwood, *op. cit.,* pp. 323–48, prints Hopkins' detailed report of his mission. Discussion of political questions at this meeting was confined to a single conversation with Molotov, in which the Foreign Minister had emphasized his distrust of Japan and his wish for the United States to warn the Japanese against attacking Siberia. Both Hopkins and the President, it is evident, were predisposed in Russia's favor; but Churchill, in trying during July to bring the Russians and Poles together, had already had a rough brush with the Soviets over the issue of the Polish boundaries. Churchill, *The Grand Alliance,* pp. 390–93.

[24] *The Grand Alliance,* pp. 433–34. Text of the definitive document in *Department of State Bulletin,* V (No. 112), 125–26. The most interesting change is the replacement of the phrase "effective international organization" by the more ambiguous expression "establishment of a wider and permanent system of general security." Roosevelt feared that the original wording would incite a quarrel within the United States over the corpse of the League of Nations. Sherwood, *op. cit.,* pp. 359–60.

[25] *Biennial Report of the Chief of Staff of the United States Army, July 1, 1943 to June 30, 1945, to the Secretary of War.* This *Report,* written in simple, vigorous prose, is destined to live as one of the great documents of military history. It is printed in its entirety in the *New York Times,* October 10, 1945. I have drawn heavily from it for this résumé of the military operations of the war.

[26] Valuable accounts of this, the Arcadia Conference, which began in Washington on December 22, 1941, and ended on January 14, 1942, are to be found in Sherwood, *op. cit.,* pp. 439–78, and in Churchill, *The Grand Alliance,* pp. 644–97. Bound across the Atlantic, Churchill prepared three papers on the future course of the war, which are printed in full in his volume. Part I, The Atlantic Front, is a powerful argument for the preparation of a joint compaign, to take place in 1942, for the possession of the

whole of French North and West Africa. Part II, The Pacific Front, analyzes the strength of Japan and foreshadows the kind of offensive campaign that was later followed against her. Part III, The Campaign of 1943, is a statement of the problem of invading Western Europe, which Churchill proposed for the summer of 1943, but which, as events turned out, did not become feasible until the summer of 1944.

The outstanding military event at this time was the stalemate suffered by Hitler's armies in Russia. While Churchill was on his way to Washington, Anthony Eden, the Foreign Secretary, was en route to Moscow. There the friction already generated over Poland became hotter when Stalin made sweeping demands on Britain respecting postwar political arrangements in Europe. Among these was the incorporation of the Baltic States in the Soviet Union. The British tie-up with the United States in the Atlantic Charter, with its stipulation that no territorial changes should take place contrary to the freely expressed wishes of the peoples concerned, gave the Churchill government the strength needed to resist the Russian demands; and when, May 26, 1942, an Anglo-Soviet treaty of alliance was signed, it contained no commitments on Britain's part to support Russian demands.

It should not escape the reader that the Soviet government was anxious to deal with the British government alone on postwar European questions; nor is it likely that, except for the American alliance, Churchill could have avoided meeting Stalin's wishes. When Molotov came to Washington at the end of May 1942, he refrained from discussion of these questions and confined himself to subdued requests for help and the creation of a second front in Europe. Nothing can be more striking than the contrast between Churchill's account of the rude, demanding nature of the Russian diplomacy toward Britain at this time and Molotov's soft-spoken approach to the United States, as recorded in Sherwood, *op. cit.*, pp. 544–80, and Hull, *op. cit.*, II, 1165–80. "Molotov's visit went extremely well," recorded Hopkins. "He and the President got along famously and I am sure that we at least bridged one more gap between ourselves and Russia." But what must now be said is that Molotov was carefully cultivating the Americans, seeking to divide them from the British, and playing upon the predisposition to extend the hand of comradeship to Russia. Since serious division of opinion existed at this time between the Americans and the British on the question of whether to invade North Africa or to attempt a cross-Channel invasion, Molotov succeeded in driving a real wedge at this point. Only on July 27, 1942, did Roosevelt reach the final decision in favor of North Africa. Sherwood, *op. cit.*, pp. 591–615. After their initial brush with Churchill, the Russians kept their own counsel on territorial questions until the Yalta Conference in February 1945.

[27] Preparations for the North African campaign entailed long and difficult diplomacy with respect to the French generals who controlled the region. Success depended on the utmost secrecy, diplomatic and military, since the French Army in North Africa recognized the authority of Vichy. After Weygand was dismissed in November 1941, we remember, Pétain came under the influence of Laval and Darlan. Through Robert Murphy and General Mark Clark, contact was made with the French army officers in North Africa and their consent to the invasion procured. Admiral Darlan, who controlled the French naval units and coastal batteries, unexpectedly turned up in Algiers after the invasion had begun. At the last moment and under duress, while virtually a prisoner of the Americans, he agreed to issue a cease-fire order to his forces which had resisted the American landings. On Christmas Eve he was mysteriously assassinated. The Nazis, taken completely by surprise, meanwhile closed in on unoccupied France, but failed to take possession of the main French fleet which, under Darlan's orders, had made its getaway from Toulon.

A detailed, documented account of this whole episode is to be found in Langer, *Our Vichy Gamble*, pp. 286–381. See also Winston S. Churchill, *The Hinge of Fate* (Boston, Mass., 1950), pp. 374–90, 432–51, 525–48, 604–47.

[28] Beginning with the Arcadia Conference and extending through the successive war councils with Churchill and others in 1943–44, the President kept Hull on the sidetrack. The Secretary complained of this neglect, but he was put off with the

answer that these meetings were concerned with military and not diplomatic issues, a statement by no means in accord with the facts. So far as the great international issues were concerned, Harry Hopkins was the President's closest adviser, and the Secretary of State was left to pick up information respecting important negotiations with Britain, Russia, and China as best he could. Hull, *op. cit.*, II, 1109–26. Although Roosevelt may have had good reasons for this procedure, the incident calls attention to a dangerous but recurrent weakness in the American type of presidential government : the fact that the Department of State may, by the Chief Executive's mere wish, be deprived of not simply participation in, but even knowledge of, major foreign policy questions.

The fractious spirit displayed by Hull in the Vichy-de Gaulle imbroglio may have been partly responsible for the President's studied neglect of the Secretary. Meeting Hull for the first time at the Arcadia Conference, Churchill noticed that he did not have the President's confidence, and over a year later Hull was still fuming against the Free French. Anthony Eden found him "a little difficult to talk to." A bitter quarrel between Hull and the Undersecretary, Sumner Welles, broke out in January 1942, weakening the State Department and leading eventually to the dismissal of Welles.

29 In addition to the purely military questions a number of diplomatic issues were raised and discussed at both Cairo and Tehran. Among these were : the future of China in relation to Britain and Russia, the place of France, the question of dismembering Germany, and Roosevelt's sketch of his ideas relating to a United Nations. Discussion of these matters is reserved for the next chapter.

The picture of Allied unity in planning the strategy of the war, presented by Marshall's *Biennial Report* of 1945, conceals the tension between the British and the Americans and, of course, the Russians that arose over differing concepts of strategy. These differences, which often provoked hard feelings and awoke traditional national jealousies, are described with understanding and imagination by Sherwood, *op. cit.*, pp. 439–809, *passim.* See also Henry L. Stimson and McGeorge Bundy, *On Active Service in Peace and War* (New York, 1948), pp. 413–612; Admiral Leahy, *I Was There*, pp. 142–267; and Churchill, *The Hinge of Fate*, pp. 740–99. The basic strategy of the war rested on Churchill's three papers presented at the Arcadia Conference (December 1941) ; and it seems clear that the United States naval chiefs, influenced like Churchill by concepts of sea power, tended to side with Churchill against Marshall and the Pentagon. Roosevelt too had a Navy point of view, hence he generally fell in with Churchill's ideas.

30 The bitter quarrels of Chiang Kai-shek and his supporter, the American general Chennault, with General Stilwell, who promoted the Ledo Road and led the invading forces from Burma, are now a matter of record. Chiang was prosecuting a war against the Chinese Communists, and it is an unanswered question whether he was more concerned with this civil conflict or with co-operation with the Allies against Japan. Roosevelt sent two special emissaries to Chungking in 1944—Vice-President Wallace in June, followed by Brigadier General Hurley in September—in bootless efforts to induce Chiang to make peace with the Chinese Communists. Sherwood, *op. cit.*, pp. 730–31, 739–40, 771–75; *The Stilwell Papers* (New York, 1948), *passim*; documents on the Wallace and Hurley missions in *United States Relations with China, with Special Reference to the Period 1944–1949* (Department of State, Washington, D.C., 1949), pp. 549–84. The latter publication is familiarly known as "The White Paper."

31 On the naval war in the Pacific consult Vols. III–VII of Samuel Eliot Morison, *History of United States Naval Operations in World War II* (7 vols. published; Boston, Mass., 1947–51). See also Admiral Leahy, *I Was There*, pp. 430–32, on secret preparations for bacteriological warfare against the Japanese and on the decision to use the atom bomb. It is Leahy's conviction that "The Japanese were already defeated and ready to surrender because of the effective sea blockade and the successful bombing with conventional weapons."

[32] Hull, *op. cit.*, II, 1165–80, 1247–73, 1451–71; Sherwood, *op. cit.*, pp. 451, 708–814; Churchill, *The Hinge of Fate*, pp. 472–502, 740–61. The London Poles were a real embarrassment to the British. By 1943 they had developed "large ambitions" to become the most powerful state in Eastern Europe. This could only be accomplished at the expense of Russia, and neither the British nor the Americans intended to support it. Sherwood, *op. cit.*, p. 710.

[33] Hull, *op. cit.*, II, 1274–91, 1570–82, 1602–24; Sherwood, *op. cit.*, pp. 695–97, 797–98, 832–33; Leahy, *op. cit.*, pp. 210–11, 259–66, 301–2. At the Second Quebec Conference, September 11–20, 1944, Secretary Henry D. Morgenthau of the Treasury submitted a bizarre plan for the reduction of Germany to the level of what was popularly called a "goat pasture." Not realizing, perhaps, what they were doing, Roosevelt and Churchill initialed the plan, but soon pigeonholed it.

[34] Sherwood, *op. cit.*, pp. 560, 785–87; Hull, *op. cit.*, II, 1292–1307; Leahy, *op. cit.*, pp. 209, 303–4; Stettinius, *Roosevelt and the Russians* (New York, 1949), pp. 189–207. At Yalta the Soviets reduced their original demand for 16 votes in the Assembly to 3, and gave their consent to three seats for the United States, if it chose. At both Tehran and Yalta, however, Stalin showed little interest in the proposed organization, and at the second of these meetings even admitted he had not studied the Dumbarton Oaks Proposals.

[35] Stettinius, *op. cit.*, pp. 112, 147–48.

[36] Sherwood, *op. cit.*, p. 867; Stimson, *op. cit.*, pp. 618–19; Stettinius, *op. cit.*, pp. 91–98. Admiral Leahy took the view that neither an invasion nor use of the atomic bomb was necessary to defeat Japan. Her defeat was encompassed by naval action. But Leahy did nothing to oppose the Army's zeal for an alliance with Russia. Leahy, *op. cit.*, pp. 311–12.

[37] Hull, *op. cit.*, II, 1309; Sherwood, *op. cit.*, p. 792.

[38] Quoted by Leahy, *op. cit.*, p. 318.

[39] Text of this document in Stettinius, *op. cit.*, pp. 351–52. Churchill was not a party to the Roosevelt-Stalin conversations respecting the Far East, but, simply to protect his position, came in on the deal at its conclusion. What his real attitude was is not known. Only the President, it is to be noted, was to "take measures" to get the consent of the Chinese.

[40] The contrast between the assumptions on which American wartime policy—military and diplomatic—in the Far East was based and the actual outcome must not escape notice. Secretary Stimson and General Marshall, representing the Army, maintained fixed opinions throughout the whole course of the war that the assistance of both Russia and China was indispensable for the defeat of Japan. President Roosevelt accepted these views and acted upon them. The costly Burma operations and the development of the transport service over the Himalayas were explained on the ground that China must be kept in the war in order to defeat the Japanese armies. But it is to be noted that neither Russia nor China had anything to do with the Japanese surrender. When Japan gave up, her armies, whether in Manchuria or in China and Southeast Asia, melted away. No large-scale engagement ever took place on the mainland.

[41] Hull, *op. cit.*, II, 1257.

[42] *United States Relations with China, with Special Reference to the Period 1944–1949*, contains the embassy reports and the documents on the Wallace and Hurley missions. Leahy, *op. cit.*, p. 289, reveals the desire of the Chinese Communist leaders to visit Washington. The White House ignored the Department of State entirely in its China policy, and sent both Wallace and Hurley to China without consulting the Secretary of State. Wallace personally intervened and persuaded Roosevelt to send him, and Hurley's appointment was due to the influence of Stimson and General Marshall, who had previously got Stilwell his command. Hull, *op. cit.*, II, 1585–87; Stimson, *op. cit.*, p. 38. Clarence E. Gauss, the regular Ambassador to China, resigned November 1, 1944, for reasons that can best be imagined, and Hurley was given his job.

Behind the scenes in Washington Chiang's two brothers-in-law, H. H. K'ung and

T. V. Soong, labored incessantly to get the ears of officials in the Treasury, War, and Navy departments, and Chiang himself sent numerous cables to various persons within the administration. On his part, Secretary Hull, while willing to stand by Chiang, wanted to take a firm hand with the Generalissimo, but was obviously thwarted. Hull told Lord Beaverbrook on July 24, 1944, that in his opinion China had "only a fifty-fifty chance to re-establish herself as a great power." Beaverbrook expressed the British view that Chiang's regime was not a real government, but was "something plastered on top of China like a button on a coat." Hull, *op. cit.*, II, 1586.

[43] Churchill, it will be recalled, advocated that the Atlantic Charter announce that the two powers favored the establishment of "an effective international organization." Roosevelt at the time shied away from so frank an expression; but with the promulgation of the Declaration of the United Nations on New Year's Day, 1942, the President assumed the lead in formulating plans for the world organization. Roosevelt conceived of the UN as virtually taking over the vital functions of defense and colonial administration from the several national states. The UN, he proposed, should control and operate a string of strategic bases around the world; and sundry colonial areas, including the islands of the Pacific, should be converted into trusteeships under the direct jurisdiction of the UN. Both Churchill and Eden considered this plan impracticable, and urged that the United States retain in outright ownership the islands that it took from Japan. Needless to say, they intended to recover the territories of the British Empire taken by the enemy. Sherwood, *op. cit.*, pp. 707–8, 716–19; Leahy, *op. cit.*, pp. 313–14.

[44] Sherwood, *op. cit.*, pp. 781–82, 858–59; Stettinius, *op. cit.*, pp. 139, 163, 170–71.

[45] Stettinius, *op. cit.*, pp. 314–15.

[46] Stettinius, *op. cit.*, pp. 151–59, 300–303, 309–18; James F. Byrnes, *Speaking Frankly* (New York, 1947), pp. 29–66. The original bone of contention over Poland's eastern boundary, the Curzon line, disappeared at Yalta. Roosevelt and Churchill both acceded to the Russian demand.

III. NEW WORLDS, NEW QUARRELS

[1] Department of State Publication 3580, *Postwar Foreign Policy Preparation 1939–1945* (Washington, D.C., 1949), contains a detailed account of the wartime planning done by the Department. Chap. viii of the UN Charter seeks to reconcile regional institutions with the general organization. Owing to its hemispheric policies and to the inter-American system arising out of these policies, the United States is in reality a strong advocate of regionalism.

[2] *Postwar Foreign Policy Preparation 1939–1945*, p. 346.

[3] *New York Times*, January 11, 1945. It will be recalled that in 1919 the Lodge reservations to the Covenant of the League insisted that the President get the prior consent of Congress before acting under the Covenant.

[4] Quoted by Robert E. Sherwood, *Roosevelt and Hopkins*, p. 870. Stettinius conceived Yalta to be an Anglo-American diplomatic triumph, and like Hopkins and others seems to have been carried away with enthusiasm for Marshal Stalin. Edward R. Stettinius, Jr., *Roosevelt and the Russians*. But Admiral Leahy felt that Stalin "definitely was not in favor of organizing the United Nations." William D. Leahy, *I Was There*, p. 304.

[5] Hopkins' records of his meetings with Stalin (and Molotov) are in Sherwood, *op. cit.*, pp. 887–912. Sherwood thinks Hopkins achieved a real victory. Stettinius, *op. cit.*, p. 321, popularizes Hopkins' own statement by concluding that "Stalin told Molotov not to make himself ridiculous." Whether Stalin really differed from Molotov will perhaps always remain a moot question. He had a very genuine wish to get along with the other two "policemen" and since one of them especially was bent on having the United Nations he saw no harm in it. There is nothing to indicate, however, that Stalin himself attached any importance to the United Nations. He understood it as something the Americans wanted, though the chances are that he did not

understand why they wanted it. His consideration of the point about free discussion that Hopkins was trying to make was too brief to be convincing.

[6] The original Rooseveltian conception of the world policemen, it will be remembered, included only four: the U.K., the U.S.A., the U.S.S.R., and the Republic of China. Neither Russia nor Britain shared the American enthusiasm for China. Stalin's choice was limited to the first three, and British diplomacy at Yalta added France. The United States got its wish to include China on the Security Council, but in spite of being warned as early as 1943 to the contrary, it failed to take into account the realities of the civil strife in that country between the Nationalists and the Communists. By "China" the United States meant Nationalist China. And when subsequently the Chinese Communists won the civil war, the American government continued to cling to its original position that only the defeated Nationalist regime might have a seat on the Security Council.

[7] The Assembly's stock began to rise in 1947 when Great Britain dumped the explosive Palestine issue in its lap. When on June 25, 1950, the Korean war started, Russia was not present at the Security Council, having boycotted that body since February 1 over the issue of expelling Nationalist China and handing over its permanent seat to Communist China. Soviet absence made it easy for the Council to vote in favor of resistance to the North Korean invaders; but at the end of July the Soviet delegate returned and threatened by his veto to destroy the effectiveness of the Council. Thus the intervention of the Assembly may well have saved the UN from complete failure so far as the Korean war is concerned, but the main question regarding the future of the UN is left just where it was. Under the Charter the Assembly does not have the authority to *initiate* enforcement actions.

[8] The Caribbean Commission, originated jointly by Britain and the United States in 1942 for the betterment of economic and social conditions in the poverty-stricken West Indies, developed even before the end of the war into a model trust territory operating independently of the UN. France and the Netherlands joined the Commission in 1946; and the West Indian Conference, meeting biennially and comprising delegations from the colonies of the four powers, was constituted an auxiliary body to give an outlet to the viewpoints of the local populations. So successful was the pioneering work of the Caribbean Commission that in 1948 a South Pacific Commission with similar objectives for the non-self-governing territories of that area was created. The same four powers, with the addition of Australia and New Zealand, comprised the membership of this new commission. *The Department of State Bulletin*, XI (No. 276, October 8, 1944), 377–79; XVIII (No. 465, May 30, 1948), 691–93; XX (No. 503, February 20, 1949), 221–26.

[9] As with the Fund, the capital of the Bank was to be paid in on a quota basis, partly in gold or United States dollars and partly in currencies of the members. The Bank also is managed by a Board of Governors whose voting power is evaluated by the amount of the quota of the respective member states. The total amount of the Fund is $8,800,000,000 and the subscribed capital of the Bank is the equivalent of $8,348,000,000. Twenty per cent of the Bank's capital may be employed in making direct loans to borrowing nations, but the remaining 80 per cent is circumscribed as a reserve fund to be used for guaranteeing loans made by private sources. This feature appears to have been introduced to satisfy the demands of the New York banks, who saw in the new World Bank a potential monopoly excluding them from the field of international lending.

The Bretton Woods Agreements became operative on December 31, 1945, by which time governments whose quotas represented 65 per cent of the total amounts had ratified. The Soviet Union had been an active participant at Bretton Woods and had signified its approval. Nevertheless, keeping its reasons to itself, the U.S.S.R. failed to ratify within the allotted time. The chasm between itself and the Western powers widened perceptibly during the interval.

[10] *UNRRA. Organization and Progress* (Washington, D.C., 1944).
[11] Hull, *Memoirs*, II, 1620.

[12] The announcement fell like a thunderbolt on both London and Moscow and came at a time when, we remember, the San Francisco Conference was entering the shoals. It is indeed regrettable that so little promotion work was done to prepare the American public for the real economic and social crisis that was to follow in the wake of the war in contrast to the immense educational activity directed at the paper formulas for peace identified with the United Nations. The British government managed to recover from the rude shock of Truman's announcement; but when Harry Hopkins went to Moscow, Stalin left him in no doubt that it had stimulated Russian distrust of American intentions. Leahy, *op. cit.*, pp. 272–73, 376–77, 409–11; Sherwood, *op. cit.*, p. 894.

[13] *The Economist*, August 17, 1946. The Agreement contained one ameliorative feature: a waiver of interest clause which conditioned the future interest payments according to the earned income of the United Kingdom. But two other stipulations proved unworkable and had to be modified: (1) a requirement that the British government had to use the credit exclusively in the high-priced American market. Inflation, already under way in 1946, absorbed more than 25 per cent of the funds. From the British standpoint, the loan was shockingly expensive and uneconomic. (2) The Agreement required the British government to make sterling, upon American demand, freely convertible into dollars. This meant that the nationals of other countries, to whom Great Britain was indebted, might change their pounds into dollars and resort to the American market. Against its will, the British government made sterling freely convertible in July 1947; and in much the same manner as a popular run on a bank during a financial panic, a disastrous "flight from the pound" ensued, only to be halted at the end of five weeks by the reimposition of the controls.

This experiment showed how badly shaken Britain's credit had become. Deterioration had set in, as a matter of fact, as far back as 1932, when shrinkage of the market abroad for British goods had forced the country to draw on its capital reserves for financing its purchases abroad. By 1938 the net annual deficit had risen to $200,000,000. With most of her invested overseas capital wiped out by the war, the deficit for 1946, the first postwar year, amounted to $1,660,000,000. Convertibility forced this up in July and August 1947 to the panic rate of $7,000,000,000 per annum. Even after the controls were reimposed the deficits continued at the rate of nearly $160,000,000 per month. United Kingdom, *Economic Survey for 1948*, Cmd. 7344.

From many directions misfortune haunted the British through 1947. Also a sizable portion of the American credit was swallowed up in the purchase of supplies for Germany. But that the British government and people were themselves guilty of overspending in their domestic economy the authoritative London *Economist* took pains repeatedly to point out. Britain, it declared on February 14, 1948, "has been living like an improvident family which, failing to make both ends meet, first spends the accumulated capital of the past, then borrows from friends—from American friends, from Canadian friends, from South African friends—and when their loans are exhausted, begins to pawn the furniture."

[14] Philip E. Moseley, "Dismemberment of Germany. The Allied Negotiations from Yalta to Potsdam," *Foreign Affairs*, XXVIII (1949–50), 487–98, and "The Occupation of Germany. New Light on How the Zones Were Drawn," *ibid.*, pp. 580–604. Moseley was political adviser to Winant in London, and writes from the standpoint of a critic of the civil affairs division of the War Department which, he feels, was to blame for defeating the work of Winant and the State Department. The latter recognized the importance of having ready a carefully considered plan for postwar Germany, and made preparations thereto. But the State Department was virtually helpless: all it could do was to act as messenger boy for the "Working Security Committee," which was made up of delegates from the State, War, and Navy departments. This body was itself a blind, since each delegation could speak and act only with the prior consent of its respective department. "This system of negotiating at arm's length, under rigid instructions and with the exercise of the 'veto'," declares Moseley, "resembled the procedures of Soviet negotiators in their more intransigent moods."

154 AMERICAN CRISIS DIPLOMACY

See also Sherwood, *op. cit.*, pp. 711–12, 713–15, 797–98, 817–19, 904–5; Hull, *op. cit.*, II, 1274–91, 1602–24; Welles, *The Time for Decision* (New York, 1944) pp. 336–64; Henry L. Stimson and McGeorge Bundy, *On Active Service in Peace and War*, pp. 556–83; Stettinius, *op. cit.*, pp. 117–34; Leahy, *op. cit.*, pp. 210–11, 301–2, 321–23. For the Morgenthau Plan see Henry Morgenthau, Jr., *Germany Is Our Problem* (New York, 1945).

15 Anthony Eden, however, changed his position. In March 1943 he agreed with Roosevelt on dismemberment. In the following August, at the first Quebec conference, he told Hull he was opposed to it. Sherwood, *op. cit.*, p. 711; Hull, *op. cit.*, II, 1236.

16 The military directive (JCS 1067) and the Potsdam protocol are reprinted in *Germany, 1947–1949. The Story in Documents* (Department of State Publication 3556 [Washington, D.C., 1950]), pp. 21–33, 47–57. A similar four-power occupation of Austria was arranged. The Big Three had previously, in 1943, agreed upon the principle of Austrian independence, and technically she was exempted from paying reparations. But nevertheless Russia secured the right to seize "German assets" in her zone, and since Hitler in 1938 had expropriated Austria's basic industries, the Soviets proceeded to do likewise.

17 Lucius D. Clay, *Decision in Germany* (Garden City, N.Y., 1950), pp. 120–23. Potsdam was in effect the Morgenthau Plan to pastoralize Germany, with the added inconsistency of providing for the compulsory resettlement in Germany of over 6,000,000 Germans from Eastern Europe. As early as March 10, 1945, *The Economist* (London) began to propound the fatal results that would flow from such a program. Characterizing the Potsdam policy as "utter lunacy," it advocated in its issue of September 8 a program of reindustrialization.

18 Text of this address in *Germany, 1947–1949. The Story in Documents*, pp. 3–8.

19 Winston Churchill first used the famous phrase, "Iron Curtain," in a great speech at Fulton, Missouri, March 5, 1946. Appealing for a "special relationship" between the United States and the British Commonwealth, Churchill with President Truman's support dramatically described the division that had taken place between the West and the Soviet sphere. At the time the American public was just beginning to awake to what had occurred. But the movement to split Europe into two separate blocs goes back to 1943 when, after Italy had surrendered, the Anglo-American powers barred the Soviet Union from sharing with them the administration of the conquered country. The division of Southeast Europe also commenced at this time with a Churchill-Roosevelt agreement giving Britain primacy in Greece. This agreement was followed by Anglo-Soviet negotiations resulting in October 1944 in an accord whereby Russia was to have predominance in Bulgaria, Hungary, and Rumania, to exercise equal influence in Jugoslavia, and to remain out of Greece. Washington was informed of this accord and protested it on the ground that it was a sphere of influence agreement. Roosevelt maintained that there was a distinction between military and political agreements. But his original bargain over Greece had had political implications—it involved support of the Greek government-in-exile—and, furthermore, the Italian policy of the Anglo-American powers, in an area where the United States led, shows that politics were inseparable from military control. See Hull, *op. cit.*, II, 1451–71, and Dwight E. Lee and George McReynolds, eds., *Essays in History and International Relations in Honor of George Hubbard Blakeslee* (Worcester, Mass., 1949), pp. 43–49.

The real issue was over the question of "free elections" in the liberated countries. To this end the Western powers got Russia to subscribe at Yalta to the high-sounding Declaration on Liberated Europe. But Stalin interpreted this declaration as merely a face-saving gesture for Britain and the United States. Each side was to discover its error.

20 James F. Byrnes, *Speaking Frankly* (New York, 1947), describes, from the standpoint of himself as the American Secretary of State, the record of the Council of Foreign Ministers. Reviewing this book, *The Economist* remarked (November 1,

1947) : "The world now lives under the sign of open disagreements openly arrived at."

²¹ Committee of European Economic Co-operation. *General Report*, Vol. I (Department of State Publication 2930, European Series 28 [Paris, 1947]). Ernest Bevin of the British Foreign Office initiated and organized this committee. The sixteen nations were: Austria, Belgium, Denmark, Eire, France, Greece, Iceland, Italy, Luxemburg, the Netherlands, Norway, Portugal, Sweden, Switzerland, Turkey, and the United Kingdom. Molotov tried, by playing on national jealousies and calling for separate "shopping lists" to be handed to the United States by each country to prevent the committee from meeting. He failed ingloriously, but the Soviet Union nevertheless kept all of the Iron Curtain countries from joining.

²² *European Recovery and American Aid. A Report by the President's Committee on Foreign Aid* (Washington, D.C., November 7, 1947). The cost estimate of this report ran considerably below that of the European Committee.

²³ The large majorities that the Recovery Program received in both the Senate and the House in March were undoubtedly due to the intensity of the feeling against communism rather than to the economic arguments on the benefits of European recovery which had originally inspired the measure. Thus Herbert Hoover, who had originally opposed the act (on economic and politically isolationist grounds), came out in its favor at the last moment and influenced much of the Republican opposition to do likewise. The Marshall Plan must be read principally in the context of American national security.

²⁴ Treaty of Economic, Social, and Cultural Collaboration and Collective Self-Defence. *The Department of State Bulletin*, XVIII (No. 462, May 9, 1948), 600–602.

²⁵ *Germany, 1947–1949. The Story in Documents*, pp. 75–80, 275–77.

²⁶ Walter Bedell Smith, *My Three Years in Moscow* (Philadelphia and New York, 1950), pp. 230–52.

²⁷ Lucius D. Clay, *op. cit.*, p. 386.

²⁸ Text of the Statute of the Council of Europe in *The Department of State Bulletin*, XXI (No. 544, December 5, 1949), 858a–62a. See also the Council on Foreign Relations, *The United States in World Affairs, 1949* (New York, 1950), pp. 110–17, 160–63; and Halford M. Lange, "European Union: False Hopes and Realities," *Foreign Affairs*, XXVIII (1949–50), 441–50.

²⁹ *The United States in World Affairs, 1949*, p. 173. For the texts of the Occupation Statute and of the Bonn Constitution see *Germany, 1947–1949. The Story in Documents*, pp. 89–97, 283–305.

³⁰ The text of this tripartite agreement on rearming Western Germany is reprinted in *Current History*, XX (February 1951), 106–7.

³¹ *New York Times*, March 7, 1951. The Bonn government appears to have given the Allies nothing of substantial value in return. It had already protested its "peaceful intentions" and promised to "eradicate" Nazism (with what sincerity the reader may judge) ; but it withheld any commitment of military support for the North Atlantic Treaty Organization, although this was what the United States at least had most wanted. The ink was no sooner dry on the agreement of March 6, 1951, than the Adenauer government began clamoring for more concessions from the West.

³² Text in Report of the Senate Committee on Foreign Relations (Exec. Report No. 8, 81st Cong., 1st sess. [Washington, D.C., 1949]). The conspicuous absentees from the treaty are Spain and Sweden. Sweden's subsequent decision to remain apart, based on her frontier position with respect to Russia, suggests the probable atttiude of the West Germans, similarly exposed. Washington's thinly disguised eagerness to draw in Spain as well as West Germany, manifested in the spring of 1951, met with cool response in London and Paris.

³³ But at the cost of some reduction in the amounts. Europe's benefits were cut to an even billion. Enthusiasts for Nationalist China, apparently more interested in restoring Chiang Kai-shek to power than in buttressing the free nations of Western Europe, muddied the waters by trying to get $175,000,000 for Chiang. They succeeded

to the extent of $75,000,000, but the President was given discretion on whether and in what manner to use it. See the section on the Far East.

[34] A Soviet note of December 15, 1950, addressed to the British and French governments, expressed this fear and charged that the Western powers were preparing a direct military alliance with the Adenauer government. A British reply denied this intention and offered a formal assurance that Britain was "determined never, at any time or in any circumstances, to allow Western Germany to be used as a base for aggression." Texts of these notes are reprinted in *Current History*, XX (February 1951), 107–10, and *ibid.* (March 1951), pp. 173–74.

[35] The report published by OEEC in 1949, at the halfway point of the European Recovery Program, predicted that in 1951–52 Europe would still have a dollar deficit of $2,300,000,000. By this time the program had cost the United States about $6,000,-000,000, but more than half of these expenditures were made in the United States. A very marked improvement in Europe's balance of "invisible" transactions, notably shipping and the tourist trade, took place in 1950. The optimistic view, expressed at the end of that year and repeated in the text above, was taken in the "Report to the President on Foreign Economic Policies" by Gordon Gray, Special Assistant to the President, printed in the *New York Times*, November 13, 1950, and also in the year-end "International Business and Financial Review" published by that newspaper in its issue of January 3, 1951.

[36] From the outset of the Marshall Plan it had been recognized that permanent European recovery was contingent upon the restoration of world trade. Various tentative approaches were made to this problem, among them a movement for a European tariff union and economic integration along nonnational lines. Mr. Paul Hoffman, the administrator of the Economic Co-operation Administration, strongly urged this upon the Europeans, but with few noticeable results. Even the small Benelux countries, committed in principle to economic integration, were a long way from achieving it. For a valuable discussion of the long-range economic problem and the relation of the United States to it see John H. Williams, "The Marshall Plan Halfway," *Foreign Affairs*, XXVIII (1949–50), 463–76.

[37] *New York Times*, December 6, 1944. Hull, *op. cit.*, II, 1451–71 furnishes details respecting these arrangements and shows the Secretary assuming a protesting attitude against what he considered a sphere of influence agreement. Roosevelt in the Greek episode foreshadowed his subsequent promotion of the Declaration on Liberated Europe by advocating three-power consultations over Balkan political problems; but Churchill convinced him that "if everybody had to consult everybody else," no decisions could be reached. The weakness in the Roosevelt-Stettinius position of December 1944 is to be found in the fact that the President had already mixed politics with military action in acquiescing in the return under British auspices of the Greek King.

[38] Sherwood, *op. cit.*, p. 864. This position, so different from the one Stettinius had assumed only two months previously, was decided upon after consultation with Anthony Eden, the British Foreign Secretary. It raises a doubt as to how much faith after all the Americans at Yalta had in the prospects for postwar Soviet friendship.

[39] Contrary to its previous announcement, the British government, apparently by prearrangement with Washington, agreed to keep its troops in Greece. The State Department under General Marshall preferred to paint the Greek civil war luridly as paving the way to a "red tide of Communist invasion." But in its historical context the struggle is tied to the Balkan wars of the past and to previous Greek civil wars. The hand of Moscow in the episode had not been found in the way the American government implied it would be. Two UN investigating commissions, one dispatched by the Security Council in December 1946 and one by the Assembly in October 1947, fixed responsibility on Jugoslavia, Albania, and Bulgaria. Russia looked sourly on, but according to the evidence she pursued a cautious line. The persevering tactics of the Greek guerrillas caused the American Mission for Aid to

Greece, sent out in July 1947, to allocate even more of the funds for military equipment than originally contemplated. Council on Foreign Relations, *The United States in World Affairs, 1947–1948* (New York, 1948), pp. 386–401, 472–80.

⁴⁰ The Soviets counterattacked on the Security Council with charges against the British for continuing to occupy Greece and Indonesia, and against the French for occupying Syria and the Lebanon. The affairs of Iran meanwhile dropped into the background until February 1949, when an attempted assassination of the young Shah, Mohammed Reza Pahlevi, precipitated a political crisis featuring the dissolution of the pro-Soviet Tudeh ("Masses") party. Moscow then made threatening gestures, including a hint that it might intervene with troops, but presently relapsed into silence. The young Shah paid a State visit to the United States, at the latter's invitation, late in the year; and though the American government studiously avoided commitments comparable to those made to Greece and Turkey, the inference was there that it might make them if an emergency demanded. What was popularly called the "Truman Doctrine" ("defense of free peoples everywhere") really meant the defense of buffer states on the periphery of the Soviet empire.

⁴¹ On the history of the Straits question see the author's article, "The Question of the Turkish Straits," *Current History*, XIII (August 1947), 65–70. Soviet policy of 1946 was a reversion to the Treaty of Unkiar Skelessi between Russia and Turkey in 1833, a treaty which Lord Palmerston by a masterly stroke of diplomacy managed to undo in 1841 and replace with a five-power treaty putting Britain again in the lead. See also the articles by Harry N. Howard, "The Montreux Convention of the Straits, 1936," in *The Department of State Bulletin*, XV (No. 375 [September 8, 1946]), 435–46; and "The United States and the Problem of the Turkish Straits," *The Middle East Journal*, I (1947), 59–72.

⁴² K. S. Twitchell, *Saudi Arabia, with an Account of the Development of Its Natural Resources* (Princeton, N.J., 1947), *passim*.

⁴³ Among the growing list of works on the subject, the two best and most comprehensive books are E. A. Speiser, *The United States and the Near East* (Cambridge, Mass., 1950) and *The Middle East. A Political and Economic Survey* (Royal Institute of International Affairs, London and New York, 1950). There is difference of opinion over the application of the terms "Near East" and "Middle East." As used by the Department of State, the Arab countries from Egypt to Saudi Arabia are included in the Near East, leaving out Turkey and Iran. But more general usage lumps all the countries of the Eastern Mediterranean, the Red Sea and the Persian Gulf as Middle East.

⁴⁴ Selig Adler, "The Palestine Question in the Wilson Era," *Jewish Social Studies*, X (1948), 303–34. At the same time the Department of State opposed the Balfour Declaration and remained anti-Zionist.

⁴⁵ *Report of the American Section* [King-Crane] *of the International Commission on Mandates in Turkey* (Paris, August 28, 1919), printed in full for the first time in *Papers Relating to the Foreign Relations of the United States. The Paris Peace Conference 1919* (13 vols.; Washington, D.C., 1942–47), XII, 751–863. This commission reached the conclusion that the indigenous Palestine Arabs wanted union with Syria, and it expressed disbelief in the feasibility of implementing the Balfour Declaration. For an interesting side light on the commission, see Adler, *op. cit.*

⁴⁶ Paul L. Hanna, *British Policy in Palestine* (Washington, D.C., 1942), is a competent history of the mandate; but the *Report of the Royal Commission*, Cmd. 5479 (London, July 1937), as a source of fundamental importance, makes fine reading. The Esco Foundation for Palestine, *Palestine. A Study of Jewish, Arab and British Policies* (2 vols.; New Haven, Conn., 1947) contains a mine of information about the country since ancient times.

⁴⁷ Sherwood, *op. cit.*, pp. 871–72.

⁴⁸ Texts of these agreements in *United States Relations with China, with Special Reference to the Period 1944–1949* (Department of State Publication 3573 [Washington, D.C., 1949]), pp. 585–96.

[49] George M. McCune, "Korea: The First Year of Liberation," *Pacific Affairs*, XX (March 1947), 3–17.

[50] Report of the United Nations Commission on Korea, August 1949 (UN General Assembly, *Official Records, Fourth Session,* Supplement No. 9), I, 32–34. Good summaries of the Korean problem may be found in the annual volumes of the Council on Foreign Relations, *The United States in World Affairs, 1945–1947, 1947–1948, 1949.*

[51] The full facts as summarized here were apparently not known in Washington until November 1946. They were rendered in a report by Edwin W. Pauley, who headed a mission sent to investigate Japanese assets in Manchuria. *United States Relations with China* (Washington, D.C., 1949), pp. 598–604. As early as September 10, 1945, however, the American embassy in Moscow correctly forecast the policy Russia would follow. *Ibid.,* pp. 122–23.

[52] *Ibid.,* pp. 131–32. Wedemeyer's report was not the first unfavorable information respecting the Nationalist regime to be received in Washington. Severely critical reports had been sent the State Department during the war years by its officers in the field. But the shirt-sleeved diplomat General Hurley, sent out by President Roosevelt in 1944, had openly espoused the cause of Chiang Kai-shek and condemned all those who criticized him as "Communists." Roosevelt, we remember, ignored the Department of State and its officers during these years, and American China policy was left in the hands of Hurley and various Army officers. It is not known who ordered the large-scale American armed intervention of 1945 against the Chinese Communists.

[53] *United States Relations with China,* pp. 311–23, sketches the military operations in that country during 1945–49. It admits that the Nationalists invaded Manchuria contrary to the advice of competent American observers, but it fails to explain why, in the face of this advice, the United States Army helped the invasion—indeed, made it possible. General Wedemeyer in his report of November 20, 1945, had recommended a temporary Soviet-American-British trusteeship for Manchuria, similar to the one intended for Korea. In view of the Korean farce, one could hardly be sanguine over a Manchurian trusteeship. The plain fact is that Russia, by virtue of geographical propinquity and superior force, was in a position to call the tune in this long-fought-over area. Furthermore, it is not to be overlooked that the Nationalists, during the short period of their occupation, acted like carpetbaggers and plundered the country unmercifully. *Ibid.,* pp. 732–35.

Direct military assistance was only part of the multitudinous forms of aid given by the United States to the Chinese Nationalists in 1945–47. Export-Import Bank credits, gifts of American surplus property in China and the Pacific islands, UNRRA funds, technical assistance, and training, the cost of which cannot be estimated, and the transfer in July 1947 of 271 naval vessels together with matériel and services helped build up the cornucopia.

[54] A foreign service report of June 1944 had condemned the megalomania of Chiang Kai-shek and criticized the Kuomintang as "a congerie of conservative political cliques interested primarily in the preservation of their own power against all outsiders and in jockeying for position among themselves." This and similar reports were branded pro-Communist by Hurley, but the fact remains that the reports of General Wedemeyer in 1945 and 1947, of General Marshall in 1946, of Ambassador Stuart in 1947–48, and of Major General David Barr, the senior American military adviser to the Generalissimo, in 1949 all substantially agree. *United States Relations with China,* pp. 133–310, 325–38, 567–70, 686–89, 758–814, 897–99.

The CC Clique was "completely dominated by two brothers, Chen Li-fu and Chen Kuo-fu, who have long been closely associated with the Generalissimo. The latter has relied on them to discipline the rank and file of the Party." *Ibid.,* p. 235 n.

[55] *United States Relations with China,* p. 247.

[56] *Ibid.,* pp. 766–814.

[57] *The United States in World Affairs, 1947–1948* (New York, 1948), pp. 199–201. The Wedemeyer Report was published in August 1949, nearly two years after it had

been written. Chiang Kai-shek knew of its contents at the time and got an assurance from Secretary Marshall that it would be suppressed. Its subsequent inclusion and publication in the White Paper, *United States Relations with China*, aimed at absolving the administration from further responsibility for China. The Nationalists were by then thoroughly beaten.

58 *United States Relations with China*, p. 319.

59 See *The New York Times*, February 15, 1950, for text and reports on this treaty. In a general way it was Soviet Russia's substitute for the 1945 agreements with Nationalist China, and contained clauses for the withdrawal of Soviet troops from Dairen and Port Arthur *after* the conclusion of a peace treaty with Japan. Superficially Mao Tsê-tung was more successful than his predecessor in extracting concessions from Moscow.

60 Department of State, *Documents & State Papers*, I, No. 1 (April 1948), pp. 32–45. This document gives expression to the same double purposes and economic absurdities previously laid down in the directives for Germany.

61 Harold S. Quigley, "The Great Purge in Japan," *Pacific Affairs*, XX (1947), 299–308.

62 *The United States in World Affairs, 1947–1948* (New York, 1948), pp. 137–48; W. Macmahon Ball, "Reflections on Japan," *Pacific Affairs*, XXI (1948) 3–19. Proof of the spiritual regeneration of the Japanese, MacArthur found, lay in their willing acceptance of his suggestion that they "renounce war" in their new constitution.

63 But the statement was so carefully worded as to give the impression that American interest in the defense of Formosa was not being denied absolutely. "In the view of the United States Government," it added, "the resources on Formosa are adequate to enable them [the Nationalists] to obtain the items which they might consider necessary for the defense of the island." This left the door open to a change of mind. For text of the statement, see *Current History*, XVIII (February 1950), p. 102.

64 Nevertheless, there is a reasonable doubt that neither Moscow nor Peiping prompted the North Korean aggression. The UN Commission in its report of June 26, 1950, strongly implied that Kim Il Sung himself pulled the trigger. Wilbur H. Hitchcock, a former member of the U.S. Military Government in Korea, offers a cogent argument to this same effect in his article "North Korea Jumps the Gun," *Current History*, XX (March, 1951), 136–44. The Korean crisis is reviewed, with accompanying documents, in *United States Policy in the Korean Crisis* (Department of State Publication 3922 [Washington, D.C., 1950]).

Index

Acheson, Dean, 134, 136
Adenauer, Dr. Conrad, 110; and de-Nazification, 155
Aid to Britain: development of the policy, 55–63; the problem stated, 47–50
Aid to China, 132, 155–56
Allied Control Council, 83, 99–100, 127
America First Committee, 49 ff.; and Lend-Lease Act, 62
Anglo-Iranian Oil Company, 122
Anglo-Japanese alliance, 3–5, 8, 12
Arabian-American Oil Company (ARAMCO), 121–22
Atlantic Charter, 69, 77, 147–48
Atlantic Conference between Roosevelt and Churchill, 23, 25, 68–70
Australia, 2–3, 29; and defense pact with United States, 140; and Lend-Lease, 63; and MacArthur, 133; and South Korea, 128
Axis, Rome-Berlin-Tokyo, 18–21, 37–38, 39–40
Azore Islands, 54; and Battle of Atlantic, 69; secret plan for occupation of, 146

Balance of power, ix–x, 2; and Japan, 10–12; and western Europe, 12–14
Balfour Declaration, 123
Battle of the Atlantic, 64–67
Belgium: German invasion of, 47, 52; liberation of, 74; recovery of, 96; and Washington Arms Conference, 8
Berlin: blockade of, 106–8; four-power occupation of, 99 f.
Borah, Senator William E., 7, 14; and Kellogg Peace Pact, 33
Bretton Woods Agreements, 93–94, 152
Brussels Pact, 106, 108, 111
Bulgaria, 102; Communists in, 114–15, 119, 120
Byrnes, James F.: and Germany, 101–2; views on Council of Ministers, 154

Cairo Conference, 73
Canada 10; and Battle of Atlantic, 69, 76; credit to Britain, 96; and Roosevelt, 45; and South Korea, 128
Caribbean Commission, 152

Casablanca Conference, 72, 75
Chiang Kai-shek, 2; at Cairo, 73; and China-India-Burma theater of war, 75; and Chinese Communists, 81–82, 129–32; on Formosa, 132, 136, 137, 138; and Japan, 19, 21, 22, 25, 26, 28; problem of, 141; wartime relations with Chennault, Stilwell, Wallace, and Hurley, 149
China, ix; and American isolationism, 16; civil war in, 129–32; as the Fourth Policeman, 78–79, 80–81; and the Himalayan Hump, 70–71, 72, 75; and Japanese policy, 18, 19, 21, 23–28; and postwar Japan, 133 f., 141; and treaty of August 14, 1945, with Russia, 81–82, 88, 126; and Twenty-one Demands, 4; and Washington treaties, 8, 11, 12, 14, 15; and World War II, 2
Chinese Communists, 81, 82; establish Chinese People's Republic and sign treaty with Russia, 132–33, 137; and Korean war, 137–40; in Manchuria, 129; problem of, 141
Churchill, Winston: at Casablanca, 72; drafts Atlantic Charter, 69; and fear of war with Japan, 23, 25; and Germany, 98 f.; his plans for the grand strategy of the war, 147–48; speech at Fulton, Missouri, 115; and threat of invasion of Britain, 55–56; and UN, 85; visit of January 1952 to Washington, 141; at Yalta, 78–79, 83
Clay, General Lucius D., 101
Collective security: and disarmament, 5–6; and Kellogg Peace Pact, 33–34; and Washington treaties, 12–14, 29
Committee to defend America by aiding the Allies, 50 ff.
Communism, x, 8; and the Cominform, 107; and East Germany, 109, 113; in France and Italy, 103, 105–6; and the Greek civil war, 114–16; and Jugoslav nationalism, 119; and Korea, 138, 142; and Munich, 36, 38; in Poland and the Balkan States, 76–77, 83–84, 87, 89, 102; see also Chinese Communists
Convoying, 66–68

161